SHAKESPEARE: A SURVEY

SHAKESPEARE:
A SURVEY

BY

E. K. CHAMBERS

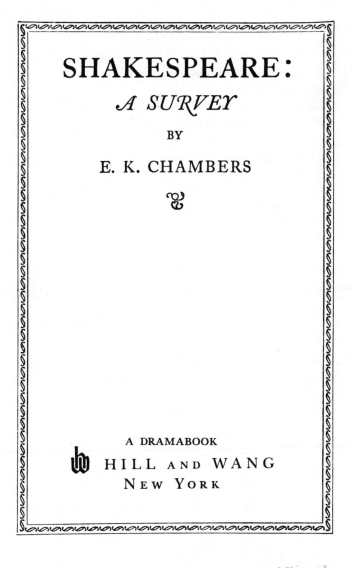

A DRAMABOOK
HILL AND WANG
NEW YORK

Published by arrangement with The Macmillan Company
ISBN 0-8090-0514-X

Library of Congress Catalog Card Number: 58-11371

Manufactured in the United States of America

FIRST DRAMABOOK PRINTING AUGUST 1958

9   10   11   12   13

PREFACE

THESE essays have already been printed as introductions to the plays for ordinary readers. They so appeared, in no logical order, from 1904 to 1908. The conditions made it natural that they should be discursive rather than systematic; and they must not be taken as representing the application to Shakespeare of a complete critical theory, or even the working out of a single line of critical enquiry. Reading them over again after a long interval, I find myself to have been mainly concerned, now with the objects and limitations of the types of dramatic expression—chronicle-history, farce, comedy, tragedy, tragicomedy—as handled by Shakespeare, now with issues more individual to the dramatist, the shifting phases of his pessimistic or optimistic outlook upon life, the apparent reflections, perhaps illusory, of his personal experience upon the mirror of his art. There is little detailed exposition of plot or characterization; still less of attempt to analyze the final mystery of magic words. But for the elimination of a few errors and inconsistencies and a shorter treatment of some of the histories, I have left the matter much as it was written. I daresay that I might write rather differently, here and there, now.

Preface

But I do not think that this would justify a re-vision. *Quisque suos patimur manes.* The maturer judgment of a man of sixty does not entitle him to erase or alter what a man of forty thought fit to record out of the innumerable trains of reflection which any contact with Shakespeare must start.

My method assumed some effective participation by Shakespeare in all the plays traditionally assigned to him and his substantial authorship of most of them. Those introductions would not have been the place, nor can this preface be the place, for a reasoned defence of that attitude. My thanks are due to Messrs Blackie and Son, the publishers of the Red Letter Shakespeare, for their courtesy in allowing me to reserve the right of republication.

E. K. C.

July, 1925

CONTENTS

Contents

SHAKESPEARE:

A SURVEY

SHAKESPEARE, we need thy solace in this day;
Not for the bugles blown about our skies,
Calling our quick-foot youth for enterprise,
To which thine Agincourt was but the play
Of children armed in spring-time; nor for eyes
That noble women bear upon their way,
Eyes that keep secret the poor heart's dismay,
Till the proud head on the wet pillow lies:
Not these! but malice up and down our streets,
The babbling tongues, the minds that cannot hold
An equal course till Time's full circle meets,
The fretful pens shod with an egoist's gold.

    Master, deep read in man's fantastic brain,
    Smile from thy sculptured stone, and leave us sane.

1916

HENRY the SIXTH

NATIONALISM came late into the English
drama. The modern imagination, consciously archaistic in temper, and stimulated by a profound and deliberately cultivated
historic sense, finds delight in the visual reconstruction of the past through a succession of
decorative scenes, linked together in no more
coherent a dramatic unity than can be furnished
by the pride of locality and the continuance of
civic tradition. Obviously the historic pageant, as
it has been represented at Sherborne, at Warwick,
at Oxford, owes much to the spectacular methods
of the middle ages. The annalistic manner, the
naive stringing of episode upon episode at the will
of the chronicle, is the same; and at the bottom
one may trace a revival of the same instinct of
popular merry-making, content to depend for
revelry upon its own untutored efforts, rather than
upon the sophisticated and exotic art of the professional entertainer. Even so, with just such a
rudimentary technique and just such a buoyancy
and feeling of play, must the citizens of mediæval
Coventry or Chester, at Corpus Christi or Whit-
suntide, have approached their annual task of
setting out, picture by picture, the long narrative
of the Fall and Redemption of Man, with its
quickly shifting scenes from the Expulsion of

Lucifer to the Day of Doom. But however much of patriotic sentiment may have been enlisted in the service of the mediæval pageants, and however much their fame may have redounded to the honour and dignity of the towns in which they were exhibited, it does not seem to have occurred to the burghers, as one would have thought might so easily have been the case, still further to glorify themselves by substituting for the familiar scriptural cycle new plays of a similar type based upon themes drawn from the local or the national chronicles. No doubt there were powerful forces to militate against any such development; the natural conservatism of established custom, the ancient connection of the pageants with the religious ceremonies of the festivals at which they were produced, the dependence of the actors upon the clerics who wrote and rewrote their texts. To these causes must perhaps be added the fact that during the half century between Agincourt and Bosworth Field, which was the heyday of the pageants, patriotism, in an England divided between the camps of the Roses, was not at its brightest. Whatever the reason, the secular mystery did not, as a fact, pass beyond tentative beginnings.

Nor was it otherwise at the coming of the Tudors. The deliberate policy of Henry the Seventh encouraged the writing of chronicles, and might have made good use of the historical drama as yet another means of inducing a pacified

England to realize its unity and its greatness. But for a time the economic conditions of the stage were unfavourable. The old habit of enormous local festival plays was dying out, and the small troops of professional actors wandering from town-hall to town-hall and from manor to manor were insufficient to sustain the burden of an elaborate spectacle, and found it easier to grapple with the less exacting demands of morality or of farce. The stage of the court and the schools, on the other hand, sought its interest either in the revival and imitation of classical comedy and tragedy or in the *Tendenz-drama* of theological controversy; and although the latter led by a curious by-path to the intrusion of such historical personages as King John and Cardinal Pandulph among the abstractions of Bale's famous allegory, it was not until the vagabond companies settled in London and for the first time established the popular drama upon a permanent theatre that the chronicle history play can really be said to have come into existence. But on the boards of the Theatre and Curtain, and during the hegemony of Tarlton and the Queen's men from 1583 to 1592, it may fairly be regarded as the dominant type; and although less artless modes followed, and the instructed stage-craft of Ben Jonson might learn to scoff at 'York and Lancaster's long jars,' it had not really lost its vogue, at any rate among the groundlings, before the closing of the theatres heralded the advent of an age in which history

3

was once more to be made and not merely to be gazed at. The prentice hand of Shakespeare found it still in its prime. To a public greedy of life and colour and movement, it stood with its alarums and excursions, its glittering armour and its purple robes, for tragedy and for romance. From murders and executions, and the ups and downs of kings on Fortune's wheel, the emotional thrill passed into the humdrum days of the shopboy and the mercer's lady. The coming and the passing of the Armada had stimulated the national consciousness, and rendered easy and natural a retrospect over the stirring moments of England's past. So had the taste of the spectators been fashioned; while playwrights, eager to meet it, found an inexhaustible mine of picturesque incident in the not too critical pages of Raphael Holinshed and his fellows. One early task of Shakespeare's was to furbish up a dramatic representation of 'York and Lancaster's long jars,' already existing in a chronicle history covering the whole of those Wars of the Roses, whose actual memory had hardly yet faded out of the popular imagination. Two mortal parts of the play, at the least, he worked over, scene after scene, with the patient labour of a journeyman; and then laid such models aside, and followed the promptings of his own spirit upon the lurid theme of *Richard the Third*. To proceed further in the straight line of chronological advance would perhaps have been indiscreet, while a Tudor still sat on the throne of

Henry the Seventh; and so in pursuit of his vein Shakespeare turned back, and after a further essay at the renovation of an old canvas in *King John*, found material not unlike that of York and Lancaster itself in that earlier period of national stress and trouble which was ultimately rendered illustrious by the sounding name of Agincourt.

The accomplishment of this second historical enterprise could hardly fail to bring before one who was by this time a master of his craft the inevitable weaknesses of the tradition in which he was working. Critical battles have been waged around the dramatic unities, and in the end it remains true that drama, if it is to accomplish its end of swaying through sympathy the emotions of the spectators, must somehow, whether it be through the unities or in any other way, achieve a unity. Which is as much as to say that literature, unlike life, must simplify its issues, and that by selection and concentration alone can it hope to grip and fasten to the predetermined mood the wandering spirit of man. And the chronicle history fails to achieve unity, precisely because it never selects, contenting itself with the artless process of translating into dramatic form the facts of the past as the chronicles give them; that is to say with all the hopeless confusion of issues, of beginnings that do not end, and of ends that do not begin, which is characteristic of life itself. One need not expect that this desultory temper should have offended against the popularity of the type. It is at all times your literary man, and not the public of the theatre, that calls for the plain issue. And the Elizabethan public, in particular, had behind it the equally desultory tradition of the miracle-plays, which were hardly yet obsolete, and on which the imagination of many playgoers had been trained. It is true that the miracle-plays, in their fullest development, had attained to a very real unity of their own, through the great cosmic cycles which embraced time and eternity in their extensive span. But it is probable that the very range of these cycles made them, on the well-known Aristotelian principle, dramatically incomprehensible as wholes; and that, even where episodes were not broken off and acted independently, it was the succession of such episodes, rather than the scheme to which they were logically subordinated, that ministered to the popular delight in street and market-place.

In any case the miracle-plays were already a survival when the chronicle history came into being, and no chronicle history fashioned on a cyclical scale is upon record. Holinshed, indeed, would have furnished ample stuff for a noble series of historical pageants stretching from the sack of Troy to the Armada itself; but the conception would hardly have been practicable within the physical limitations of Elizabethan theatres and Elizabethan companies. As a rule the chronicle histories content themselves with such unity, often artificial enough, as the limits of a particular reign

6

may suggest; and the principle finds expression in such titles as *The Famous Victories of Henry the Fifth* or *The Troublesome Reign of King John*. Shakespeare did not, of course, handle so primitive a type of drama without some attempt to reduce the formless structure to unity. Following instinctively upon lines which the great Attic dramatists had worked out before him, he seems to have endeavoured to treat the majority of his historical plays, less as independent units, than as acts or moments in some long succession of historical events better capable than those of a single reign of being represented as a process with a definite beginning, middle, and end. Thus in the tetralogy of York and Lancaster, which is made up of the three parts of *Henry the Sixth* and of *Richard the Third*, the whole tangled web of half a century's chronicles is arranged along a great curve of embittering civil strife, from the first outbreak of faction after the death of Henry the Fifth to its final extinction in the union of the white rose and the red upon Bosworth Field. Certainly the unity so obtained is more a formal than a real one; an acknowledgement of the need for some such principle in the chronicle history, rather than a solution of the problem of attaining it. *Henry the Sixth* is still artless and chaotic enough, in all conscience, and if *Richard the Third* arrives at greater coherency, this is largely at the expense of a breach of continuity in general tone and temper between it and its predecessors in the series. If

7

there is a single dramatic intention common to the four plays, it is a political one, in the constant sense of disunion as the one fatal element in national life, and of the implied contrast, which the chronicles themselves were indeed written to suggest, between the rudderless state of an England deprived of its natural leader and the glorious possibilities of a Henry of Monmouth or a Henry Tudor. The flame of patriotism burns still in the scenes which celebrate the prowess of Lord Shrewsbury, and Thomas Nashe records the response which these scenes evoked when they were produced, probably with Edward Alleyn in the part of Shrewsbury, upon the boards of the Rose in the spring of 1592:

How would it haue ioyed braue Talbot (the terror of the French) to thinke that after he had lyen two hundred yeare in his Toomb, he should triumph againe on the Stage and haue his bones new embalmed with the teares of ten thousand spectators at least (at several times) who, in the Tragedian that represents his person, imagine that they behold him fresh bleeding.

In the desire to make the dead past live again, rather than in any psychological formula of the tragic or the comic vision, lies the real meaning of the chronicle play.

Sentimental persons have sometimes professed to be shocked at the inglorious part assigned to Joan of Arc in *Henry the Sixth*, and have consoled themselves with the reflection that Shakespeare was dependent upon his sources and that, if he depicted the Maid as a wanton and a practiser with evil spirits, this was only because he found her so represented in the chronicles and had no material for arriving at a truer historic judgment. Certainly the process of rehabilitation was not before Shakespeare, and the argument is sound as far as it goes. But it rather begs the question by assuming that Shakespeare or any other English national playwright would have cared very much whether he was unjust to a French heroine or not. It was the quality of England, not of France, that he set out to celebrate, and it may be admitted that patriotic fervour is by no means always touched with the quixotic generosities of a Sidney, and is frequently accompanied by the very natural desire to make out its enemies as no better than they ought to be.

RICHARD the THIRD

WITH *Richard the Third* Shakespeare completes his nonage. It is a masterpiece, but a masterpiece from the same hand which contributed, to how small or great an extent it is impossible to tell, but in any case prentice-wise, to the final shaping of those typical dramas of a pre-Shakespearean epoch, the three parts of *Henry the Sixth*. It resumes the past, rather than preludes the future; and although the continuity of development is never broken, you shall hardly trace the lineaments of the creator of Macbeth and Iago in those of the youngest and most brilliant graduate in the school of Marlowe and Kyd. To say that there is nothing of Shakespeare's personality in *Richard the Third* would be a paradox, for assuredly his sign-manual is upon scene after scene; and indeed it is the principal object of this essay to isolate and fix an element in the composition of the play wherein Shakespeare's personality most strongly declares itself. But at most it affords his individual variation upon a traditional manner of the English stage, which had its roots in the miracle-plays and moralities, and had already been brought to a high state of elaboration by his immediate predecessors. It was written while the golden key to the unexplored gardens of enchantment which he was to make his own had still to be found.

This criticism holds, whether you regard the diction and handling of the dialogue or the greater matters of structure and dramatic intention. Here, in such scenes as that in which the two queens and the mother of Richard toss the tennis-ball of their passion in alternate speech, is the culmination of that rhetorical style, full of antitheses and piled-up parallelisms, to which Shakespeare found his way in the process of revising the naive crudities of *The Contention of York and Lancaster*, and which was soon to pass through the crucible of the lyric mood in his coming essays at tragedy in *Romeo and Juliet* and *Richard the Second*. The weakness of the method is already apparent in the falsetto which is its inevitable accompaniment; and the melodramatic power of certain effects hardly compensates for the straining of the lungs and for the iteration of vituperative epithets until they lose their edge. This is a part of the burden of Shakespeare's inheritance which perhaps he never wholly succeeded in throwing off.

In conception, as in style, *Richard the Third* is a summary of the serious drama of the later eighties. It completes the York and Lancaster tetralogy, and, although diverging widely from the lines laid down in the three parts of *Henry the Sixth*, is in many points only intelligible by reference to these. It is thus an organic outgrowth of chronicle history, just as chronicle history itself was an adaptation of mediæval pseudo-dramatic methods to a new subject-matter. The filiation is obvious.

The distinction lies in the fact that the latest stage of the development affords drama in the true sense, as well as chronicle history. It is not content merely to give a visualized representation of successive events, but endeavours to arrange these as a single action with a beginning, middle, and end, and to interpret the pageant in the light of profound and interesting moral ideas. In *Richard the Third*, indeed, the moral ideas are hardly more an expression of Shakespeare's own personality, than the elements of style. He has not as yet even shaped them to his own uses, but has taken them over bodily, and perhaps without any very profound concern, from his masters Marlowe and Kyd. The day when he will return to them and re-read the old problems in his own fashion has not come. At present they mean to him only material for his growing skill as a dramatic workman. Even Marlowe and Kyd themselves, in their handling of moral ideas, owed almost as much to the moralities that went before them as the chronicle histories owed to the miracle-plays. The experience and speculation of the Renascence had as yet modified the ornament rather than the temper of European thought; and, although the Battle of the Vices and the Virtues was no longer the literary mode, its spirit survived in the preoccupation of that phase of Elizabethan tragedy, of which *Richard the Third* is a late and not the least characteristic example, with the broadest issues of good and evil. Two dramatic motives, indeed, almost entirely dominate it. One is that of retaliation, the call of blood for blood, finding its lower expression in such revenge plays as *The Spanish Tragedy* or *Titus Andronicus*, and its higher in some vague half-pagan conception of Nemesis, of a sleepless destiny inexorably linking sin to retribution. The other, closely related to the first, is that of the life according to Machiavel, whose cold-blooded doctrines of state-craft, squaring with some lurid practices of the times, had evidently impressed the Elizabethan imagination with the notion of an ethical monster, akin to the 'superman' of our modern Nietzsche, who shall dare to say to his soul, 'Evil, be thou my good!' and shall prosper accordingly until the predetermined day for the thunderbolt to fall upon him. That these two motives furnish forth the dramatic life of *Richard the Third* calls, I think, for no demonstration. Richard's stupendous rise and towering fall, the bevy of ghosts crying *'Vindicta! revenge!'* who serve to symbolize the retributive character of the catastrophe, are of themselves sufficient to class it as a Nemesis play. Nor is it less easy to trace in Richard himself the familiar outlines of the Machiavellian man, such as the earlier dramatists had conceived him. You may know him by the deliberation and self-consciousness of his villainy. 'I am determined to prove a villain,' says Richard. It is precisely in this *parti pris* of evil that the essential quality of the dramatic type consists. Just so does Barabbas, in *The Jew*

of Malta, hug himself upon the surpassing degree
of his own infamy—

> Now tell me, worldlings, underneath the sun
> If greater falsehood ever has been done?

Just so, too, does Aaron in *Titus Andronicus* utter
his heart in more crude out-bursts of self-
gratulation and self-condemnation—

> Even now I curse the day, and yet, I think,
> Few come within the compass of my curse,
> Wherein I did not some notorious ill;

and again—

> If one good deed in all my life I did,
> I do repent it from my very soul.

Nor does the tradition end with Richard. Even
in Shakespeare's latest plays the Machiavellian
villain lingers. Iago, and Iachimo too, do but wear
this rue with a difference. As for Richard himself,
one may trace the growth of Shakespeare's conception of the character as far back as *Henry the
Sixth.* In the earliest scenes he is but one among
other gallant lads, the strenuous supporter, first
of his father's, then of his brother's claim to the
throne. It is not until the middle of the third part
that a soliloquy suddenly lets the spectator into
the secret of his ambitions and his temperament.
He dreams on sovereignty and knows himself a
born plotter—

> Why, I can smile, and murder while I smile,
> And cry 'Content' to that which grieves my heart,
> And wet my cheeks with artificial tears,
> And frame my face to all occasions.

> I'll drown more sailors than the mermaid shall;
> I'll slay more gazers than the basilisk;
> I'll play the orator as well as Nestor,
> Deceive more slily than Ulysses could,
> And, like a Sinon, take another Troy.
> I can add colours to the chameleon,
> Change shapes with Proteus for advantages,
> And set the murderous Machiavel to school.
> Can I do this and cannot get a crown?

This is followed up by another speech, after the stabbing of King Henry, in an even more pronounced Machiavellian tone—

> Then, since the heavens have shaped my body so,
> Let hell make crooked my mind to answer it.
> I have no brother, I am like no brother;
> And this word 'love,' which greybeards call divine,
> Be resident in men like one another,
> And not in me. I am myself alone.

It is to be observed that these passages have no equivalent in the chronicles and no dramatic value in *Henry the Sixth* itself, which ends with the coronation of Edward. They point already to an intended *Richard the Third* much on the lines of the existing play. And the fact that they appear, one wholly and the other in germ, in *The Contention* is one of the strongest arguments of those who detect the hand of Shakespeare in the unrevised as well as the revised plays.

There is one aspect of Richard's personality as foreshadowed in these passages of *Henry the Sixth* which calls for especial attention. He describes himself not merely as a 'murderous Machiavel,' but in particular as an accomplished dissembler, one able to 'frame his face to all occasions,' a Ulysses, a Sinon, a Proteus. The same note is repeated in *Richard the Third* itself. Richard prides himself on achieving his ends, 'all the world to nothing,' with no weapons on his side, 'save the plain devil and dissembling looks.' Lessoning Buckingham in intrigue, he asks—

> Come, cousin, canst thou quake, and change thy colour,
> Murder thy breath in middle of a word,
> And then begin again, and stop again,
> As if thou wert distraught and mad with terror?

And Buckingham replies—

> Tut, I can counterfeit the deep tragedian,
> Speak and look back, and pry on every side,
> Tremble and start at wagging of a straw,
> Intending deep suspicion. Ghastly looks
> Are at my service, like enforced smiles;
> And both are ready in their offices,
> At any time, to grace my stratagems.

This is moderately true of Buckingham, whose dissembling is, as a matter of fact, somewhat amateurish; it is pre-eminently true of Richard himself. Richard is, indeed, a consummate actor. The whole secret of his success lies in the adroitness with which he plays upon the ambitions and weaknesses of those whom he intends to make his puppets, in the audacity with which he flings himself into the appropriate utterance of sentiments the most foreign to his nature. And how he revels in it, in his command of himself, in his betraying silences and ironical speech, in the fine sense of dramatic values with which he chooses the moment to strike his blows. Exactly in this consists Shakespeare's personal variation upon the stock Machiavellian theme. His Richard is a monster, like Barabbas or Aaron, and not merely an example of ordinary human frailty. He makes evil his good; but, as I read him, it is not so much for the sake of the evil itself, as for sheer joy in the technique of villainy, in the contriving of the nice adjustment of springs and wires whereby evil comes about. He does not really want the crown, but he does want the world to bustle in; and, scene after scene, he goes last off the stage, twisting his misshapen body in glee, not at the fruit but at the success of his machinations. What a roll his triumphs make! Edward persuaded to imprison Clarence on a false insinuation of treason; Clarence himself and the 'simple gulls,' Hastings, Derby, and Buckingham, made to believe that this imprisonment is the work of the queen's kindred; these in their turn lulled into false security until they are suddenly stricken down; Hastings ruined by a baseless and plausible accusation of witchcraft; Anne wooed and won in the very presence of murdered Henry's corpse; Buckingham befooled by idle promises and thrown aside when he is useless; the suffrages of the citizens gained by an impudent assumption of pious humility; through all the maze of intrigue the ready resource of the accomplished actor never fails him

17

for a moment. His methods are simplicity itself. He leans much upon the affectation of being an honest, well-meaning man, whose motives are sadly misjudged, and who sometimes cannot refrain from anger at the wrongs done to him by others—

> Because I cannot flatter and speak fair,
> Smile in men's faces, smooth, deceive, and cog,
> Duck with French nods and apish courtesy,
> I must be held a rancorous enemy.
> Cannot a plain man live and think no harm,
> But thus his simple truth must be abused
> By silken, sly, insinuating Jacks?

He has no ambition. He had rather be a pedlar than a king. Above all he is religious. The scene in which he appears between two bishops, with a prayer-book in his hand, to gull the mayor of London, is only one of several in which he takes delight, as he himself puts it, to—

> Clothe my naked villany
> With odd old ends stolen out of holy writ;
> And seem a saint, when most I play the devil.

Of course it all comes to an end. You cannot cog for ever with heaven. From the beginning there have been some who have seen through him; mostly women. He may tell them that he is too childish-foolish for the world, if he will; but they know him too well, who have borne with him from the womb, or shared the fearful trepidation of his bed. Even his vaunted dissembling ultimately fails him. In his last bout he is palpably outwitted. Red with the blood of her sons, he woos Elizabeth for her daughter, even as at an earlier moment, red with the blood of her husband, he had wooed Anne. 'Relenting fool, and shallow, changing woman!' he sneers. But after all, Elizabeth is the deeper dissembler. She is already far in the plot with Richmond, and, although her daughter shall be a queen, she shall assuredly not be Richard's queen. With the change in the tide of his fortune, Richard's nerve leaves him. Evil dreams beset him more and more, sure tokens of the unavoided doom of destiny that is closing him round. He has met his match when death, the most finished of tragedians, steps towards him on the stage of Bosworth Field.

I have already hinted that Shakespeare, at the period of his career at which he wrote *Richard the Third*, does not impress me as being primarily interested in moral ideas. Richard as Machiavel and Richard as the chosen victim of Nemesis are only moderately convincing. On the other hand, Richard as an actor is convincing enough; and in this side of his hero's personality I think that Shakespeare was very much interested indeed. He was, of course, an actor himself; perhaps had not very long been one; and his adventurous mind, with its usual restless energy, was eagerly pursuing the psychological secrets of his craft. 'Myself have seen his demeanour no less civil than he excellent in the quality he professes,' says Henry Chettle, in almost undoubted allusion to the 'upstart crow,

beautified with the feathers' of poets, whom poor
embittered Greene had gibed at as 'in his own
conceit the only Shake-scene in a country.' Some
obscure passages in the *Sonnets* have been interpreted as signifying that, in certain moods at least,
the mummer's life was not wholly to the taste of
the ambitious young man whom the brilliant Earl
of Southampton honoured with his friendship—

Alas! 'tis true, I have gone here and there,
And made myself a motley to the view,
Gored mine own thoughts, sold cheap what is most dear,
Made old offences of affections new.

It is perhaps possible to take 'motley' somewhat
too literally. But that a sensitive and self-centred
spirit should rebel against a profession which a
subtle writer of our own day has numbered with
that of the 'daughters of joy' is not unlikely, after
all; and the status of a 'vacabond' may have had
its sting for one whose father had been bailiff of
Stratford and claimed coat-armour, and who had
more than a touch of the *bourgeois* in his blood.
But it was only in certain moods, one may be
assured. In others the fascination of an art unequalled in its control over the shifting souls of
men must have been strong upon him; nor is the
least proof of this in the fact that he chose to turn
a play, conventional enough in its structure and
its theme, into a professional note-book full of the
nicest and most penetrating observation.

The COMEDY of ERRORS

LATIN comedy, filtering down for the most part through Italian channels, has left its mark upon more than one of Shakespeare's plays. But it is in *The Comedy of Errors* alone, with its atmosphere of slaves and courtesans, its breathless dialogue, its strained domestic relations, its unity of action upon an open street between the convent and the house of Antipholus, that one may find any close reproduction of the manner of Plautus and of Terence. In view of the vogue which the powerful influence of the schoolmasters upon the development of the drama in England during the first two-thirds of the sixteenth century had given to both these writers, it is hardly worth while speculating how far, if at all, Shakespeare went directly to the fountain-head for his play. That *The Comedy of Errors* derives from the *Menaechmi* is obvious. It is equally obvious that it is not a translation of the *Menaechmi*, but a free adaptation of the ingeniously entangled situation which its model afforded; and it is probable that one at least of the new complications introduced, the addition to the twin Antipholuses of the twin Dromios, owes its suggestion to another play of Plautus, the *Amphitruo*. There is no particular reason to suppose that Shakespeare knew William Warner's translation of the *Menaechmi*, the publication of which in 1594 was probably an effect rather than a cause of the production of the play. The book may have been circulating with other of Warner's Plautine versions 'for the use and delight of his private friends' at an earlier date, but it is to be suspected that, had it come into Shakespeare's hands, the scanty verbal resemblances between it and *The Comedy of Errors* would have been increased. The Latin of Plautus is not easy; but even if Shakespeare's private scholarship were unequal to the task, of which there is no proof, and if, which is extremely unlikely, he had never had an opportunity of seeing the *Menaechmi* performed in the original or in a translation by London schoolboys, there were probably scores of persons among his acquaintance who could readily tell him so much of the plot as was required to serve his turn. It is a hazardous conjecture, and therefore has been made with much confidence, that a play performed at court by the choir-boys of St Paul's on the 1st of January, 1577, under the title of 'the historie of Error,' represents an earlier composition subsequently worked up by Shakespeare. That is, I think, too much to hang upon a similarity of name. 'Truth is one,' says Plato, 'but there are many kinds of error.' *Cuiusvis hominis est errare*, says the Latin grammar. But one recognizes the spirit in which English literary history has not infrequently been written.

Shakespeare or another has of course introduced into the story certain elements which are quite alien to Plautus. There is the emotional interest, the note of romance, such as we find it in *The Merchant of Venice*, derived from the travels of Ægeon in search of wife and family, his condemnation, and the triple ἀναγνώρισις which drenches the rather violent humours of the closing scene in sentiment. Such a situation is common form in Elizabethan comedy, just as it was common form in the tragedy of Euripides, but it will be admitted that the dramatic spirit had travelled long mediæval roads before it could find its place among the situations of Plautus. Similarly it is a modern, rather than a Latin conception of the position of the wife in comedy, that determines the stress laid throughout the play upon the jealousy of Adriana, which again and again strikes a serious chord in the very midst of riot and horse-play, and finally leads up to the little sermon delivered by the Abbess to the foolish wife, for which the intrigue is stopped at a critical moment. Adriana admits that she has dwelt upon her wrongs, in season and out of season—

It was the copy of our conference.
In bed he slept not for my urging it;
At board he fed not for my urging it;
Alone, it was the subject of my theme;
In company, I often glanced it;
Still did I tell him it was vild and bad.
 Abbess. And thereof came it that the man was mad.
The venom clamours of a jealous woman
Poisons more deadly than a mad dog's tooth.

The commentators have been struck by the incongruity of this insistence upon the ethical issue with the general temper of the play, and have explained it after their fashion as due to the reaction of Shakespeare's own domestic circumstances upon his art. They regard him as preoccupied, both in *The Comedy of Errors* and in *The Taming of the Shrew*, with the relations of husband and wife and the interpretation of the marriage vow, because he too had married in haste and repented at leisure, and had suffered at bed and board from the tongue of Anne Hathaway, until he had been forced to solve his problem by a hasty flight upon the London road. Poor Anne Hathaway, of whom after all we know nothing but that she had a honeysuckle name, and was some years older than Shakespeare, and was kind to him before marriage, and received a legacy of his second-best bed! I shall not pursue that controversy. At any rate it is clear that, whether he had learnt the lesson by experience of his own fire-side, or by experience of the stormy fire-sides of his friends in comparison with that peaceful one which he so rarely visited in Stratford, Shakespeare was very much convinced, when he wrote *The Comedy of Errors*, of the sound practical truth that indiscretion in the expression of jealousy is by no means a way to remove the causes of jealousy; and that he was careful so to order his play as to give pointed utterance to this conviction. So much does the theme, in its serious aspect, turn upon jealousy, that when one finds the record of a play, new at a date about which *The Comedy of Errors* may very well have been written, acted by a company with which Shakespeare almost certainly had other relations, and bearing the title of *The Jealous Comedy*, one is tempted to ask whether this and *The Comedy of Errors* are not one and the same. Here, again, one cannot build much upon nothing but a name, and I am certainly not going to insist upon the identification. If the date which it indicates is correct, *The Comedy of Errors* is probably Shakespeare's first comedy, and so much, indeed, one might readily maintain on general grounds, and particularly upon the liberal use of verse, regular and doggerel, in clownish scenes, for which he had already learnt, by the time he came to write *The Two Gentlemen of Verona* and *Love's Labour's Lost*, that the proper medium is prose. One must not, of course, forget the possibility that the play may be a *remaniement*, and if so may contain elements of style as well as of subject-matter which cannot be safely regarded as being of Shakespeare's own fashioning. Here, however, we again approach the dangerous regions of conjecture.

In so far as it is concerned with jealousy and the ethical problems which hinge upon jealousy, *The Comedy of Errors* has an undeniable claim to the title which it bears. It is comedy in the true sense of a criticism of life, which is at heart profoundly serious, and employs all the machinery of wit or humour, with the deliberate intention of reaching through the laughter to the ultimate end of a

25

purged outlook upon things. Let an audience shake its sides at the plight into which a scold is brought by the railings of her tongue, and it is odds that they will go away with the conviction that the wiser course is not to rail. Whether they will actually cease to rail is perhaps hardly the concern of the dramatist, whose will to propagate his own vision of things is not necessarily identical with the pang with which the missionary aches for souls. From one point of view, then, *The Comedy of Errors* is to be classed as a comedy. But the label hardly applies to it as a whole, since, as I have already pointed out, the ethical element, no less than the element of romance, in the play has been imported into the original design under the promptings of the Elizabethan mood. Stripped of these ornaments, the interest declares itself as almost entirely one of plot, arising out of a succession of ingeniously interwoven situations brought about by the facial resemblances of the two pairs of twin brothers and the accident of their coming together, unknown to each other, in the same city. Too much praise cannot be given to the technical skill with which the idea is worked out; nor can it be denied that in this respect many improvements have been made in the original scheme of the *Menaechmi*. The supplementing of the Antipholuses by the Dromios quadruples the possibilities of misunderstanding, and the fun grows fast and furious, as error is piled upon error. If the rehandling of the Plautine structure is to be attributed to Shakespeare himself, he was already a master of stage-craft. To this particular type of drama it is possible to give the name of farce rather than of comedy, if certain distinctions are observed. Farce, indeed, is a term which has been used by literary historians in two rather different shades of meaning. In one acceptation, derived from its use as applied to *Maître Pathelin* and other examples of fifteenth-century French dramatic humour, it does not so much connote something other than comedy, as a variety of comedy itself. It is a matter of temper and *milieu*. Farce is comedy translated from the speech and manners of a cultivated society into the speech and manners of the *bourgeoisie*; or perhaps it would really be more historical to say that comedy represents a development out of farce, due to the sharpening of the wits and the refinement of the moral issues which accompany or form part of the growth of a cultivated society as distinct from a *bourgeoisie*. Such farce is a comedy of the ruder vices and the more robust virtues, a comedy in which fisticuffs, literal and verbal, take the place of rapier-play. In Shakespeare it is represented, magnificently enough, by *The Taming of the Shrew* and *The Merry Wives of Windsor*. And its primary dramatic interest is still, as in other forms of comedy, an interest of character, whatever other elements, of buffoonery or intrigue, may be added to this. In *The Merry Wives of Windsor*, there is both buffoonery and intrigue; in *The Taming of the Shrew*

27

buffoonery, but, so far at least as the main Petruchio and Katherina story is concerned, no intrigue. But the second application of the term farce is to a dramatic form which is sharply differentiated from comedy by the fact that in it the interest of character is wholly replaced by an interest of plot. The conception of farce in this sense may be defined as the deduction of a logical conclusion from absurd premises. The playwright starts with some impossible assumption, which you must take for granted; however unconvincing, however grotesque, it is beyond your criticism. From this he proceeds, without any further breach of the probabilities, to show what follows, and to work out a resulting tissue of absurdities, all inherent in the initial situation. I do not say that all farcical plots actually respect this scientific analysis of their structure, but they will be found to be the more successful, the more closely they conform to it. If, therefore, I call *The Comedy of Errors* a farce, it is not, as in the case of *The Merry Wives of Windsor* or *The Taming of the Shrew*, the temper of its ethics that I have in mind. There is nothing particularly farcical about the marital relations of Antipholus and Adriana or the sensible didactics of the Abbess. Farce has indeed generally a more brutal touch in such matters. There is horse-play, of course; but that is common to both types of farce. It is rather the plot of *The Comedy of Errors* that seems to me to answer very closely to the definition of a farcical plot. The initial assumption is of a personal similarity between two brothers so close as to extend to their raiment, and to deceive even those with whom they are most familiar. Given this, all the episodes of the play, however ridiculous the situations they involve, unwind themselves plausibly and naturally enough. One qualification must however be made. There is a weak point. Antipholus and Dromio of Ephesus did not know that they had twin brothers. They had been separated as children from Æmilia by rude fishermen of Corinth almost immediately after the shipwreck. But Antipholus and Dromio of Syracuse did know. They had been brought up by Ægeon until they were eighteen years of age; and had only left him with the expressed intention of seeking out their brothers. One can hardly suppose that Ægeon had failed to tell them of the extraordinary likeness which had existed between the children. This being so, it is almost incredible that, when they found themselves being obviously and constantly mistaken at Ephesus for persons not themselves, the solution of the puzzle should have failed to suggest itself to them. The same criticism applies, in the last scene, to Ægeon, who, when he found himself repudiated by the son and slave whom he thought he knew, must surely, after his long narrative to the duke a few hours before, have guessed that these could only be the son and slave whom he did not know. There are therefore in reality two assumptions, not one, made in the play; an assumption of physical resemblance so close as to be mistaken for identity, and an assumption also of a very singular kind of oblivion in at least two of the personages. One such assumption is, as already explained, of the very essence of the game, but against a second we are entitled to protest. Had it not been for this lack of economy in hypothesis, *The Comedy of Errors* would have presented the very pink and perfection of a farcical plot.

TITUS ANDRONICUS

MOST competent students of *Titus Andron-icus* will admit that such interest as their work upon the play affords is to be found in the region of comparative rather than in that of absolute criticism. To a mind whose conceptions of tragedy have been largely formed upon the later practice of Shakespeare himself, there is nothing to claim the tragic analysis in so raw a tale of blood and revenge, culminating in the nightmare scene wherein the mutilated stumps of Lavinia hold the basin over which Titus, with the one hand left him, cuts the throats of her ravishers. The situations, as they unroll themselves in breathless succession, would be wholly sickening, were they not at the same time so remote from reality as to become merely grotesque. Not yet has Shakespeare, if it was Shakespeare who prepared this meal of horrors, learnt the authentic touch upon pity and upon fear; we are far indeed from the passionate thrill of Lear as he beholds the good green world in which he has rioted toppling around him, and from the sad and gracious harmonies of Desdemona's death-chamber.

Baffled by the absence of greatness, the critics have fastened upon the gossip of a somewhat irresponsible dramatist of the end of the seventeenth century, who seems to have heard it in the green-room that the play was not in substance Shakespeare's at all, 'but brought by a private Author to be Acted, and he only gave some Master-touches to one or two of the Principal Parts or Characters.' About the issue so set controversy has alternately leaped and smouldered for more than a century past. Quite recently it has flared forth again with the renewed vigour of a phœnix, and in a way that impresses one, not so much with the failure of each disputant in turn to convince, since that might only mean that sufficient material for the solution of their common problem is lacking, as with the abstinence of them all alike from any attempt to think out and apply a logical method of investigation. A survey of the accumulated literature of the subject is disconcerting, in the evidence which it affords of the small extent to which literary history, or at any rate the literary history of England, has come into contact with the scientific spirit. This is, one may suppose, primarily due to the fact that it has never, at the more important universities, become a matter of academic discipline. The activities of scholarship have been diverted to other fields of enquiry; and into the void thus left has pressed a crowd of journalists and idle antiquaries, who have come to their task with an imperfect equipment of training, and have pursued it under the stimulus rather of partisanship than of research. They have generally started from a sentiment; either the sentiment of conservatism, which resents the questioning even of a literary tradition as a dangerous disturbance of the foundations of things; or the sentiment of what may be called Shakespeareolatry, which resents the ascription to 'our Shakespeare' of anything which the sentimentalist chooses to consider unworthy work, as being of the nature of an insult to his genius. They frame such an hypothesis as the sentiment may suggest to them; and proceed to support it with that combination of rhetorical appeal and unconscious manipulation of evidence which the theologians have elaborated into a system under the title of apologetics. Meanwhile the inductive method, of which it is of the very essence that it is disinterested and leaves the hypothesis to be suggested by the facts themselves, is neglected, or is regarded as an instrument belonging to the natural sciences and somewhat beneath the dignity of literature.

If the problem of the authorship of *Titus Andronicus* can be unravelled at all, it can only be by setting to work in a wholly different temper. For indeed it is not really an isolated problem, but a mere fragment of one far wider, which embraces a large mass of anonymous dramatic work produced in the decade preceding 1594, and involves a minute consideration of the conditions of dramatic production during that period. It will not be difficult to show that this is necessarily so. The arguments to be weighed in investigating Shakespeare's share, if any, in the play turn almost entirely on the determination of differences and relationships of style. There is a certain amount of external evidence available, indeed; but it serves rather to define than to resolve the issue. The title-pages of the 1594 and 1600 editions of *Titus Andronicus* contain lists of the theatrical companies by whom it was in succession performed. A comparison of these with the entries in Henslowe's *Diary*, and of those again with the German and Dutch adaptations of the play, suggests the conclusion that the extant text dates from the beginning of 1594, and represents a revision then made of an older play, which had been produced in the spring of 1592, and is called by Henslowe *Titus and Vespasian*. The revision must have been substantial, since Henslowe seems to have treated the result as a new play; and an allusion by Ben Jonson makes it possible that the 1592 version itself was in the same way a substantial revision of something earlier still. So far it is possible to arrive without raising the question of authorship at all. But even as regards that the external evidence is not silent. *Titus Andronicus* was named in Meres' list of Shakespeare's plays given in his *Palladis Tamia* in 1598; and it was included in the First Folio edited by his fellows Heminges and Condell in 1623. It is eminently characteristic of the forensic manner in which the whole controversy has been conducted, that those who question Shakespeare's authorship have exhausted their energies in endeavouring to suggest that Meres may have been ignorant, and Heminges and

Condell dishonest. This is abusing the plaintiff's attorney with a vengeance. Admit the contention, and the authorship of nearly the whole of the pre-1594 drama falls into chaos; since, whatever deductions must be made from the value of the evidence of Meres and of Heminges and Condell, it is at least far stronger than any that can be produced for Kyd's authorship of *The Spanish Tragedy*, or for Marlowe's authorship of *Tamburlaine*, or for Greene's authorship of *Orlando Furioso*, or for Peele's authorship either of *The Arraignment of Paris* or of *The Battle of Alcazar*. As a matter of fact, it cannot be shown that a single play is ascribed to Shakespeare either in *Palladis Tamia* or in the First Folio, of which he was not in some sense, although perhaps only as collaborator or reviser, the author; and this being so, the consensus of the two authorities is obviously very strong evidence indeed. But of course it is not absolutely conclusive; and it is theoretically possible to conceive a triumphant demonstration, on grounds of style alone, not only that Shakespeare cannot possibly have designed the structure of the original play, but that he cannot possibly have written that revised text of the original play which appears, from such indications as are available, to be what we have before us. The only points I want to make now are, firstly, that no such demonstration has yet been approached; and secondly that, in its absence, the presumption must be that Meres and Heminges and Condell did not err. Even then, of course, you have the alternative of regarding Shakespeare, either as the original author, or simply as the reviser of the play. Ravenscroft's gossip, for what it is worth, is in favour of the latter hypothesis; and this is not inconsistent with the general probabilities as to Shakespeare's first essays at dramaturgy.

The method generally adopted by those, who have been unwilling to recognize Shakespeare's sweet Roman hand in *Titus Andronicus*, has been that of direct approach. That is to say, they have selected elements of diction, phrase and rhythm from the play, and have endeavoured to show that parallels to these are less frequently to be found in what they regard as Shakespeare's undisputed works, than in those of some other of his contemporaries. The application of this method has obviously led to very inconclusive results, since its exponents have in turn ascribed the play to Kyd, Marlowe, Greene, Peele, and Lodge, and the latest of them appears to think that contributions of all or nearly all of these, as well as of Shakespeare himself, either as original writers or as revisers, have to be disentangled in the complicated web of the piece. A literary equation comprising five or six unknown quantities is likely to remain a puzzle. Clearly the ill-success of a method may mean either that the problem is insoluble, or that the method itself has been badly worked, and not necessarily that it is inherently unsound. And the stronger objection to the method of direct approach is the *a priori* one, that it attempts to proceed upon grounds of style without any preliminary enquiry as to what elements of style are evidential and what are not. Surely there are all sorts of questions that must be asked before any importance can be attached to the fact that some particular locution used in *Titus Andronicus* does not reappear in plays written by Shakespeare after 1594 and does reappear, say, in *The Battle of Alcazar*. You have to determine, on the side of Shakespeare, what portions of his early style were permanent and what passed away; and again, how far at the beginning he had a style of his own at all, and how far he reproduced, consciously or unconsciously, the style of his predecessors; and in the latter case, whether it was their printed works only, or his memory also of those that trod the stage, which influenced him; and whether the process of revising an old play made any difference, so that he is less himself with a model before him, than when he is writing with a free hand on a sheet of blank paper. And then, as regards the other dramatists, you have to ask, whether they also have distinctly recognizable styles of their own, and if so, what are the elements really characteristic of each, and what are the elements, if any, which belong to a common stock of vocabulary and metaphor upon which every writer of the time drew as a matter of course, and which therefore cannot be used as evidence of authorship at all. And are the known writers of the time sufficient to account for all its anonymous plays? Or are there other personalities, as undefined as was Kyd's a few years ago, to be formulated, and kept in view when this or that anonymous play has to be assigned? And what were the methods of collaboration and revision? And what amount of revision was held to justify the reviser in claiming a play as a new play and as his play? It is very likely that many of these questions can never be answered; but I think that an answer to them is necessary, before such a question as that of the authorship of *Titus Andronicus* can be seriously approached in any other fashion than that of guesswork. And assuredly, if the investigation is to be undertaken at all, it must be undertaken, as I have already suggested, disinterestedly; in abstraction from each and all of the particular difficulties, which its results may ultimately help to clear up, and not in the light of this or that preconceived hypothesis about any one or more of these. So alone will there be a chance of its being conducted according to the principles of right reason, and in security from the bias which inevitably arises from the forensic desire to prove a case. The labour entailed would be considerable, and only to be faced by the co-operation of many scholars. And the results might be negative, should the indubitable work of the dramatists concerned prove insufficient to form the basis of a sound induction; but in that case we must be content to leave the anonymous plays anonymous, and not to cavil at the authority of Meres and of Heminges and Condell as to *Titus*

Andronicus. For it is only on the basis of convincing arguments as to style, derived from such an induction, that scepticism as to that authority can become permissible.

The TAMING of the SHREW

AN age which flatters itself, so far at least as its formal professions of faith are concerned, that it has rounded Cape Turk, must needs make it a point of honour to take offence at the theme and temper of *The Taming of the Shrew*. The Odyssey of the fair lady of Padua is certainly conceived in a spirit which suggests the author of *The First Blast of the Trumpet against the Monstrous Regiment of Women* rather than the author of *The Subjection of Women*. And if you have wept for the hunted Diana, you can hardly refuse to shed a tear for the humiliation of Katherina, for the impetuous haggard tamed to wear the hood and jesses of the secular tyranny of man. Wedded against her will to her 'mad-brain rudesby,' bemoiled with the mire of her bridal journey, railed at from bed and board, her gown rejected for an apple-tart and her cap bemocked for a porringer, compelled at last to show herself ridiculous in the public road and obsequious at home, she, no less than her nineteenth-century sister, stands for all time as a type of the wrongs done to her much-enduring sex. You do not need her final sermon, with the symbolical placing of her head beneath the foot of the genial ruffian who has subdued her, to point the obsolete and degrading moral:

> Such duty as the subject owes the prince,
> Even such a woman oweth to her husband.

It is perhaps the duty of the critic to explain how all this can be true, as no doubt it is true, beyond all possibility of cavil, and how the play can still remain, as it clearly does remain, a well of hearty and not unwholesome laughter. It is not, I think, sufficient to say that the paradox affords an example of Shakespeare's immortal humour triumphant in the handling of an unsympathetic plot for which Shakespeare is not himself responsible. The attempt to brand as non-Shakespearean everything, which in style or ethics fails to come up to a preconceived and wholly sentimental ideal of the national dramatist of England, is one which is responsible for the introduction of a good deal of confusion into English literary criticism. It is plain enough that *The Taming of the Shrew* is of the nature of a revision of an earlier play, which was published in 1594, probably about the time at which the revision was done, under the title of *The Taming of a Shrew*; and further that, while the revised play only occasionally reproduces the actual wording of the original, it throughout follows it very closely in its structure and the ordering of its incidents. It is therefore the author of *The Taming of a Shrew* rather than the author of *The Taming of the Shrew* who is primarily responsible for fixing those relations between Petruchio and Katherina to which exception is taken. But it is by no means so clear that Shakespeare is thereby cleared even of primary responsibility. It is, in fact, one of the most difficult outstanding problems of Shake-

41

spearean scholarship to determine on the one hand how much Shakespeare wrote of *The Taming of the Shrew*, and on the other how little, if any, he wrote of *The Taming of a Shrew*. It is closely cognate to that other problem of *Henry the Sixth*. The rest of the earlier play may be neglected, but the Ferando and Kate scenes in it read like a first draft of the Petruchio and Katherina scenes of its successor, just in the same way in which the Jack Cade scenes in *The Contention of York and Lancaster* read like a first draft of the similar scenes in *Henry the Sixth*. Both *The Taming of a Shrew* and *The Contention of York and Lancaster* appear to have originally belonged to a company of actors passing under the protection of the Earl of Pembroke; and one is almost forced to the alternative, that either Lord Pembroke's men had the advantage of a forgotten writer who possessed considerable comic power and to whom Shakespeare was content to owe no little debt, or that Shakespeare himself began his dramatic career by contributing to plays for these men, and that, when he made use of the Ferando and Kate and the Jack Cade scenes at a later date, he was doing no more than reclaim his own. I do not pretend to decide between these hypotheses. Nor, for my present purpose, is it necessary to do so. For if Shakespeare did not conceive the relations of the shrew and her tamer, he at least adopted them, and bent all the resources of his invention to give them laughable expression; and thereby I fear he must be held to have assumed responsibility, and laid himself open to any ethical criticism which they may entail.

It is a further question, how far the ethical critic has really a *locus standi*. There is more than one way of meeting him. Obviously, one may appeal to the historic sense, and say that it is absurd to bring Shakespeare to the bar of a sentiment which has in the main been evolved since his day. This is, no doubt, true, so far as it goes. The doctrine of the equality of the sexes, as an ethical principle, would not have meant very much to an Elizabethan. And the saying that Shakespeare 'was not of an age, but for all time' is about as true as many another mortuary phrase. Like every other vital writer, he is instinct with the spirit of his age, and vital largely because he is instinct with it; and, without the historic sense, his ethical standpoint is in many respects incomprehensible to those who come after him. His attitude towards Shylock in *The Merchant of Venice* is, of course, a crucial instance. But I do not know that the appreciation of this takes one very far, critically, in understanding *The Taming of the Shrew*. For, as a matter of fact, *The Merchant of Venice* and *The Taming of the Shrew*, although Heminges and Condell classed them both as comedies, belong to wholly different dramatic types. The moral ideas of *The Merchant of Venice* are essential to its structure. It is a drama of emotions, a tragicomedy; and it is precisely out of its moral ideas, out of the conflict of Love and Hate which it sets forth, that its emotions arise.

The Taming of the Shrew

The Taming of the Shrew, on the other hand, is not a drama of the emotions at all. It is a comedy, or more strictly a farce, in the true sense. It approaches its theme, the eternal theme of the duel of sex, neither from the ethical standpoint of the Elizabethan pulpiter nor from that of the Pioneer Club. It does not approach it from an ethical standpoint at all, but merely from that of humorous and dispassionate observation, which is at least one of the permitted attitudes of Thalia towards all the facts of human life. The humour of strange bedfellows; that is its burden. Petruchio of Verona is as peremptory as Katherina Minola is proudminded. Let us see how these two curst characters hit it off in the rough-and-tumble of matrimony. The clash of temperaments and the inevitable domination in the long run of the stronger furnish forth a situation and a process, which surely bear regarding in their laughable aspect without any evocation of ethical theories as to the heaven-determined position of the husband in the domestic hierarchy. Art is entitled to make such abstractions from the totality of things. That the point is not a sociological one is shown by the fact that it would be in no way lost if the positions were inverted, and the dominating will given to the wife instead of the husband; as indeed was done by John Fletcher, whose *The Tamer Tamed* presents Petruchio *en secondes noces*, the butt of a verier shrew than either Katherina or himself. Such an inversion would naturally be unthinkable if an

44

ethical judgment, feminist or anti-feminist, were involved. Perhaps Shakespeare has left some handle to the misunderstanding in giving prominence to Katherina's sermon, as if it were the key-note of the whole play and expressed the dramatist's moral summing-up of the conflict he has depicted. Katherina speaks it; but she is Petruchio's mouthpiece, not Shakespeare's; and she should recite her lesson on the boards with a wry face which shall make it clear that it is but the last triumph of Petruchio's famous medicine for a curst wife. Petruchio meanwhile must applaud and clink his glass, in appreciative glee at his own astonishing masterfulness.

It must be admitted that the treatment of the central theme in *The Taming of the Shrew* has a brutality about it. Brutality, especially in sexual matters, is quite in the tradition of farce, and one of the notes which serve to differentiate it from other sub-varieties of comedy. For farce, properly regarded, is not a thing disparate from comedy, but rather a mode of it, comedy as it appeals to intellects which are far from being tickle of the sere and need a compelling stimulus to clap them into horse-laughter. Of course it is necessary to distinguish. The Early Victorian writers for the stage have led us to look upon farce as a type of drama whose humour is wholly external, due to absurdities of situation arising by logical development from some impossibility assumed as a starting-point. We have forgotten to expect from it that outlook upon real life which is very properly recognized as suitable to true comedy. *The Comedy of Errors*, in which the complete facial identity of the two pairs of brothers affords the initial impossibility, is perhaps the only play of Shakespeare's that really answers to the formula of farce so defined. Yet it would be difficult to class either *The Taming of the Shrew* or *The Merry Wives of Windsor*, to say nothing of the underplots in many of the tragicomedies, as anything but farces. And if one goes back a little further than the Early Victorian order of ideas, one finds that the farce of complicated situation has neither the sole nor the original right to claim the title. Farce, as it may be traced from the very dawn of the history of drama, was primarily not a drama of incident and intrigue, but a drama of the outlook upon life, just as much as comedy itself. You may call it *bourgeois* comedy, or comedy of the market-place, if you will. It differs from typical comedy in two ways; firstly, not by the absence of outlook upon life, but by an outlook upon life definitely brutal or cynical, instead of sympathetic or at most ironical; and, secondly, in that it proceeds at a greater distance from the normal facts of life, of which it presents an extravagant or burlesque perversion, instead of merely a humorous or whimsical arrangement. It is also more universal. Fine comedy has emerged but here and there in the literary history of the civilized peoples of Europe. It demands a special organization of humanity, a quick-witted urban folk, trained in the arena of the *salon* to applaud the give-and-take of dialogue and to discern nice shades in the surface of things. Meredith has analysed it:

There are plain reasons why the Comic poet is not a frequent apparition; and why the great Comic poet remains without a fellow. A society of cultivated men and women is required, wherein ideas are current and the perceptions quick, that he may be supplied with matter and an audience. The semi-barbarism of merely giddy communities, and feverish emotional periods, repel him; and also a state of marked social inequality of the sexes; nor can he whose business is to address the mind be understood where there is not a moderate degree of intellectual activity.

But the broad leer of farce is everywhere, and scholars and courtiers have never disdained to be clapped from time to time on the back with the same jests that have tickled the ribs of boors and citizens. Farce, crude and obscene, was the stock-in-trade of the innumerable army of mimes who drove tragedy and comedy from stage after stage of the Roman Empire. The politer modes of literature were whelmed in the night of the dark ages; but farce, one may shrewdly suspect, survived, to burst forth in extraordinary exuberance during the fourteenth century, together with that *fabliau* to which, in actual subject-matter as well as in spirit, it is so closely related. In the earlier English drama of the sixteenth century, farce comes only second to didactic allegory in popularity. And so the tradition is handed on to the immediate predecessors of Shakespeare himself. Throughout

47

its history the themes of farce have not varied essentially. Certain topics have proved inexhaustible; the tricks of ill-reputed trades, such as that of the miller; the warfare of the townsman and the clerk; the greed and hypocrisy of priests and friars; the ingenious wiles of miching rogues, a Pathelin, an Autolycus. And above all it has made its merriment of the duel of sex, in that marital form in which the common consent of all peoples has agreed to find the duel of sex most amusing. The beaten wife and the hen-pecked husband, the cuckold and the shrew, are among the oldest of its conventions; and in painting the battles and the reconciliation of Petruchio and Katherina, Shakespeare was merely, one may be sure, reproducing for the thousandth time a situation at which many a mediæval green or castle hall, no less than many a theatre of Antioch or Byzantium, had often laughed its fill.

The TWO GENTLEMEN of VERONA

No play of Shakespeare, to my thinking, bears upon it such obvious marks of immaturity as *The Two Gentlemen of Verona*. It is not his first play, for at least the journey-work on the three parts of *Henry the Sixth* and on *Titus Andronicus* must have preceded it. It is not even his first comedy, if, as is possible, *The Comedy of Errors* may be identified with *The Jealous Comedy* of Henslowe's list. But in *Henry the Sixth* and *Titus Andronicus* his task seems to have been little more than that of polishing and rewriting, scene by scene, existing texts; while even in *The Comedy of Errors* the classical model of the *Menaechmi* provided him with a scaffolding to work upon, and saved him from the necessity of confronting those problems of structure which are the most ticklish of all for the prentice hand. *The Two Gentlemen of Verona* really declares itself as immature because it is Shakespeare's first essay at originality, at fashioning for himself the outlines of that romantic or tragicomic formula in which so many of his most characteristic dramas were afterwards to be cast. Something which is neither quite tragedy nor quite comedy, something which touches the heights and depths of sentiment and reveals the dark places of the human heart without lingering long enough there to crystallize the painful impression, a love story broken for a moment into passionate chords by absence and inconstancy and intrigue, and then reunited to the music of wedding-bells; such is the kind of dramatic scheme which floated before him, when he first set pen to paper in making a play of his very own. And the difficulties which the conception entails, in bringing about a happy ending that may find acceptance without proving demonstrably untrue to the facts of human nature, were perhaps greater than he had dreamed. Certainly, neither in *The Two Gentlemen of Verona*, nor in some later plays, whose handling is in the main surer and more masterly, did he altogether overcome them. Consider the last scene in the greenwood near Milan. Since the end of the second act, Proteus has earned our gathering detestation. He has been successively false to Julia, to Valentine, to the duke, to Thurio. The wanton attempt to force the unprotected girl who has repelled his dishonourable advances puts a climax on his iniquities. No audience can help wanting to see him punished; he must needs be wholly unsympathetic. And suddenly the natural development of the situation stops. The uplifted hand of poetic justice fails to strike. Within the space of not more than sixty lines, Proteus is converted by Valentine's reproaches; Valentine not merely forgives him, but makes the impossible offer to resign to him his own claim on Silvia's affections; and apparently the gift is only averted by the revelation of Julia and the discovery by Proteus that after all there is nothing in Silvia's face that he cannot spy more fresh in that of Julia. One recognizes that tragicomedy must have its reconciliation; but surely this is a reconciliation, in its almost cynical brevity and lack of psychology, to leave one gasping. Yet I do not know that it is really more amazing than the reconciliation of *Much Ado About Nothing*, in which the despicable Claudio is first offered a cousin in substitution for Hero, and finally recovers the very bride whom his disloyal acceptance of an incredible slander has well-nigh done to death; or than the reconciliation of *Measure for Measure*, in which the lechery and the hypocrisy of Angelo are rewarded with the hand of the much-wronged Mariana. Intent, as it would seem, on putting humanity into the puppets of romance, Shakespeare failed to observe that, as one result of the process, the conclusions of romance would cease to convince.

The sentimental bankruptcy, then, of *The Two Gentlemen of Verona*, although doubtless a more practised hand might have palliated it, is not by itself an infallible sign of an early play. But there are other signs to be noted. One is to be found in the abuse of verbal ingenuities. Shakespeare never quite lost his taste for these, but in *The Two Gentlemen of Verona* they are at once excessive in number, and of a puerility which may be exampled by the astounding puns upon 'ships' and 'sheep,' 'laced muttons' and 'lost muttons,' the 'tide' and the 'tied,' and other gems of speech which bedeck the conversation of the pages, to whom, after the fashion of Lyly's recently published comedies, the play looks for its comic relief. There is another in the lack of adroitness which allows the characters, as in *The Comedy of Errors*, and even, a little later, in *A Midsummer Night's Dream*, to fall into pairs. A Proteus and a Valentine, a Julia and a Silvia, a Launce and a Speed, do not provide a grouping of sufficiently varied interest. And there is a third in the constant appearance of motives which recur in later plays, with the suggestion that Shakespeare regarded the introduction of them into *The Two Gentlemen of Verona* as having been of the nature of a tentative experiment, that did not disqualify him from making further use of their tested capabilities when designing more mature and considered work. I do not of course lay stress on the fact that Julia, like Portia, and Rosalind, and Viola, and Imogen, sets forth upon her audacious adventure in—

> Such weeds
> As may beseem some well-reputed page,

for that indeed is common to the whole world of Elizabethan drama; and when it is realized that the women's parts were played by boys, the frequency of the device explains itself. But one may remark the similarity between the discourse of Julia with Lucetta over her lovers and that of Portia with Nerrissa in *The Merchant of Venice*. Launce reappears, hardly bettered, as the Launcelot of the same play. Romeo uses the ladder of ropes, just as Valentine designed to do, and harps upon the ill word 'banished,' just as Valentine did; while the forest near Milan, where they swore 'by the bare scalp of Robin Hood's fat friar,' cannot but recall that forest of Arden where another band of outlaws would 'fleet the time carelessly as they did in the golden world' in *As You Like It*. Apart alike from what is merely anticipatory and what is merely colourless in the play stands the figure of Sir Eglamour, the knight vowed to chastity, and the chivalrous aider of distressed women. He is slightly sketched enough, but is romantic in a sense in which Shakespeare does not normally read romance. I do not recognize a character of quite the same type in any later play.

After all, *The Two Gentlemen of Verona* is interesting, not so much for its strictly dramatic content as for what it implies, for the evidence it affords of what Shakespeare was preoccupied with when he wrote it. One is commonly told that Shakespeare is the most objective of writers, and that is of course true in the sense that, beyond most other men, he had the gift of dispassionate observation and the power of projecting himself into all kinds of personalities most alien to his own. But I will never admit it to be true if by it is meant that he is not also subjective, that no reflex of his own personality is to be found among the creatures of his fashioning, and no shadow there of the experiences and ambitions which swayed and moulded the life of their creator. After all, even the most objective of writers cannot build cast-iron doors across the chambers and galleries of his brain. A poet will write of what interests him, whether within or without; nor is there any reason to suppose that Shakespeare was less interested in himself than in other people. Personally I find it impossible to read *The Two Gentlemen of Verona* except in the light of the *Sonnets*, some of which at least must be almost exactly contemporary with the play, and which portray clearly enough the temper of mind in which Shakespeare came to its composition. I do not claim to have any special key to the mysteries of the *Sonnets*. I do not know to whom or of whom they were written, or how far they are an actual record and how far an imaginative transcript of the facts that underlie them. I only know that there is heart's blood in them, and that to treat their passion as a mere literary exercise is to betray a more than average insensibility to the nature of poetic utterance. That, when no longer quite a young man, Shakespeare fell seriously into love; that love brought him little satisfaction and much disturbance in other relations of life, especially in that of friendship; that he came away with an experience behind him and the bitter taste of disillusion in his mouth; I do not see that you can infer much less than this, and I do not see that you would know much more, if you could add the lady's name and the worldly rank of the man for whom it pleased her to throw over a poet. One can hardly be surprised, however, that the first play written by Shakespeare after so disconcerting an adventure should bear some traces of his discomfiture. In *The Two Gentlemen of Verona* it is clear that he has been given furiously to think about love. Love, indeed, viewed professedly in the abstract, but pursued with a commentary not wholly free from personal bias, is the central theme of the play, the staple of conversation not only for the principal personages, who are lovers, but also for their apes and echoes, and occasionally shrewd critics, the page-boys. And if the maxims and reflections which the contemplation of love inspires at every turn and corner of the dialogue are not wholly free from a suspicion of commonplace, perhaps that is precisely because they are of the class which is suggested afresh to men in every generation by the common yet eternally new experience. Ordinarily, indeed, the references to love in *The Two Gentlemen of Verona* reproduce pretty faithfully the familiar range of ideas and even the traditional phrases of Elizabethan sonnetting. There is the same insistence upon the inevitable and arbitrary character of the passion, the same tendency to make—

> A couplement of proud compare
> With sun and moon, with earth and sea's rich gems,
> With April's first-born flowers and all things rare,
> That heaven's air in this huge rondure hems;

the same extravagance of hyperbole, as when Valentine fears for his mistress—

> Lest the base earth
> Should from her vesture chance to steal a kiss,
> And, of so great a favour growing proud,
> Disdain to root the summer-swelling flower,
> And make rough winter everlastingly.

As a rule you will not take it all too seriously. But from time to time the mask of lightness is withdrawn and a haggard face looks out. A profoundly convinced, even bitter, personal note sounds through. To this Shakespeare, Love has in reality proved a mighty lord; he has actually known what hell it is—

> To be in love, where scorn is bought with groans;
> Coy looks with heart-sore sighs; one fading moment's mirth
> With twenty watchful, weary, tedious nights.
> If haply won, perhaps a hapless gain;
> If lost, why then a grievous labour won;
> However, but a folly bought with wit,
> Or else a wit by folly vanquished.

Above all, one may fairly recognize in Proteus, Proteus the passionate and the perjured, not perhaps a 'portrait' of the false friend and supplanting lover, whoever he may be, of the *Sonnets*, but at least an image which would not have been drawn, or at any rate not in such deeply bitten lines, had not the friend of the *Sonnets* given Shakespeare cause to drink his potions of siren tears.

And now it may be noted that the presence of this personal element in the play gives a peculiar emphasis to that romantic unreality in the ending which has already been considered. It is because

Shakespeare knew his Proteus, and knowing him, painted him as he was, without taking the trouble to keep him within the lines of the romantic convention, that the purely conventional and unconvincing repentance and forgiveness which await him in the Milanese forest appear to us things to be so much resented. Had he been a mere puppet, we should not have grudged him a puppet's reward. But the man is more than the poet; and it were ungrateful to complain that Shakespeare has introduced a bit of Shakespeare's humanity into *The Two Gentlemen of Verona*, even at the cost of destroying the flawless perfection of a work of art.

LOVE'S LABOUR'S LOST

LITTLE in Shakespeare is more tedious than certain parts of *Love's Labour's Lost*. Among the verbal antics of 'the pedant, the braggart, the hedge-priest, the fool and the boy,' which form the background of the play, if you occasionally stumble upon a recognizable jest, you more often wander, a disconcerted alien, through impenetrable memorials of vanished humour. Even in the light-hearted scenes in which the skirmishing girls of France uphold the battle of sex against their flouted Navarrese lovers, although the spirit of mirth is undeniably there, the actual savour of mirth has not seldom, for a modern reader, evaporated from the dialogue. One is sometimes tempted to hold that a difference in the sense of humour is the last barrier between age and age, which even the most highly-trained historic consciousness never quite succeeds in overleaping. But the judgment will bear a yet further refinement. Humour has its roots after all in elements of the strange composition of man which are constant enough; his vanity, his mutability, his serious preoccupation with trifles, from shells and feathers to laces and scarves, his ineradicable tendency to pass himself off on himself and on others as that which he is not. These things remain, and, age by age, the remorseless comic spirit makes its game of them. But, by their very nature, their manifestations, or at least their urban manifestations, with which comedy has most to do, are transitory. Follies of speech, follies of dress, fantasies of youth, fantasies of lovers in love with love; they come and go, lighter than a puff-ball, and as they pass into oblivion, the wit and irony of the pursuing humourist pass too. 'A jest's prosperity lies in the ear of him that hears it.' You must laboriously exhume, with the aid of the scholiast, what split the sides of Aristophanes and his audiences; and even the London of Elizabeth, or, for the matter of that, the London of Victoria, was alive to absurdities which, for the twentieth century, belong to the region of archæology. When one is dealing with humour in its dramatic expressions, there is yet another factor to be borne in mind. Fashion is largely an affair of externalities, and in mocking these the dramatist can always count upon the co-operation of the mime. But the gestures and the intonations of the mime die upon the stage where they were born, and the more faithful a comedy is in its ironical representation of contemporary fine manners and other modes of affectation, the less of it survives upon the printed page. Yet when all allowances have been made, alike for the efflux of time and for the withdrawal of the personality of the mime, the honest chronicler is still obliged to admit the existence of a simple and primitive quality in the humour which reigned at the court of Gloriana, a willingness to be tickled by certain verbal quips and jingles and by certain personal retorts more direct than epigrammatic, at which a later and perhaps more sophisticated taste declines to be arrided. A social organization may fairly be set down as rudimentary in which it moves laughter that a gentleman should enquire 'What time a' day?' and a lady should find no better reply than, 'The hour that fools should ask.' Such repartee passes current still, but not above the fourth form. 'Good wits will be jangling,' says the Princess; and one can only recall the words in which Ophelia describes Hamlet's disordered reason—

Like sweet bells jangled, out of tune and harsh.

Taken as a whole the plays of Shakespeare perhaps suffer less from the remoteness of the social manners they imply than those of many other men; certainly less than those comedies, such as *Epicoene*, in which Ben Jonson deliberately strove to fix and transfix the flying humours of the town. Shakespeare, indeed, is not primarily a satirist, and when he does turn to satire, he is apt to find his material not so much in urban manners and the vagaries of the court, with their unstable equilibrium, as among those more conservative elements of society whose habits of life and habits of thought time does not so readily devour. That is why he has, in the words of a great modern humourist, a laugh 'broad as ten thousand beeves at pasture'; for a Mistress Quickly, a Dogberry, a Justice Shallow, live still, long after an Armado or a Parolles has become alms for oblivion. The

60

large proportion of dead matter in *Love's Labour's Lost* has led some to suppose it the first and not wholly successful essay of Shakespeare's prentice hand. It is an early play, of course, and no doubt Shakespeare's personal sense of humour ripened and mellowed after he had written it. But I should be disposed to ascribe what might be called, in the special sense suggested here, the 'urbanity' of its temper to the direct influence of the distinctly urban and courtly comedies of Lyly, several of which were printed when the performances by the singing school of St Paul's came to an end in the early 'nineties. Ultimately the group of grotesques who make a background to *Love's Labour's Lost*, and especially the Pedant and the Braggart or *Miles Gloriosus*, owe their derivation to the standing types of Italian comedy, which itself reaches back to the conventions of the Latin stage. But the immediate resemblance of Armado and Moth to the Sir Thopas and Epiton of Lyly's *Endimion* has often been observed; and Lyly's rendering of the airs and graces of the court doubtless served Shakespeare as a literary model for much of the intolerable smart talk dear alike to his pages and to their masters and mistresses.

Shakespeare's debt, such as it is, to Lyly does not, however, prevent him from aiming the shafts of his wit, in *Love's Labour's Lost*, at certain literary tendencies of which Lyly stood then, and stands now, as the obvious representative. I do not, of course, mean that either Armado or Holofernes is to be supposed, in the strictest sense, to parley euphuism. Much learned ink has been spilt in analysing the technical features of the prose of *Euphues* and in demonstrating that Shakespeare does not directly reproduce them in the play. It is, no doubt, so. The vogue of a mannerism of style is no less fleeting than that of the cut of a doublet, and it is the *Arcadia* of 1590 rather than the *Euphues* of 1579 that Armado burlesques, when he rakes together his double-barrelled epithets, or periphrases of 'the posteriors of the day, which the rude multitude call the afternoon.' For Holofernes, on the other hand, one need hardly trouble to seek an exemplar, since there is no age of literary history in which the pedants have not 'been at a great feast of languages and stolen the scraps.' Yet it remains true that the inflation of Armado and the pedantry of Holofernes only represent the extravagances of that effort after the deliberate cultivation of language in which Lyly was certainly, for the Elizabethans, an honourable pioneer. Apart from its extravagances, this effort, with its wholesome determination to use words, not as dead counters, but as living organisms, comes near to the secrets of style. Like all forms of literature in which style is made a conscious object of pursuit, it has its subtler dangers in the possibilities of an elaboration of phrase out of all proportion to the exposition of matter which the phrase is intended to adorn. That the sonnetteers, to whom in the main Lyly's task of cultivating style passed, were

not always careful that the thing said should be
equal to the way of saying it, must be admitted;
and this finer weakness of what in the broader
sense is to be called euphuism, as well as its more
obvious liabilities to parody, is touched upon in
Love's Labour's Lost, when Berowne declares his
disillusion with—

> Taffeta phrases, silken terms precise,
>   Three-piled hyperboles, spruce affectation,
> Figures pedantical;

and announces his intention to woo thereafter—

> In russet yeas, and honest kersey noes.

That Shakespeare himself, especially in his son-
netteering days, was not wholly in a position to
throw stones at the abusers of taffeta phrases
without danger to his own habitation, does not
disallow his criticism; for it has always been held
an amiable quality of your true humourist to show
some observance of courtesy to the follies at which
he tilts.

But with Berowne we pass from the background of the play to its main action, and here,
with an exception, as I have noted, for some of the
small change of sexual debate, the comedy rings
sound enough and is by no means tedious. The
king and his book-men, withdrawn from the world
into a philosophic austerity that is destined to
lower its colours at the first summons from a troop
of petticoats without, furnish ideal stuff for the
comic spirit, which is always merciless to such
schemes of life as fail to take into account the

working of the primitive instincts. One may observe the resemblance between the motive and that of the vanquished rebels against love in *Much Ado About Nothing*, a resemblance which has led to the not unreasonable conjecture that an early version of the later play may have been the vanished *Love's Labour's Won*. The distinction between 'Lost' and 'Won,' indeed, very exactly indicates the divergence, in the issue, between the two love-stories. Amongst the recluses of Navarre, Berowne, the mocker, wears his rue with a difference. He belongs to the Mercutio type of character, in which some have found a special reflection of at least one aspect of Shakespeare's own personality. Just as Mercutio goes to his death with a humourous sense of the absurdity of the cause for which he would not dream of hesitating to fight, so, though naturally he has less at stake, Berowne enters into the affectation of his fellows with the very clearest consciousness of the unreality of his inhuman undertaking. The King's first act, after the bond is signed, is to waive the strict letter of it, 'on mere necessity,' in order to permit of the reception of the embassy from France; and Berowne comments—

Necessity will make us all forsworn
Three thousand times within this three years' space;
For every man with his affects is born,
Not by might mastered, but by special grace.

Well, the bond does not last long, when the Princess and Rosaline and Katherine and Maria come upon

64

the scene. The students quickly change to sonnetteers, and it is diverting enough when each in turn discovers the apostasy of the others, and confesses his own. And after all, in spite of his common sense, Berowne no more escapes the snares of the comic spirit than the rest of them. He may not have thought himself secure from the ordinary frailties of human nature, but somehow he certainly had, like Benedick, thought himself secure from the one big misadventure of falling in love. And yet, in ten minutes, he is the hopeless captive of Rosaline's bow and spear—

> And I, forsooth, in love! I, that have been love's whip,
> A very beadle to a humorous sigh,
> A critic, nay, a night-watch constable,
> A domineering pedant o'er the boy,
> Than whom no mortal so magnificent!
> This wimpled, whining, purblind, wayward boy,
> This senior-junior, giant-dwarf, Dan Cupid,
> Regent of love-rhymes, lord of folded arms,
> The anointed sovereign of sighs and groans,
> Liege of all loiterers and malcontents,
> Dread prince of plackets, king of codpieces,
> Sole imperator and great general
> Of trotting 'paritors—O, my little heart!—
> And I to be a corporal of his field,
> And wear his colours like a tumbler's hoop!

But the comic spirit has not finished his sport with the lords of Navarre when he has set them to writing sonnets. Love, once gravely rejected, is now as gravely pronounced supreme—

> For valour, is not Love a Hercules,
> Still climbing trees in the Hesperides,

Subtle as Sphinx, as sweet and musical
As bright Apollo's lute, strung with his hair?
And when Love speaks, the voice of all the gods
Make heaven drowsy with the harmony.

The lyric touch recalls Marlowe and his choice
glorification of Hero—

Hero the fair,
Whom young Apollo courted for her hair.

And yet after all it is but one affectation exchanged
for another; the affectation of sentiment set at
nought for the affectation of exaggerated sentiment. The fantastics have learnt to woo, but they
have not yet learnt to win. Their heads are still in
the air and their feet tread no solid earth. They
blunder on, with high-flown rhymes and sought-
out compliments, which, as Berowne, still a shade
more acute than his fellows, comes to realize, are
but 'as bombast and as lining to the time,' and
deliver them over an easy booty to 'the tongues of
mocking wenches.' At the very first encounter,
they are 'all dry-beaten with pure scoff.' And
suddenly, with the announcement of the death of
the Princess' father, the merriment of the comedy
turns to seriousness, just as does that of *Much Ado
About Nothing* in the immortal scene in which the
passionate Beatrice bids Benedick to 'Kill Claudio!'
The crestfallen lovers learn that the condition of
success in love is to come into touch with life; and
for Berowne the mocker is set the special task
to spend a twelvemonth in a hospital, and there—

With all the fierce endeavour of his wit
To enforce the pained impotent to smile.

One must not resent the intrusion of this deeper note; for Thalia is at heart the most serious of the Muses, and if she play the game imposed upon her to the end, she is surely entitled, for epilogue, to doff the grimacing mask, and honestly to speak out her own moral.

ROMEO and JULIET

THE legend of immortal lovers was almost closed when Shakespeare wrote his *Romeo and Juliet*. From the fable and the history of antiquity had come Paris and Helen, Troilus and Cressida, Hero and Leander, Antony and Cleopatra; from the fable and the history of the middle ages, Tristan and Iseult, Lancelot and Guinevere, Paolo and Francesca, Abelard and Heloise, 'that learned nun,' and, to our modern imagination at least, Sigurd and Brynhild and Aucassin and Nicolette. In the dawn of the Renascence, Petrarch had set his Laura there and Dante his Beatrice. Into that goodly company Romeo and Juliet pass as by right divine; and to-day, with the possible exception of Faust and Marguerite, they are still the latest comers. Richard and Lucy Feverel, Pelléas and Mélisande, are only privileged to linger near the gates; for the process of literary even more than of ecclesiastical canonization is strict in its requirement of the hundred years' probationary interval.

Immortal lovers belong to the passionate romantic tradition, and assuredly the romantic note is clear enough in Shakespeare's play. The characteristic tragedy of his ardent youth—for even if he is responsible for *Titus Andronicus*, you will not call that characteristic—it accepts a secular theme, and stands apart from the great group of tragedies which he wrote ten years later, with their obstinate personal questionings and probings into the mystery of life. It is a tragedy of lyric emotion, not a tragedy of philosophic insight. The convention of star-crossed lovers is familiar to all romance; and what *Romeo and Juliet* claims to do is only to give this convention yet another new setting. In a different sense, of course, it is personal enough. Like all the plays of this period, it reflects something of that disturbance in Shakespeare's own emotional life, of which the more direct, although far from clear, record is in the *Sonnets*. Shakespeare has been, at the age of thirty or thereabouts, in love, and it has proved a rather serious matter. He has come through the fire and is more or less whole again, no doubt; but he still remains much preoccupied with his puzzling and not altogether satisfactory adventure. Both *A Midsummer Night's Dream* and *Romeo and Juliet* are attempts on the part of a reflective and youngish man to state life in terms of the force by which he has been nearly tripped up and is still obsessed. That the statement is a somewhat conventional one may perhaps be explained by the fact that many other youngish poets have shared the experiences by which it is prompted. Of course, the two plays differ entirely in their way of putting things. In *A Midsummer Night's Dream* the problem is seen from the comic point of view. Life as the sport of love is a bewildering fantasy, a game of hide and seek. But

A Midsummer Night's Dream is an after-thought, written while the poignancy of the experience faded, and the sense of humour asserted itself. Certain elements of it seem like a deliberate travesty of *Romeo and Juliet*. The comic point of view is not wholly absent from the tragic and probably earlier play. It is embodied in the irony and the audacious license of Mercutio's talk. Love to Mercutio, as to the author of *A Midsummer Night's Dream*, is one of—

> The children of an idle brain,
> Begot of nothing but vain fantasy,
> Which is as thin of substance as the air.

But it must be observed that the love at which Mercutio tilts is less the romantic passion which is the subject of the play, than the mere shadow and foil of that passion, the boyish fancy which occupies the unawakened heart before the true love comes. Rosaline must endure Mercutio's jesting, but Juliet is beyond its reach, and as the plot thickens, the jesting itself passes into tragedy, and Mercutio's voice is heard no more. Essentially the temper of *Romeo and Juliet* is a high and serious one. Love comes into life like a sword, touching here a man and there a woman, and scorching them with a terrible flame. The boy and girl lovers are doomed souls from the beginning. They are raised into the highest heaven, merely that an envious fate may pluck them down again. Love is a mighty power, but destiny is mightier still, and cruel. And the conflict of these Titanic forces, crushing the young lives between them, is the issue of the tragedy.

The pity and the terror of it are heightened by the rapidity of the action and by the presaging gloom which, in true Shakespearean fashion, hangs about its earlier moments. The oncoming of love is a sudden splendour, without help and without preparation. *Ecce deus fortior me, qui veniens dominabitur mihi.* Romeo has been an amorist, posing before the mirror of his own self-consciousness, with tears and sighs and early morning walks and an affectation of solitude and the humorous night. He was for the numbers that Petrarch flowed in, has rhymed 'love' and 'dove,' and nick-named Cupid with paradox and artful phrase. All this has meant nothing; it has been but fantasy, born of leisure and the romantic imagination. With the first sight of Juliet all this vanishes. The pale hard-hearted wench Rosaline becomes as though she were not. Romeo remains a poet still, with a turn for the romantic embroidery of his emotions which contrasts with the direct simplicity of Juliet's self-abandonment. But the quality of his poetry has changed; it has put off empty conceits, and at once rings out sincere in the magnificent and characteristically Elizabethan hyperbole of—

O, she doth teach the torches to burn bright,

and in that exquisite image, remembered from a Stratford morning—

So shows a snowy dove trooping with crows,
As yonder lady o'er her fellows shows.

71

To borrow a pregnant distinction of Coleridge's, Romeo has passed from the sphere of fancy to the sphere of imagination.

But the shadow of the end is already upon it all. Even as he puts on his mask to enter Capulet's house, Romeo is struck with a grim foreboding—

> My mind misgives
> Some consequence, yet hanging in the stars,
> Shall bitterly begin his fearful date
> With this night's revels, and expire the term
> Of a despised life closed in my breast
> By some vile forfeit of untimely death.

Even during the first rapture of answering love, the sinister anticipation finds its echo in Juliet's breast—

> I have no joy of this contract to-night;
> It is too rash, too unadvised, too sudden,
> Too like the lightning, which doth cease to be,
> Ere one can say 'It lightens.'

How swiftly it all passes! There is one brief and memorable dialogue in the pauses of the dance, darkened almost immediately by the thought of the feud between the houses; one cool night of pomegranates and the moon and the soft Italian air. And then the blow falls with the death of Tybalt, and Juliet and her Romeo become the shuttlecocks of fate, which, as ever, finds battledores ready to hand in meaningless accident and human stupidity. The insolence of a hot-headed boy, the ambition of worldly parents, the blundering of a messenger, the tremors of an ancient friar; such are the instruments which bring about the catastrophe. But they are only the instruments. For Shakespeare, at this moment of his thought, things could not have ended otherwise. As he sees love, in the distorted glass of his own unlucky experience, it is of its essence that it should issue tragically. As usual, he is his own best commentator, and a passage in *A Midsummer Night's Dream* sums up the whole temper of *Romeo and Juliet*. It stands as an edict in destiny, Lysander tells you, that—

> The course of true love never did run smooth.

Love is magnificent, the very transformation of the soul; but something perverse and devastating always clings to it—

> Making it momentany as a sound,
> Swift as a shadow, short as any dream,
> Brief as the lightning in the collied night,
> That, in a spleen, unfolds both heaven and earth,
> And ere a man hath power to say 'Behold!'
> The jaws of darkness do devour it up.
> So quick bright things come to confusion.

That is the tragedy of youth, with its insatiable thirst for happiness and its easy and overwhelming discouragement—

> So quick bright things come to confusion.

The intensity of such a tragedy as *Romeo and Juliet* is the result of concentration, and every element in the play, which does not directly bring the two lovers and their fate before the audience, none the less derives its meaning from its relation to the central theme. I have already pointed out

73

how Romeo's earlier fancy for Rosaline serves as a foil for the real passion which was lying in wait for him, and how Mercutio voices the comic aspect of love in contrast to that tragic aspect which is here the dominant inspiration of the poet. Most of the other subordinate characters are designed to add to the significance of the background. They stand for readings of love different from that of the idealist. To Paris, as to Romeo himself in his unregenerate days, it is a sentimental exercise; to Juliet's parents, part of the customary business of a well-ordered and honourable family life; to the nurse, a gross affair of the physical senses. The dramatic function of the friar is perhaps a little more difficult to formulate. He has sometimes been taken as less an actor in the tragedy than its spectator and critic; a kind of chorus, whose business it is to fit it with a moral; and this is found in the speech in which he advises Romeo to 'love moderately,' because—

These violent delights have violent ends.

Of such a theory it can only be said that, if it correctly expounds the moral of the play, this is a singularly futile one, since it must be obvious that both the love and the love's disaster are presented as things entirely beyond the power of their puppets to cause or cure by any deliberate act or abstention of their own. There is, of course, no reason whatever why there should be a moral at all. *Romeo and Juliet* is a tragedy, not a comedy; and the burden of a tragedy is always an emotion, not an idea. So far as it has ethics, they are implied, and do not call for deliberate statement. Moreover, the friar is by no means sufficiently detached from the action to be capable of being regarded as a mere chorus. It is, after all, the failure of his scheme which leads directly to the final woes. I take it that he is not so made a main agent without intention, and that the object is to increase the spectator's sense of an irresistible destiny warring against the lovers. The wisdom of age is no more able than the ardour of youth to withstand the courses of the stars.

Intense tragedy often ends upon a softened note. This is a matter of dramatic psychology. The overwrought nerves demand the cadence. One recalls the benison of the goddess at the end of the *Hippolytus*, and the exquisite close of the *Samson Agonistes*—

> Nothing is here for tears, nothing to wail
> Or knock the breast; no weakness, no contempt,
> Dispraise or blame; nothing but well and fair,
> And what may quiet us in a death so noble.

Similarly *Romeo and Juliet* finishes upon 'a glooming peace.' All is not matter for sorrow. There is an obvious gain to set against the loss in the reconciliation of the houses over the grave of the 'poor sacrifices of their enmity.' And also, surely, there is the consciousness that the splendour of love in life is not wholly obliterated, even when life and love are blotted out together. We have seen Romeo turned from a boy into a man by love,

75

and the white-souled Juliet into a breathing, passionate, daring woman. The exaltation of this endures, so that after all it would seem as if it were love and not destiny that is the indomitable force. Here again, one can best interpret Shakespeare by himself, by one of the noblest and most monumental of the *Sonnets*—

Love's not Time's fool, though rosy lips and cheeks
Within his bending sickle's compass come;
Love alters not with his brief hours and weeks,
But bears it out even to the edge of doom.

Love's not Time's fool! Some such sense of the ultimate value of ideal love survives the sense of the apparent ruin of ideal love in *Romeo and Juliet*.

A MIDSUMMER NIGHT'S DREAM

SHAKESPEARE'S conception of the fairy
world is taken, partly from romance, partly
from beliefs of the folk which were already
in his day beginning to pass into the shadowy
region of old wives' tales. Oberon and his eastern
realm are to be found in *Huon of Bordeaux*; and
every English country-side knew of the little green
dwarfs who dwelt in the earth-knolls and danced
by night in the fairy rings, and of Robin Good-
fellow, the tricksy house spirit, who performed
domestic labours for cleanly maidens, and played
malicious pranks upon slatterns or upon such as
neglected the simple observances which he regarded as his due. Shakespeare's own fairies,
which have impressed themselves upon the imagination of the world after Shakespeare, differ
both from the fairies of romance and the fairies of
tradition in the important feature of their infinitesi-
mal size. He has turned them from merely small
men and women into elemental spirits, in touch
with all the dainty and delicate things of earth and
air, capable of lighting torches at the glow-worm's
eyes and warring with rere-mice for their leathern
wings. He has further, in *A Midsummer Night's
Dream*, introduced a classical touch by borrowing
the name Titania for the fairy queen from Ovid.
Ovid uses it as an epithet of Diana, 'the Titan-

born'; and the identification of Diana with the leader of the fairy rout is one that is familiar to mediæval writers on the supernatural.

On *a priori* grounds, one might perhaps have expected that an unacademic writer, coming straight from the heart of Warwickshire, would have kept closer to the lines of the old folk beliefs about the 'good people,' and would even have shared in the habits of thought and imagination from which those beliefs took their rise. It is certainly not so with Shakespeare, who, for good or for evil, is a thorough child of the Renascence, and exhibits not only the Renascence love of quaint lore plundered from every quarter, but also the Renascence positive spirit, for which such lore has little meaning otherwise than as material for deliberate poetic craft. He takes his superstitions from learned and literary sources, just as he takes his natural history from the bestiaries, no less freely than from his own observation. Even when his material is of English origin, it is not always clear whether he has drawn it from reminiscences of his own Warwickshire boyhood or from some popular book, such as Reginald Scot's *Discovery of Witchcraft* or Harsnet's *Declaration of Popish Impostures*. It must not be assumed, therefore, that Shakespeare's use of the supernatural for dramatic purposes implies a belief in its actual and objective existence. Where it is not merely imposed upon him by his historical sources, it seems to serve one of two ends. Either it attunes the minds of the audience to a tragic or ironical issue, as for example in the terrible dreams of Richard Crookback before Bosworth Field; or it is a symbol, introduced by the poet as a recognition of a mystery, an unexplained element in the course of human affairs upon earth. This is its really important function in some of the greatest plays. It is Shakespeare's confession of ignorance, of the fact that in his observation of life he has come just there upon something which baffles analysis, something which is, but which cannot be quite accounted for. Thus in *Macbeth* the witches symbolize the double mystery of temptation and retribution; in *The Tempest* the magic arts of Prospero and the spiritual forces which are at his beck and call symbolize the mystery of an overruling Providence, and perhaps at the same time something of the mystery of the creative poetic imagination. The agency of the fairies in *A Midsummer Night's Dream* is capable of a similar explanation.

Of course the play is primarily a court revel. It was doubtless written for a wedding, and possibly for a wedding at which Elizabeth was present. It has the profusion of dance and song, the picturesque staging and pretty costumes, the sprinkling of courtly compliment, the piquant contrast of poetry and clowning, which were the delight of the nobles and maids of honour who assembled at Gloriana's palace of Greenwich. But at the same time it is a true comedy, a deliberate picture of life

79

as life reveals itself to the shrewd insight of the comic spirit. The theme is love—an obvious theme for a wedding play, even if it were not the one about which Shakespeare's imagination was principally exercised at the moment. He had written *The Two Gentlemen of Verona*, and had either written or was on the point of writing *Romeo and Juliet*, with its tragic burden of two lives ruined and at the same time ennobled by love. Even in *Romeo and Juliet* the comic as well as the tragic view of love is present. It is incarnate in the critical wit of Mercutio. But in *A Midsummer Night's Dream* it has undisputed sway. We have no longer to do with Dante's 'lord of terrible aspect,' but rather with the roguish little Cupid of Ovid, the irresponsible child-god, with his blinded eyes and his erring arrows. 'Hast been in love?' says the young shepherd to the old one in *As You Like It*, then—

> How many actions most ridiculous
> Hast thou been drawn to by thy fantasy?

Love, as interpreted by the comic spirit, is a certain fine lunacy in the brain of youth; not an integral part of life, but a disturbing element in it. The lover is a being of strange caprices and strange infidelities, beyond the control of reason, and swayed with every gust of passion. He is at odds for the time with all the established order of things, a rebel against the authority of parents, a rebel against friendship, a rebel against his own vows. This is love as it figures in comedy, and in the presentation and analysis of this lies the point of the play.

Bearing then in mind this central idea of the lawlessness and the laughableness of love, one may observe how carefully, for all the apparent whimsicality of structure, it is kept to the front in the working out of the plot. As is generally the case in Shakespeare's comedies, this is composed of several stories, which are woven together with remarkable ingenuity. You have the story of Theseus' wedding, the story of the Athenian lovers, the story of the quarrel of Oberon and Titania, the story of the handicraftsmen's play, and finally the story or interlude of Pyramus and Thisbe. It is the first of these which serves as the link that holds all the rest together; for it is at Theseus' wedding that Hermia's fate is to be decided; it is to celebrate this that the fairies have come from the farthest steppe of India, and it is for this that Bottom and his fellows are painfully conning their interlude. But the most important story from the point of view of the comic idea, and the one to which most space is devoted, is that of the Athenian lovers. As Ten Brink has pointed out in his excellent study of the play, the motive of this story is varied from that of Chaucer's *Knightës Tale*. In the *Knightës Tale* the friendship of Palamon and Arcite is broken by their common love for Emilia. This corresponds very closely to the relation of Proteus and Valentine in *The Two Gentlemen of Verona*. But both in *The Two Gentle-*

men of Verona and in *A Midsummer Night's Dream*
Shakespeare has complicated the situation by introducing a second woman, and in *A Midsummer
Night's Dream* he has still further modified it by
making the broken friendship that of the women,
not that of the men. In this friendship broken by
love we get, then, one illustration of the central
idea. But there are others in the story. There is
Hermia's defiance of her father and of Athenian
law for the sake of Lysander; and above all there
is the extraordinary inconstancy which both
Lysander and Demetrius display in the bestowal
of their affections. Demetrius has deserted Helena
for Hermia before the play begins; and in the
course of the night in the wood, Lysander goes
over to Helena and back to Hermia, and Demetrius in his turn goes back to Helena without any
apparent rhyme or reason. Surely the central idea
of the play is carried to a point that is almost farcical.
At the crisis of the play, when the cross-purposes
are at their maddest, one can only re-echo Puck's
criticism—

Lord, what fools these mortals be!

Shakespeare does not, on this occasion, look to
psychology to body forth his meaning. In *Romeo
and Juliet*, he shows us the difference which love
makes, in the actual characters of the lovers as they
blossom out before us. But it is a commonplace
that the lovers of *A Midsummer Night's Dream* are
faintly sketched and barely differentiated. Helena
is tall and fair and timid: Hermia is little and dark

and shrewish. Demetrius is crabbed and Lysander is languid. It is difficult to say much more. They are but the abstract Hes and Shes of the conventional love-story. But this want of characterization is of little importance, because symbolism comes in to take the place of psychology. The transferences of affection which form the principal revolutions of the story are represented as due to supernatural agency, to the somewhat randomly exercised power of the fairies. Moreover, taking perhaps a hint from Lyly, Shakespeare invites us to consider the whole thing as a dream. Here is the significance of the title. It is life seen through a glass darkly; such a vision of life as a man might have on Midsummer Night, the one season of the year around which Elizabethan superstition gathered most closely, when herbs were believed to have their especial virtues, and strange beings to be abroad. And yet it is not all a dream, or, if a dream, it is one which passes very easily into actuality. For these inconstancies, of which Oberon's love in idleness is the cause, are after all not really different in kind from the initial inconstancy of Demetrius to Helena, for which no such reason is proposed. And again, when Demetrius is by magic restored to his first love, the effects of this continue on into the waking life as a quite natural thing which provokes no amazement. So that in fact, as far as the story of the lovers is concerned, the introduction of the supernatural element does not bring about anything

83

which would have been impossible or improbable without it. The magical love in idleness really does nothing more than represent symbolically the familiar workings of actual love in idleness in the human heart. Boys in love change their minds just so, or almost just so, without any whisper of the fairies to guide them. Romeo left his Rosaline quite as suddenly as Lysander left his Hermia. Here, then, is the function of the supernatural in *A Midsummer Night's Dream*. The mystery, so to call it, the inexplicability which is bound up with the central idea of the play, is the existence of that freakish irresponsible element of human nature out of which, to the eye of the comic spirit, the ethical and emotional vagaries of lovers take their rise. And that this element does exist is recognized and emphasized by Shakespeare in his usual way, when he takes the workings of it in the story and explains them symbolically as due to the interference of fairy agency.

Now, in humanity the disturbing element of love in idleness is generally only a passing fever. There is a period of *Sturm und Drang*, and then the man or woman begins to take life seriously, and is ready to submit to its discipline and to accept its reasonable responsibilities. And so by the side of Lysander and Demetrius we have the grave figure of the Athenian duke, Theseus. Theseus has had his wayward youth; he has 'played with light loves in the portal,' with Perigenia and Aegles and the rest; ay, and in the glimmering night even with Queen Titania herself. Moreover, in his passion for Hippolyta he has approached her through deeds of violence; he has 'won her love, doing her injuries.' But now, like the Henry the Fifth of whom he is a prototype, he has put away childish things; he stands forth as the serene law-abiding king, no less than the still loving and tender husband. Thus the story of Theseus' wedding not only, as has been said, serves to hold the plot together, but also contributes its share to the illustration of the central idea.

When we turn to the fairies, we find that what enters into human life only as a transitory disturbing element, is in them the normal law of their being. They are irresponsible creatures throughout, eternal children. They belong to the winds and the clouds and the flowers, to all in nature that is beautiful and gracious and fleeting; but of the characteristics by which man differs from these, the sense of law and the instinct of self-control, they show no trace. Puck, the fairy jester, is a buffoon of spirits, whose sport it is to bring perplexity upon hapless mortals. Oberon and Titania will be jealous and be reconciled to each other a dozen times a day, while for culmination of their story you have the absurd spectacle of a fairy in love with an ass. So that in them is represented, as it were *in vacuo*, the very quality of which it is the object of the play to discern the partial and occasional workings in the heart of humanity.

In the story of the handicraftsmen, the central

85

idea does not find any direct illustration. The story is required, partly to introduce the interlude, but still more to provide that comic contrast which was always an essential feature of a mask, or a play written on the lines of a mask. It is ingeniously interwoven into the fairy story by making Bottom the instrument of Oberon's revenge upon Titania. And it is in the person of Bottom that the whole humour of the thing consists. He is, with the possible exception of the Nurse in *Romeo and Juliet*, the first of Shakespeare's supreme comic creations, greater than the Costard of *Love's Labour's Lost* or the Launce of *The Two Gentlemen of Verona*, as the masterpiece is greater than the imperfect sketch. From beginning to end of the play his absolute self-possession never for a moment fails him. He lords it over his fellow-actors, as though he, and not Quince, were poet and stage-manager in one; he accepts the amorous attentions of a queen with calm serenity as no more than might naturally have been expected; nor does he ever, either before or after his transformation, betray the slightest suspicion of the fact that he is after all only an ass. It has often been thought that in the rehearsal scenes Shakespeare was drawing upon the humours of such rustic actors as might have ventured a Whitsun pastoral at Stratford-upon-Avon; yet one fears that the foibles of the green-room are much the same in the humblest and the loftiest walks of the profession, and who shall say that the poet is not poking good-humoured fun at some of his fellows of the Lord Chamberlain's company?

Finally, with the interlude, we come back to the central idea once more. For in the ill-starred loves of Pyramus and Thisbe, their assignation, their elopement, and their terrible end, we have but a burlesque presentment of the same theme which has occupied us throughout. It is all a matter of how the poet chooses to put it. Precisely the same situation that in *Romeo and Juliet* will ask our tears, shall here move unextinguishable laughter. And so the serious interest of the play dissolves in mirth, and while the musicians break into the exquisite poetry of the epithalamium, the playwright stands and watches us with the smile of wise tolerance on his lips.

RICHARD the SECOND

RICHARD THE SECOND has, beyond its actual dramatic quality, a singular interest for those who care to study the development of Shakespeare's dramatic methods. With *Romeo and Juliet* and *A Midsummer Night's Dream*, it belongs to the period of a deliberate literary experiment. For the space of a tragedy, a comedy, and a history, Shakespeare essayed to write drama in the lyrical vein, with his singing robes on, with an abundance of passionate and highly coloured speech, and with the aid of rhyme and other devices of lyrical utterance. Afterwards he desisted from this way and sought another manner, more varied and flexible, and therefore more sensitive to the rise and fall of emotion which necessarily underlies dramatic expression. I do not know whether *Richard the Second* has ever been set to music and furnished forth the book of an opera; but it would lend itself to such treatment, and even as it stands it calls less for acting in the naturalistic sense, than for a rhetorical and measured declamation. Richard's own part, in particular, at least after the wheel of fortune has begun to carry him downwards, is one long and elaborated recitative of profound and subtle pathos.

To say that the play is lyric is by no means to say that it is not dramatic also. On the contrary, every element in it is carefully subordinated to the strictly dramatic end of throwing into powerful relief the strong contrast and conflict between the two principal characters, Richard and his cousin and supplanter, Henry of Bolingbroke. This conflict has its political aspect, since the play is, primarily, a study in kingship, and, beyond that, it has its personal aspect, since, even more fundamentally, the play is a study in human nature, and sets in opposition the two types of personality between which, from the beginning, the inheritance of this world has been divided. *Richard the Second* is, of course, the first act in the trilogy which leads up to the portrait of Shakespeare's ideal and heroic king, in *Henry the Fifth*. Henry has every right to sovereignty, the right divine of birth, and the human rights of efficiency and of that sympathy with the instincts and emotions of his folk, the attaining to which is the real explanation of his unprincelike and wayward youth. Like the summer grass, he has grown to kingship—

Unseen, yet crescive in his faculty.

Neither Richard the Second nor Henry the Fourth realizes more than a fraction of this tripartite ideal; and therefore each, politically, is a tragic failure. Richard, indeed, has nothing but the irony of the right divine; he is neither efficient nor sympathetic. Bolingbroke is efficient enough, but a self-seeker, and to the end the stain of disloyalty and usurpation mars his kingship. This is the outline of

Shakespeare's political philosophy as it finds expression in the trilogy.

It need hardly be said that the antithesis between Richard and Bolingbroke goes much further than politics; it rests upon one of the ultimate distinctions amongst mankind, that of the practical and artistic temperaments, the men of deeds and the men of dreams and fancies. The personal beauty of Richard, on which much stress is laid in the play, is but the map of his delicate intellect and flower-like imagination. He delights in music, in a spectacle, in the pomp and circumstance of his state. He is an orator, with a wonderful flow of eloquent words which runs like a river through scene after scene. He has his intuitions, and can read the hearts of men, although he cannot control them. Like so many of the personages whom Shakespeare the actor made, he is himself a born actor. He loves a dramatic effect. He is in his element, sitting in the high seat at Coventry and throwing his warder down just at the critical moment when the champions are levelling their spears in the lists. Even in his downfall, it gives him a thrill to take the stage in Westminster Hall and slowly to disembarrass himself of his crown with speeches of studied pathos, while the lookers-on are divided between admiration for the artist, pity for the man, and irritation at the *poseur*. He has no morals and no real feeling for anyone but himself; yet his sensitiveness of soul enables him to hold the hearts of those with whom he enters into personal relations, the queen whose bed he has wronged, the young nobles who plot in his cause, the menial who with much ado gets leave to see his face in prison. In return he has a fund of ready sentiment, which goes out not only to human beings, but also to 'roan Barbary' and to the literal earth of his native land. And when action is called for, it is always sentiment that he succeeds in substituting. The shocks of misfortune stimulate him only to a more and more subtle exercise of his incomparable imagination. He becomes an interested spectator of his own ruin, dressing it out with illuminating phrases and exquisite images, and so turning it into a thing of beauty and of sorrow for himself and the audience; but he makes no effort to avert it, and falls back upon a mystical consciousness of his divine right, and a half-belief in the probability of some incredible divine intervention in his favour. Never at any time does he come face to face with facts; but always sees them through the beautiful and distorting medium of his own dramatic fancy. The uncompromising popular judgment, with its short cuts to truth, sums him up, roughly enough, as 'the skipping king'; and, in Shakespeare's psychology, he stands for the type of the artist.

Against Richard, Bolingbroke presents the incarnation of efficiency. He has no gifts or graces; the courtesy which wins him popularity is a matter of deliberate attitude, not of instinct. He speaks few words; none unconsidered or without a definite practical end. You recognize in him 'the still strong man in a noisy land'; one who knows how to bide his time, and moves irresistibly, with something of the terrible precision of a machine, towards his predetermined end. The antagonism between him and Richard declares itself from the beginning, and both are conscious of it. His attitude towards the king during the early part of the play conceals a covert threat; at the end, though the less effective rôle is his, he keeps his temper, and treats the tirades of the victim, whose days he has already numbered, with a contemptuous and studied brevity. Of course *Richard the Second* does not give us by any means the whole of Bolingbroke. Within its limits he is thoroughly successful. In the conflict with Richard, efficiency has its full triumph over imagination. The completion of the picture is left for the second part of the trilogy, discovering his weakness in the want of sympathy which leads him to offend the hot-blooded nobles and to misjudge the finely-tempered nature of his own son. Usurpation, moreover, must pay its price, and *Henry the Fourth* yields the mysticism of Richard its posthumous justification in the persistent sense of guilt which makes Henry's crown sit uneasy upon his head, and drives him to plan the expiation of that crusade to the Holy Land which he is never destined to accomplish. It is not until the second generation that the curse of Richard's spilt blood has worked itself out.

This, however, is to anticipate. The dramatic

intention of *Richard the Second* as a single play must be distinguished from the dramatic intention of the total trilogy of which it forms only one stage. And within *Richard the Second* the issue between Richard the dreamer and Bolingbroke the 'crown-grasper' is a clear one. The sympathies of the audience, naturally enough, swing and sway with the progress of the action. The design of the dramatist requires that they shall be against Richard during the period of his tyranny, and shall gradually be won to his side from the moment when his fortunes begin to decline. This is almost inevitable, since it is of the essence of tragedy that the tragic fate should be intelligible and should none the less awake pity and awe. It is a little more difficult to say whether any ultimate judgment upon the puppets by their interpreter is involved. Mr W. B. Yeats, in his book called *Ideas of Good and Evil*, seems to have no doubts about the matter, and decides without hesitation that Shakespeare, as an artist, put the children of light before the children of this world, and was personally in touch with the ineffectual dreamer Richard, rather than with his 'efficient' rival. He says—

I cannot believe that Shakespeare looked on his Richard II with other than sympathetic eyes, understanding indeed how ill-fitted he was to be King, at a certain moment of history, but understanding that he was lovable and full of capricious fancy, 'a wild creature' as Pater has called him.... He made his King fail, a little because he lacked some qualities that were doubtless common among his scullions, but more because he had certain qualities that are uncommon in all ages. To suppose that Shakespeare preferred the man who deposed his King is to suppose that Shakespeare judged men with the eyes of a Municipal Councillor weighing the merits of a Town Clerk....He saw, indeed, as I think, in Richard II the defeat that awaits all, whether they be Artist or Saint, who find themselves where men ask of them a rough energy and have nothing to give but some contemplative virtue, whether lyrical phantasy, or sweetness of temper, or dreamy dignity, or love of God, or love of His creatures.

Mr Yeats goes on to dwell upon Henry the Fifth, and Shakespeare's attitude towards the hard practical qualities which made Henry so conspicuous a success exactly where Richard was so conspicuous a failure—

To poise character against character was an element in Shakespeare's art, and so, having made the vessel of porcelain Richard II, he had to make the vessel of clay Henry V. He makes him the reverse of all that Richard was. He has the gross vices, the coarse nerves, of one who is to rule among violent people, and he is so little 'too friendly' to his friends that he bundles them out of doors when their time is over. He is as remorseless and undistinguished as some natural force, and the finest thing in his play is the way his old companions fall out of it broken-hearted or on their way to the gallows; and instead of that lyricism which rose out of Richard's mind like the jet of a fountain to fall again where it had risen, instead of that phantasy too enfolded in its own sincerity to make any thought the hour had need of, Shakespeare has given him a resounding rhetoric that moves men, as a leading article does to-day.... Shakespeare watched Henry V, not indeed as he watched the greater souls in the visionary procession, but cheerfully, as one watches some handsome spirited horse, and he spoke his tale, as he spoke all tales, with tragic irony.

Mr Yeats's views upon life are always interesting and often illuminating; but one may perhaps be pardoned for regarding the passages which I have quoted as affording a rather typical illustration of certain weaknesses of the current ideal of 'temperamental' criticism, as compared with that older conception of which Matthew Arnold was the high priest, and of which the primary virtues consisted in 'keeping one's eye on the object' and 'seeing things as they are.' Matthew Arnold's rigorous teachers, never, one fears, succeeded in seizing Mr Yeats's youth. I am quite sure that Mr Yeats himself, in judging kings or ploughmen, would always give the palm to imagination over efficiency; and for all I know, if human characteristics are reducible to ultimate standards of value, he may be perfectly right. Πολλοὶ μὲν ναρθη-κοφόροι παῦροι δέ τε Βάκχοι. But after all it is not Mr Yeats's vision of life, or mine, that is in question, but Shakespeare's. And I do not for a moment believe that in reading Shakespeare he has succeeded in keeping his eye upon the object. Shakespeare, if I am not mistaken, was the last man likely to underrate the hard practical qualities which go towards efficiency. For a poet, he had the firmest grasp upon the central facts of life. After all, he was not a Celtic idealist, but an honest burgess of Saxon Stratford; and, in spite of some conventional phrases about the immortality of his

95

verse in the *Sonnets*, he shows singularly little desire unduly to magnify his office as artist. One has even sometimes a lurking feeling that he thought himself extremely lucky to have made enough by his pen to enable him to settle down for the evening of his life on an equal footing with the prosperous and unimaginative tradesmen who had earned their comfortable fortunes by meeting the very practical needs of his native borough; and that, perhaps, his first investment in tithes gave him a thrill which he never afterwards re-captured even in creating Imogen. I do not, of course, quite believe this, but I do believe that Shakespeare, who saw all round life, saw it on the whole very normally, and that he weighed his men and women just a little more in relation to the central purposes of the world than Mr Yeats does or is inclined to admit that he did. Naturally he under-stood his Richard the Second and his Falstaff, as well as his Henry the Fifth, and understanding must always imply some measure of sympathy. Yet I find it difficult to think that his ultimate judgment upon them differed essentially from that of any clear-sighted and broad-minded Elizabethan student of history who did not happen to be a poet.

KING JOHN

FOR the sake of the wild and whirling words of Constance and the boyish pathos of Arthur's struggle against death, it is possible that *King John* may always continue to have its share of devotion from readers of Shakespeare. The sentimentalism of commentators is apt to find in the play a reflection of the natural sorrow of the poet at the death of his own son Hamnet. But the sentimentalist is a dangerous leader in the slippery ways of literary biography. *King John* may very well have been already written when Hamnet died in August, 1596. Moreover, the psychological theory implied is a fantastic one. The grief of Constance rings true enough; but, after all, her hint of woe is common, and it must certainly not be assumed that a dramatist can only convince by reproducing just those emotions which he has seen at play in his own household. It is safest to regard the tragic figure of the weeping mother as based rather upon broad human sympathies than upon personal experience; but whatever its origin, the part of Constance, like that, almost contemporary, of the unkinged Richard the Second, affords an ideal mouthpiece for the flood of splendid emotional declamation, which is one of the finest and most enduring qualities of the Elizabethan stage.

> And, father cardinal, I have heard you say
> That we shall see and know our friends in heaven.
> If that be true, I shall see my boy again;
> For since the birth of Cain, the first male child,
> To him that did but yesterday suspire,
> There was not such a gracious creature born.
> But now will canker sorrow eat my bud,
> And chase the native beauty from his cheek,
> And he will look as hollow as a ghost,
> As dim and meagre as an ague's fit.
> And so he'll die; and, rising so again,
> When I shall meet him in the court of heaven,
> I shall not know him. Therefore never, never
> Must I behold my pretty Arthur more.

This has the authentic thrill in it; but there is much in *King John* which is far away indeed from such fine rhetoric. Rarely, for example, did Shakespeare write anything more frigid than the casuistries of Pandulph, with their baffling and bewildering reliance upon verbal ingenuities.

> It is religion that doth make vows kept;
> But thou hast sworn against religion,
> By what thou swearest against the thing thou swearest,
> And makest an oath the surety for thy truth
> Against an oath. The truth thou art unsure
> To swear, swears only not to be forsworn;
> Else what a mockery should it be to swear!
> But thou dost swear only to be forsworn,
> And most forsworn, to keep what thou dost swear.

But, whatever the merits or demerits of *King John* as regards phrasing and the handling of individual episodes, there can be no doubt that there is hardly any mature play of Shakespeare the total dramatic effect of which is so disappointing. Something of the epic chronicle, it must be admitted, hangs about all the Histories; but for the most part, whatever room may be left for alarums and excursions and other irrelevancies, there is nevertheless some intellectual core, some recognizable attempt to body forth a central idea in dramatic form. But what is the intellectual bearing of *King John*? Plainly it is conceived as a tragedy, but wherein does the tragedy consist? Is John himself the villain or the hero? Are we, as in *Richard the Third*, face to face with the Nemesis that waits upon wickedness in high places? And if so, why do many of the scenes, and in particular the closing lines, with their emphasis upon England's dissensions as the cause of England's woes, seem to strike another note, and to point out not John, but those who plot against John, as the workers of the tragic evil? One fears the answer is, that no answer can be given, and that the infirmity of double purpose here suggested is indeed inherent in the backboneless structure of the piece. The explanation of this want of grip and dramatic unity in *King John* is probably to be found in the fact that Shakespeare has put, and perhaps from the conditions under which he worked was only in a position to put, but little of himself into the play. Standing aloof as it does from both of the two great tetralogies into which the bulk of the poet's dramatic comment upon English history was cast, that of York and that of Lancaster, it is hardly more than a bit of hack work. Herein, indeed, it stands upon much the same footing as *Henry the Sixth* itself, in the two latter parts of which, at least, Shakespeare seems to have been but learning his trade by rewriting, scene for scene, the two parts of the older chronicle play known as *The Contention of York and Lancaster*. Quite similarly it is probable that *King John*, from the points of view alike of the actors, of the booksellers, and of the dramatist himself, was not an independent creation, but only a revision of another old chronicle play, still extant under the title of *The Troublesome Reign of King John*. A comparative reading leaves the relation between the model and the copy clear enough. Obviously Shakespeare has advanced enormously in authority and in manipulative dexterity since he was set to tinker at *The Contention*. So far as the rewriting of the dialogue is concerned he takes a very free hand, and only here and there retains a turn of speech of his predecessor. Moreover he omits many scenes and liberally clips others, with a view to compressing the matter of two performances within the limits of one; and of course the gain in dramatic concentration and vigour is considerable. But when all is said and done, the old play remains the model; and indeed, so far as structure goes, the parallelism is quite complete. Somewhat different value is given to the motives and situations in *King John*, but there is hardly one which *The Troublesome Reign* did not originally dictate.

The Troublesome Reign, although not without its merits, belongs wholly to the chronicle history *genre*, and it is not surprising to find that it already displays that invertebracy of purpose of which one is inclined to complain in *King John*. It appears, from internal evidence, to have been written about the time of the Spanish Armada, and is representative enough of the heightened national and Protestant feeling which that enterprise had not unnaturally evoked. It should be noted that, even in *The Troublesome Reign*, John was not making his first appearance as a dramatic figure upon the English stage. On the contrary, he was already an ancient tradition. Half a century before, at the very beginning of the English Reformation, a 'matter touching King John' had been played at Cranmer's palace, in which he was glorified to all good Protestants as 'the beginner of the putting down of the Bishop of Rome.' Probably the interlude presented on that occasion was the *Kynge Johan* of that uncompromising controversialist, Bishop John Bale of Ossory, of which a later version, revised after the accession of Elizabeth, is preserved. In this singular piece, which marks the transition between the morality and the chronicle history, there is no mention of Arthur and his claims. John is depicted as a zealous reformer, persecuted and finally poisoned by the Pope and Pandulph, with the aid of Sedition and Dissimulation, and in after days avenged by 'that Duke Josue, which was our late King Henry,' in the guise of Imperial Majesty. There is no evidence that the author of *The Troublesome Reign* knew *Kynge Johan*, and it is not very likely, as the earlier play remained in manuscript until recent years. But for him too John is primarily the champion of England against the Pope, and as such the national hero of a Protestant age. There are some humorous scenes, omitted by Shakespeare in the process of adaptation, in which the Bastard ransacks the treasure-coffers of convents and monasteries, with the result of finding 'fair Alice the nun' locked up in the abbot's chest and Friar Laurence in that of the abbess; while at the end the dying John utters a harangue in which he foretells the coming of—

> A kingly branch,
> Whose arms shall reach unto the gates of Rome,
> And with his feet tread down the strumpet's pride,
> That sits upon the chair of Babylon.

Such was the temper of 1588, in which sleeping antipathies had been fanned again into fierce blast by the coming of the Armada. But the old playwright had not the art of Bale to select only such elements from history as might serve to further his dramatic purpose. Apparently taking his material wholesale from the chronicles of Holinshed, he inserts into his heroic framework the whole sanguinary story of the plot to murder Arthur, in which the king plays so far from heroic a part, regardless of the reaction which this must needs have upon the sympathies of the spectators.

Shakespeare, as has been said, adopts the full structural outlines of his predecessor, and with them this historic incongruity in the presentment of the principal character which is so destructive of all true dramatic unity. But he alters the distribution of the emphasis, pruning the obsolete Protestantism, and bringing the Arthur theme with its capacities for emotional treatment into the foreground of his design, where it repeats the somewhat melodramatic pattern already made use of in *Richard the Third*. The limitations of the adapter do not, of course, allow this process to be complete. During large tracts of the play John, or the English spirit which John is made to typify, is still conceived in the heroic vein. The theological rancour has in the main disappeared, in spite of the king's defiance of the 'usurped authority' of the Pope, and his expressed determination—

> That no Italian priest
> Shall tithe or toll in our dominions.

But the note of nationalism is there still, and if the play looks back to *Richard the Third*, it looks forward just as much to *Henry the Fifth*. It contains the first of those glorifications of the island realm which Shakespeare, as often as not, prefers to put in the mouth of a foreigner. It is Austria who vows—

> That to my home I will no more return,
> Till Angiers and the right thou hast in France,
> Together with that pale, that white-faced shore,
> Whose foot spurns back the ocean's roaring tides,

> And coops from other lands her islanders,
> Even till that England, hedged in with the main,
> That water-walled bulwark, still secure
> And confident from foreign purposes,
> Even till that utmost corner of the west
> Salute thee for her king.

Even so does John of Gaunt himself extol, in *Richard the Second*—

> This royal throne of kings, this sceptred isle,
> This earth of majesty, this seat of Mars,
> This other Eden, demi-paradise,
> This fortress built by Nature for herself
> Against infection and the hand of war,
> This happy breed of men, this little world,
> This precious stone set in the silver sea,
> Which serves it in the office of a wall,
> Or as a moat defensive to a house,
> Against the envy of less happier lands.

There is an Anglo-Saxon ring, too, in the description of the triumphant evening of battle upon which, as from a day's sport in the chase—

> Like a jolly troop of huntsmen, come
> Our lusty English, all with purpled hands,
> Dyed in the dying slaughter of their foes;

and in that of the light-hearted gentlemen who cast their fortunes with John's expedition in the eternal spirit of knight-errantry—

> Rash, inconsiderate, fiery voluntaries,
> With ladies' faces and fierce dragons' spleens.

It is perhaps from a consciousness of the ambiguous place which John must necessarily fill in the play, that Shakespeare throws a large share of the burden of his nationalism upon the Bastard. This tall man of his hands, with his blustrous humours and his shrewd mother-wit, is clearly intended to be typical of the stout Anglo-Saxon race. He has the blood of her kings, even though it came to him a little o'er the hatch, and the very spirit of Plantagenet; and in his large composition there are tokens of the greatest of her heroes, Richard Cœur-de-lion himself. So he stands for England throughout. The sins of his king do not, as in the case of some greater nobles, turn him from loyalty to his country. It is he who throws down the glove of undying defiance to the foreign invader, and as the curtain falls voices the watchword of England's peace—

> This England never did, nor never shall,
> Lie at the proud foot of a conqueror,
> But when it first did help to wound itself.
> Now these her princes are come home again,
> Come the three corners of the world in arms,
> And we shall shock them. Nought shall make us rue,
> If England to itself do rest but true.

But in a drama faults of structure are irreparable, even by a Shakespeare; and neither Constance nor the Bastard can really redeem the incoherent patchwork from ineffectiveness.

The MERCHANT of VENICE

THE melancholy of Antonio is a perpetual undertone in the gaiety and the tribulation of *The Merchant of Venice*. It claims your pondering in the first significant words of the play; nor is its meaning, there or elsewhere, clearly or explicitly set forth. Solanio and Salarino, with the natural assumption of poor men, that a rich man must be at least as much concerned about his riches, as themselves are at their want of riches, have an obvious explanation ready to hand; and Antonio merely replies that it is not his merchandise that makes him sad. Gratiano, since he must always be talking, thinks, or pretends to think, that his friend is deliberately affecting the serious pose proper to persons of importance; and him too Antonio puts by with a smile. Gratiano is not of those to whom one reveals the heart's secrets. So that you are left to guess whether there is a heart's secret here at all, or whether Antonio is sincere when he declares that he is no more able than another to tell what stuff his melancholy is made of, whereof it is born. The current explanation has it that he is quite sincere, and that a vague uneasiness stands for a premonition of the disaster which is shortly to overtake him. Such a device falls altogether within Shakespeare's dramatic methods. If one cites only plays contemporary with *The Merchant of Venice*, there is the prophetic foreboding of the little queen in *Richard the Second*, when her lover and king has gone forth on his light-hearted expedition to Ireland—

> Some unborn sorrow, ripe in fortune's womb,
> Is coming towards me, and my inward soul
> With nothing trembles:—

and there is the ironical inverse of the same situation when Romeo steps out into the morning, and tells us that his bosom's lord sits lightly in his throne, five minutes before he is to learn that Juliet sleeps in Capel's monument. Yet a difference is to be observed. *Richard the Second* and *Romeo and Juliet* are to issue tragically; and therefore the preluding touches which tune the spectator to the sense of tragedy are justified. They have their appointed and logical place in the pattern. With *The Merchant of Venice* it is otherwise. Heart-strings shall be wrung in the process of the story; but it is not, as a whole, written in the key of tragedy. It stands under the domination of Portia, the first and most triumphant of Shakespeare's questing heroines; and its atmosphere is throughout in harmony with Portia's sunny hair, and Portia's sunny wit, and Portia's sunny temper, rather than with the grey twilight of Antonio's mood.

A formal analysis of the central dramatic intention—the *idée mère* of the play—can only confirm one's immediate feeling that its stage must not be hung with black. Heminges and Condell classed it with Shakespeare's comedies, and it claims to be, upon every page, a 'comical history.' But 'comedy,' like most other literary terms of art, has but a shifting connotation, and one is hardly dispensed from enquiring in what precise shade of its significance it is here to be taken. In the long history of the soul of man, the dramatic instinct seems to have worked its way to two or three types of outlook upon the world which it mirrors; and for each of them the ambiguous term 'comedy' has its distinct meaning. There is the drama of amusement, the drama of ideas, and the drama of emotion. The drama of amusement asks the name of comedy for the give and take of dialogue and the tangle of intrigue with which it entertains the spectator. But the drama of amusement is too purely external to take rank as art in the higher sense in which art is before all things an expression of the personality of the artist. The higher drama, on the other hand, differentiates itself, according as it expresses one or other side of such a personality. It is the medium through which the dramatic artist conveys to the audience his ideas about life, or it is the medium through which he conveys to them his emotions about life. Comedy, in what I accept as the primary sense of the word, is the characteristic form taken by the drama of ideas. Such is the comedy of Aristophanes and of Molière. It has its roots in the fearless and outspoken comment of the κῶμος, the revel rout, or of the κώμη, the village rout.

In its urban forms it is still essentially an analysis, a criticism, of life. And, therefore, it is really no paradox to say that comedy is often one of the most serious and even didactic of utterances. The comic dramatist has reflected upon life and condemns it. He lays his finger upon its follies and weaknesses. He strips it bare for you, a wheel of fortune, a dance of fools, a show of jerking puppets. His cap and bells hides this deliberate intention. His bauble conceals a scalpel. 'He uses his folly as a stalking-horse, and under the presentation of that he shoots his wit.'

Is it, then, this primary type of comedy to which *The Merchant of Venice* belongs? Are we to find in it the critical outlook, the play of bitterness or of humour or of irony upon life? Up to a point the intention of the piece can, no doubt, be so formulated. Take it as a series of variations on the obvious comic theme of the hollowness of appearances; and the choice of the caskets, the deception of Shylock, even the disguise of the wives and their stratagem with the rings, fit naturally enough into such a design. Nor can one fail to notice how well a good deal of the dialogue lends itself to such an interpretation. Gratiano chaffs those—

> That therefore only are reputed wise
> For saying nothing.

Arragon scorns 'the fool multitude that choose by show.' Bassanio sermonizes upon 'beauty purchased by the weight,' upon golden locks that are 'the dowry of a second head,' 'the beauteous scarf veiling an Indian beauty,' and upon other illustrations of his thesis that 'the world is still deceived with ornament.' Certainly here is one element in the structure of the play. But as certainly, I think, when you have disengaged and fixed this element, you have not really accounted for the whole. For you have not accounted for the other element of emotion; and although, no doubt, as you watch *The Merchant of Venice*, you feel the gathering conviction that 'the outward shows are least themselves,' yet after all this feeling is only subordinate to the swing and sway of your sympathies with the trapping of Antonio and the rout of Antonio's oppressor by Portia's divine and generous wit. In virtue, then, of its emotion, the play falls outside the range of comedy in the sense in which comedy is the vehicle of the drama of ideas; since to such comedy it is vital that it should remain unemotional, should see all things in the dry light of reason unperverted by the heart, and should hold the sympathies aloof that its flight may be all the more deadly to the brain.

It is probable enough that *The Merchant of Venice* has a divided purpose. Literary types rarely offer their pure form in concrete examples. But in the total impression left by the play it is the emotional and not the critical attitude towards life which predominates. And it is the principal ambiguity of the term 'comedy' that it stands not only for the characteristic expression of the drama of ideas in the sense already defined, but also for one variety of that other type of drama which is not of ideas but of emotions, since in it the artist is endeavouring to transfer to the audience not his own judgments, but his own emotional states, through the medium of their sympathies with the woes and exultations of the characters whom he fashions for the purpose. This secondary sense of the word is to be explained in part by the influence of mediæval usage, which had forgotten its theatre, and had come to regard comedy and tragedy, not as names for specific dramatic types, but as names for emotional narratives coming respectively to happy and to sad endings. When, at the Renascence, emotional drama grew up again on the basis of mediæval narrative, it became the natural heir of the same distinction. The stress of emotion is common to Elizabethan tragedy and Elizabethan comedy, but while in tragedy it issues in pity and terror and the funeral procession, in comedy it gathers only to pass away and dissolve in triumph and laughter and the clash of marriage-bells. For such emotional or romantic comedy, as distinct from comedy proper, 'tragicomedy,' which the Elizabethans themselves sometimes used, is perhaps the happiest term.

If, then, *The Merchant of Venice* is to be regarded as primarily a tragicomedy, a drama of emotional stress with a happy ending, and only secondarily a comedy, a drama of the criticism of life, the next question which claims an answer is: What precisely is the emotional issue which is raised and which demands our sympathies in the play? It is probably true of all emotional drama that it tends to present its issue as a conflict, for this is an obvious and natural scheme for the arrangement of human characters set over against each other and answering speech by speech upon the narrow boards of a stage. It is certainly true of the Elizabethan drama, which had always behind it the tradition of the morality, with its serried array of vices and of virtues, warring for the soul of man. The theme of *The Merchant of Venice*, in particular, is readily to be formulated as a conflict. It is a conflict in the moral order, between the opposing principles of Love and Hate. That Shylock, whetting his knife upon his soul, stands for the principle of Hate is plain enough. Hate, indeed, is almost the first word that we have from his mouth—

> I hate him for he is a Christian.

And when he thinks himself on the point of victory and is pressed to give a reason for his action, he will give none—

> More than a lodged hate and a certain loathing
> I bear Antonio.

Of course Shylock's hate is to be explained and traced to its roots, some of which, at least, lie rather in what he has suffered than in what in himself he is. Shakespeare aimed to make a man, and by no means a mere moral abstraction. But it is impossible to understand the play without careful guard against that favourite modern heresy of interpretation which sees so deep into the heart of Shylock that, in fact, it converts him from the villain into the hero. One recalls Heine and the pale, fair English girl with large black eyes, who shared his box at Drury Lane, and at the close of the Fourth Act 'fell to weeping passionately, several times exclaiming "The poor man is wronged!"' Heine, I suppose, saw the performance of Edmund Kean, and Kean appears to have been the principal culprit in a transvaluation of dramatic values, which is to be explained at least as much by the inveterate craving of the leading mime for a 'sympathetic' part, as by the influence of an humanitarian age that has learnt to feel for oppressed nationalities and has forgotten to dislike usury. I am not concerned to deny that Shakespeare himself was led by the logic of facts, and in the teeth of his own dramatic arrangement, to give some handle for this misunderstanding of Shylock. One cannot forget the famous vindication of Hebrew humanity with which the wanton raillery of the silly Salarino gets its answer. Certainly Shakespeare saw all round his Shylock. But the play becomes a chaos if the qualifications of Shylock's villainy are allowed to deflect the perception of the fact that after all it is he and none other who stands for the villain in its structure. One must, of course, exercise a little of the historic imagination in judging of an Elizabethan play. There has been a certain evolution of the moral sentiments in the course of three centuries. To the modern *ethos* Antonio spitting upon the usurer's gaberdine is almost a more distasteful figure than the usurer himself, and the notion that even a proven criminal may justly be compelled to change his religion as the price of his life is intolerable. But one is not to suppose that the Elizabethan audience saw things after this kind. I do not think there is much in the theory that *The Merchant of Venice* was directly motived by the trial and execution of the Jew, Roderigo Lopez, on charges of plotting against the life, not only of Don Antonio of Portugal, but even of Elizabeth herself. But it may, anyhow, be assumed that the temper of the play chimed in with a popular sentiment towards the chosen people which, in England at least, hardly finds an echo to-day outside the limits of Whitechapel. Nor is the interpretation of Shylock the only case, even in this single comedy, in which the historic imagination is called for. Put Jessica or Bassanio to the test of the finer ethical ideals, and you will find it difficult to justify the conduct of the one in robbing her father's jewel-chest to pay the expenses of her elopement, or the conduct of the other in setting out to retrieve his wasted fortunes by the adventure of a gilded bride, until you remember that *The Merchant of Venice* is not in the realistic manner, and that, with whatever sound humanity it states its main issue, it makes no effort to depart from many of the world-old conventions of romance which it found in its sources among the *novelle*. For Bassanio it may perhaps be added, that 'fair speechless messages' had already passed between his eyes and Portia's in the days of his bravery, and that he may not have been quite so worldly an adventurer as he chose to represent himself as being to Antonio.

One cannot fail to see that, if Shylock embodies the principle of Hate, Antonio and Portia between them embody that of Love. Antonio will put his 'uttermost' at the service of his friend, and even when he is in the snare, will hold all debts cleared between them if he might but see Bassanio at his death. Portia, in her turn, has, as Lorenzo tells her—

> A noble and a true conceit
> Of god-like amity.

For love's sake she defers the consummation of her wedding rites and essays a doubtful enterprise to purchase—

> The semblance of her soul
> From out the state of hellish cruelty.

Her glorification of 'the quality of mercy' in the trial-scene is the spiritual counterpart to Shylock's dogged insistence on the rights of Hate; and her ultimate triumph, all the more perhaps for the obvious legal quibbles on which it is based, is nothing else than the triumph of Love, in the deliberate preference of equity to rigid justice. For moral and epilogue of the whole you may take the exquisite lines which she speaks as she treads once more her terraces of Belmont in the white moonlight—

> How far that little candle throws his beams!
> So shines a good deed in a naughty world.

And what of Antonio's melancholy all this while? What place has it in the happy ending which this most delectable lady has brought about, with all its after-mirth? Antonio, as I read him, does not put off his melancholy. He bows his thanks over Portia's hand, and stands silent and gravely smiling through the greater part of the frolic with the rings. Even the return of his argosies, inevitable in the winding up of a tragicomedy, leaves him still, I fancy, a sombre figure in the background. For, in fact, Antonio's melancholy preceded the loss of his riches, and I think that it has had very little to do with that, or with the fear of death either, all the time. At the beginning of the play he was going to lose something much dearer to him than riches, his friend Bassanio. Bassanio had just broken to him his intended marriage, and this it was that made him sad. He was not likely to explain to Gratiano or Salarino, but directly they had gone out he turned to Bassanio and showed on what his mind was running in the quick enquiry—

> Well, tell me now what lady is the same
> To whom you swore a secret pilgrimage,
> That you to-day promised to tell me of.

Consider, again, the scene described by Salarino at Bassanio's embarking, still before any question of the miscarriage of his vessels can have come to his ears, how—

> His eye being big with tears,
> Turning his face, he put his hand behind him,

And with affection wondrous sensible
He wrung Bassanio's hand; and so they parted.

'I think he only loves the world for him,' says Salarino. Bassanio was merely voyaging a few miles from Venice, but it was to his wedding, and Antonio knew well how hardly the closest intimacies of bachelors survive the coming of a woman's love.

A critic, for whose opinion I have the highest respect, argues as against this explanation of Antonio's melancholy that 'Shakespeare would not have left such a main motive of the play to the imagination of his audience.' But it is not a main motive of the play at all. On the contrary, as I have shown, Antonio's whole attitude is out of harmony with the sunny atmosphere which reigns throughout, and which has its justification in the happy ending to which the audience are presently to be wafted. I am inclined to doubt whether this particular point in the play was intended for the audience at all, and is not rather the intrusion of a personal note, an echo of those disturbed relations in Shakespeare's private life of which the fuller but enigmatic record is to be found in the *Sonnets*. Shakespeare, too, like Antonio, had lost a friend, and had lost him through a woman; nor does it seem to me to be inconsistent with any view which Shakespeare can be supposed to have taken of his art, that he should reserve something behind the arras of a play for his own ear, for the secret consolation of his private trouble.

HENRY the FOURTH

In *Henry the Fourth* chronicle history becomes little more than a tapestried hanging, dimly wrought with horsemen and footmen, in their alarums and their excursions, which serves as a background to groups of living personages, conceived in quite another spirit and belonging to a very different order of reality. Shakespeare set out in the beginning to tell of 'old, unhappy, far-off things, and battles long ago'; but he turned, with a growing mastery of realistic delineation and an unabated interest in all that lay before his eyes, to interpolate his narrative with scenes that bore no tincture of antiquity, and to show the very age and body of the time his form and pressure in vivid transcripts of contemporary life as it was lived from day to day in a Midland country-side or in the crowded streets of London town. Not since Chaucer painted, one by one, his pilgrims as they issued beneath the low archway of the Tabard in Southwark, had literature deigned to put upon record so ample a breadth of the varied web of English society. Here a group of carriers grumble to each other as they pack their horses by the light of a lanthorn in order to reach Charing-cross before nightfall. Here a leisurely country gentleman talks with his bailiff of the sowing of the headland with red wheat and the merits of a local dispute, or regales his friends with a last year's pippin and a dish of caraways in the quiet of his scented orchard. And in the narrow passages of an Eastcheap tavern drawers bustle to and fro scoring pints of bastard in the Half-Moon; Hostess Quickly gossips with Mistress Keech the butcher's wife, who has come in to borrow a mess of vinegar for a dish of prawns; and a gang of riotous youths, with a disreputable old knight in their midst, drink limed sack and profit by the attentions of Mistress Dorothy Tearsheet and her fellow-pagans, to the enlivening accompaniment of Sneak's noise.

In its turn all this revel of local colour and rapidly-shifting detail becomes the setting of a single great comic figure, and thereby the plays attain the unity, which their intermediate position in the dramatic cycle that begins with *Richard the Second* and ends with *Henry the Fifth* makes it difficult for them to accomplish in any other way. Instead of the dynamic unity of an emotional issue set and resolved in the course of the action, they have the static unity of a pervading humorous personality. Sir John Falstaff represents the top of Shakespeare's achievement in the creation of an immortal comic type. Individual in the fullest sense, since general characteristics meet and mingle in him as in a veritable creature of flesh and blood, he is none the less typical and symbolical in that these general characteristics reach in him their most complete and monumental expression.

In such a figure literature provides a standard to which ever after we refer half-insensibly our judgments not only of art but of humanity. We none of us know a Falstaff; but we all of us know persons some at least of whose traits find in Falstaff their archetype and quintessence. Shakespeare never produced anything else quite so great as Falstaff and in the same vein. Bottom the weaver, Juliet's nurse, Hamlet's gravedigger, Sir Toby Belch; these and many others are genuine comic types, in the sense here explained, but they are all of lesser composition. Nor can the Uncle Toby, the Doctor Primrose, the Caleb Balderstone, the Sam Weller, the Mrs Elton, the Mrs Poyser, of later writers equal this masterpiece. His sole rival is a contemporary, the ingenious gentleman, whose lineaments it is to be hoped we all of us also find among those of our acquaintances, Don Quixote de la Mancha.

Shakespeare's imagination, no less than that of his audiences, lingered affectionately around this creation. Falstaff pervades both parts of *Henry the Fourth*; and if the heroic ideals of *Henry the Fifth* could hardly have endured the disillusion which a contact with so very unideal and unheroic a personality must needs have entailed, yet the insistence of royal as well as of popular taste was strong enough to compel the revival of the favourite as a centre to the riotous and *bourgeois* mirth of *The Merry Wives of Windsor*. Of all the children of Shakespeare's brain, Falstaff and his satellites are alone thus privileged to prolong their existence beyond the limits of the play which gave them birth. *The Merry Wives of Windsor* is, of course, unmixed farce; and throughout the conception of Falstaff owes most of its elements to the shaping hand of this first and ruder incarnation of the comic spirit. To tickle the gross ears and shake the lusty sides of Queen Bess and the groundlings is his primary function; and to this end he resumes in himself all the familiar qualities of which, since before the dawn of recorded things, farce has made its inexhaustible and unvarying sport. He is a sot, a lecher, a coward, a cheat, a braggart, and a hypocrite. And since it is by means of the visible and physical infirmities of frail humanity that farce most easily calls up the unquenchable guffaw, Falstaff is not only eternally thirsty, but also incredibly and ridiculously fat. His size lends half the point to his adventures, when he 'lards the lean earth as he walks along' after the encounter with his fellow-robbers on Gadshill, or at Shrewsbury calls upon Prince Henry to bestride him if he sees him down in the battle. 'And I had but a belly of any indifferency,' he tells us, 'I were simply the most active fellow in Europe; my womb, my womb, my womb undoes me.' It is eminently characteristic of the direct and unsophisticated methods of farce that allusions to Falstaff's fatness largely take the place of repartee at the Boar's Head tavern, and furnish forth half the merriment of the table. Prince Henry, in particular, is never tired of the theme. 'A tun of man,' he calls Falstaff, and 'barebone,' and 'sweet creature of bombast,' and 'bed-presser,' and 'horseback-breaker,' and 'huge hill of flesh,' and 'martlemass,' and 'this wen,' and 'globe of sinful continents,' and 'that trunk of humours, that bolting-hutch of beastliness, that swollen parcel of dropsies, that huge bombard of sack, that stuffed cloak-bag of guts, that roasted Manning-tree ox with the pudding in his belly.' With some justice, perhaps, does the victim complain that his tormentor has 'the most unsavoury similes,' and is, indeed, 'the most comparative, rascalliest, sweet young prince.' Of himself Falstaff speaks more tenderly as 'plump Jack,' and, although he admits that he was 'born with a white head and something a round belly,' he is in the main disposed to explain his physical condition as a consequence of his emotions. 'A plague of sighing and grief! it blows a man up like a bladder.' The prince, however, has an alternative and perhaps more plausible hypothesis, that it is due to 'drinking of old sack, and unbuttoning thee after supper, and sleeping upon benches after noon.' It need not be said that the taste for sack, hardly less than corpulence, lends itself admirably to the purposes of farce. It is understanded of the people, and one may be sure that the actor who played Falstaff got his laugh every time that he drained his cup or called for another on the plea that he were a rogue if he drunk that day. And there is a humour, perhaps beyond the reach of the groundlings, in the old toper's philosophical commendation of the virtues of a good sherris-sack, on the strength of which he declares, 'If I had a thousand sons, the first humane principle I would teach them should be, to forswear thin potations and to addict themselves to sack.'

For after all you have not exhausted Falstaff, when you have called attention to those broad and obvious features of his composition which fit him to walk the easy stage of farce. Comedy is differentiated from farce, not merely by the more temperate gusts of laughter which it awakes, but also by the fact that it calls the brain to its assistance, and finds material for its diversion, less in the visible infirmities of the body and soul of man than in the underlying inadequacies and inconsistencies of motive and ideal which a subtle psychological analysis lays bare. In the portrayal of Falstaff the moods of comedy and of farce are curiously interwoven. The comic spirit is busiest with him when he is aroused to an uneasy consciousness that his earthy mode of life requires some sort of justification. This justification generally takes the form of depreciation of other persons on whom he chooses to lay the responsibility for his degradation. 'And I have not forgotten what the inside of a church is made of, I am a peppercorn, a brewer's horse. The inside of a church! Company, villainous company, hath been the spoil of me.' With characteristic impudence he upbraids Prince Henry himself. 'Thou hast done much harm upon me, Hal. God forgive thee for it! Before I knew thee, Hal, I knew nothing; and now am I, if a man should speak truly, little better than one of the wicked.' Or it is the 'costermonger times' that are out of joint, and simple virtue can hardly hold its own. 'In the state of innocency Adam fell; and what should poor Jack Falstaff do in the days of villainy?' An extra cup of sack readily works him up to the heights of self-pity. 'Go thy ways, old Jack; die when thou wilt! If manhood, good manhood, be not forgot upon the face of the earth, then am I a shotten herring. There live not three good men unhanged in England, and one of them is fat and grows old. God help the while! A bad world, I say!' All this is not wholly insincere. In his salad days, when he was page to Thomas Mowbray, Duke of Norfolk, and might pass a jest with John of Gaunt himself, Falstaff had doubtless bright dreams which time and sack have woefully falsified. But his remorse is not to be taken too seriously; it is long since it has been much more than a last refinement of luxury. And obviously one cannot suppose that there is any sincerity at all in his grave statement to the Lord Chief Justice that, for his voice, he had 'lost it with hallooing and singing of anthems.' There are some indications that, as the plays were originally produced, there was a stronger element of conscious hypocrisy in Falstaff, which was subsequently expunged. The character is said to have once borne the name of Sir John Oldcastle, a famous fifteenth-century Lollard; and the picture drawn of him seems to have incurred the disapproval of the Puritans, and to have led to the intervention of Oldcastle's powerful representative, Lord Cobham. 'Oldcastle died a martyr,' says the epilogue, 'and this is not the man.'

There is stuff for comedy, again, in the fact that Falstaff's intellectual faculties have survived the shipwreck in which morality and even ordinary decent living have come to ruin. His quick wits are always ready to save him from some dire humiliation, to the brink of which he has been led by his cowardice or his greed. His mental resource is inexhaustible. No man is his master at a verbal retort, or in the gentle art of making the worse appear the better cause. Again and again he is on the point of being cornered, and succeeds in turning the tables on his adversary by some deft counter-attack or astounding license of mendacious assertion. Henry and Poins spend whole scenes in an elaborate intrigue to confound him over the imaginary highwaymen at Gadshill, and after all he eludes them with a roar of laughter and a hearty, 'By the Lord, I knew ye as well as he that made ye!' Charged before the Chief Justice by Mistress Quickly with an ancient unpaid debt, he leaves the court gasping with the calm defence, 'My lord, this is a poor mad soul; and she says up and down the town that her eldest son is like you.' And did dishonesty ever find a more complete apology than in his surprised, 'Why, Hal, 't is my vocation, Hal! 't is no sin for a man to labour in his vocation'? His strength lies in his utter ἀναίδεια. Provided that he come off best in a bout of verbal fence, he is ready to accept any moral judgment that may be formed of him with the most serene indifference. And so comedy disputes him for her own with farce. Farce is a rough and tumble, but it is precisely in such contrasts within the soul as those here indicated that comedy takes most delight. The most profoundly serious of the Muses, she has always, throughout the long ages of literary history, made it her grave function to be preaching sincerity by the ironic exposure of shams.

Let us put it to the credit of Falstaff that he had a genuine affection for the wayward young prince who condescended to be his boon companion. The blow that fell, when the crowned Henry renounced all knowledge of him and his fool-born jests, struck not merely at his purse, but at his heart. To Master Shallow his explanation is glib enough, as usual. Nevertheless he has had his death-sentence. In *Henry the Fifth* he passes away, meanly, behind the scenes; and Ancient Pistol speaks his epitaph, 'His heart is fracted and corroborate.'

MUCH ADO ABOUT NOTHING

TRAGEDY, comedy, tragicomedy, farce; these and such like terms as these are not merely the bloodless inventions of a literary historian enamoured of labels and ambitious to classify the creations of art, as naturalists classify the flowers of the field or the birds of the air. They do actually answer to something in the soul of things, and denote, in however rough and summary a fashion, real distinctions of kind among the methods by which, throughout the ages, the dramatist has accomplished his eternal aim of persuading a reluctant and self-centred audience to feel as he feels and see as he sees. Each kind has its own laws, or, if you will, its own atmosphere and its own temper or attitude towards life; and it is by remaining obedient to those laws or remaining sensitive to that atmosphere and that temper, that the dramatist achieves the unity of impression which is the essential condition of his triumphant appeal. Each kind moves, as it were, in its own plane, keeps its own distance from the observed facts of human life, imposes its own assumptions and makes its own abstraction from the heterogeneous motives to be discerned as partially and imperfectly operative in that life. Dramatic consistency really means keeping in the plane; and the penalty of leaving the plane is the

127

loss of dramatic illusion, always, where so much of visual realism and so much of psychological convention have to be reconciled, in perilously unstable equilibrium. It is no doubt a fault of the Elizabethan drama, to be set against its remarkable humanity and its unbounded wealth of poetic invention, that, not having come to reflect upon the artistic conditions of its own existence, it too often fails to keep the plane. Its instinct is to be comprehensive, not to select or to reject, but to hold up its mirror at shifting angles to the whole uncoordinated welter of things. Elements of tragedy, comedy, tragicomedy, and farce are thrust together, without due care for the subordination of one to another, until the total effect of many a play is dissipated, and such dramatic result as it achieves is episodic, an affair of magnificent sections of dialogue and moving single incidents, rather than of a designed and coherent whole. Even Shakespeare's is, more often than not, a wasteful and irregular greatness, although to greatness all things be permitted; nor will you readily find a more typical example of precisely that inconsistency of purpose and, as it were, clashing of dramatic planes, of which I have spoken, than in one of the acknowledged masterpieces of Shakespeare's sunniest period, a play pulsing with vitality of every possible kind, *Much Ado About Nothing*. Singular that Mr Swinburne, most inspired and most errant of critics, should have selected among the qualities of the play those of 'absolute power of composition, faultless balance and blameless rectitude of design,' for especial praise. Such a judgment is only, one fears, maintainable if exclusive attention is paid to the technical and, no doubt, extremely adroit linking of scene to scene, without regard to the more important matter of the juxtaposition of dramatic values thereby entailed.

What must, I suppose, be regarded as the central motive of *Much Ado About Nothing* falls within the conception of tragicomedy in that aggravated form of which the degenerate modern examples have earned the depreciatory name of melodrama. A gallant and noble youth, Count Claudio, is betrothed to a beautiful and irreproachable lady, Hero. The course of true love is forbidden to run smooth by the machinations of Don John, a thorough-paced villain of the deliberate Machiavellian type dear to the Elizabethan imagination. Don John is a dark and sinister figure, one—

> Whose spirits toil in frame of villainies,

and whom at any moment you expect to hear say, like Barabbas in *The Jew of Malta*,—for the first but not, unfortunately, for the last time—'I must dissemble.' Don John's plotting throws a cloud of suspicion on the fair fame of Hero. Claudio rejects her at the steps of the altar. She is believed to be dead of grief and shame. Then, through mean instruments, the falsehood is revealed; the lady's innocence is proclaimed; she is discovered

129

to be living after all; and is restored to the arms of the lover with whom she is to live happy ever after. The scheme is perhaps justified by the fine emotional handling of the scene in the church, and by the pathetic dirge sung over the wronged Hero while she is still thought by Claudio to be dead. But it is obvious that it belongs throughout to the melodramatic plane; and if you marvel at the insufficient evidence on which a grave slander against a spotless woman is accepted, or express a doubt whether Claudio's conduct was really such as should have been compensated by the recovery of his bride, the only possible answer is that these things are integral parts of the melodramatic formula, and cannot be disturbed without risk of the whole ancient edifice tumbling to the ground. Any closer psychology would have been inconsistent with the distance at which melodrama makes its very abstract rendering of life. The critical justification, within its limits, is sound enough. A melodrama is a melodrama, and can only hope to escape detection and retain its illusion by following the conventional lines which have been set for melodrama from before the beginning of time.

But if the tale of Hero and the slanderous tongues is structurally the backbone of *Much Ado About Nothing*, it is none the less clear that it is far from exhausting the dramatic interest of the play. Side by side with the tragicomic theme arranged to trap your emotions, there is also a theme of pure comedy lying in wait for your laughter in the paradox of the relations between Hero's cousin Beatrice and Claudio's friend Benedick. In the working out of the action Beatrice and Benedick come to figure even more largely than Claudio and Hero themselves; and from their names, it may be noted, the play seems at an early date to have derived an alternative title. Beatrice and Benedick are jesters at love, caught in the net of love and condemned in the face of all men's mockery to betray themselves as the inconceivably ready victims of the divinity, whose colours they have flouted and whose reasonable service they have forsworn. Such are the chosen sport of the comic spirit, whose virtue it always is, through the garlands of laughter with which it bedecks the surface of life, to lay its finger upon the follies and absurdities of those who hold themselves aloof from the natural and wholesome laws which lie at the foundations of life. Shakespeare had handled the theme before, when he drew in *Love's Labour's Lost* the picture of the Eveless Eden of Navarre, whose flaming bulwarks fell at the first flutter of a troop of approaching petticoats. Berowne and Rosaline are but faint sketches beside Benedick and Beatrice. Shakespeare came to *Much Ado About Nothing*, which some believe to be *Love's Labour's Won*, with a far finer sense for the delicious entanglements of intrigue, and a ripened humour which makes the eaves-dropping scenes in Leonato's orchard a joy for ever. This one may maintain, and yet be willing to admit

131

that the wit-combats of the protagonists sometimes leave one aghast at the Elizabethan notion of repartee, and inspire a firm conviction that no element in human culture is quite so fleeting in its transformations as the sense of what is funny in the give and take of dialogue. Benedick entreats Beatrice to remain obdurate in her desire never to hear a man swear he loves her, since 'so some gentleman or other shall 'scape a predestinate scratched face'; and the lady retorts, 'Scratching could not make it worse, and 't were such a face as yours were.' With such subtle quart and tierce of mind did they cross the dialectic foils in Messina.

It is wit that evanesces, not humour, and since, while in Benedick and Beatrice wit and humour alternate, Dogberry and Verges are of humour compact throughout, it follows that, although the brilliancy of the former pair is in places a little tarnished, that of the latter must always remain pure gold. This is, in truth, of the dramatist's most authentic mintage. Like Bottom the weaver, like Christophero Sly, like Mrs Quickly, like Justice Shallow, like a score of other immortals, Dogberry and Verges are as eternal smiles upon the face of earth itself, the mellow fruit of that deliberate realistic observation of the Anglo-Saxon idiosyncrasies of speech and thought, as they revealed themselves to him in burgess and rustic, which links Shakespeare to Chaucer, and of all his innumerable gifts is perhaps his most inalienable birthright.

But I came to bury Cæsar, not to praise him. One must needs pay tribute of homage both to Benedick and Beatrice and to Dogberry and Verges when the occasion offers. Yet the critical question remains to be faced; how are these elements of pure comedy related to the tragi-comedy which is the main substance of *Much Ado About Nothing*, and how far is this relation consistent with that unity of impression which a great play should, undeniably, create? Structurally, no doubt, the dove-tailing is, as Mr Swinburne pointed out, faultless. The constables and their clumsy following not merely come in pat to effect the final rehabilitation of Hero; they also provide a scene of dramatic irony in which Leonato is on the point of prematurely discovering the plot against his daughter's peace before it bursts, but for the lack of time or the patience necessary to disentangle their stupidities. The gulling of Benedick and Beatrice, again, comes in simply and legitimately as a pastime between the betrothal of Hero and her wedding, and the merging of the two plots in the scene in which Beatrice bids her protesting lover to kill Claudio is as perfect a piece of dramatic workmanship as can be imagined. But I am not thinking so much of external structure as of harmony of atmosphere and the preservation of the tragicomic or melodramatic plane. And I do not see how it can be maintained that this does not suffer woefully from being cut across by the wholly different plane to which the comic elements of the drama belong. Benedick and Beatrice may be structurally subordinate to Claudio and Hero. This does not prevent them from being a very living man and a very living woman, and as such infinitely more interesting than the rather colourless lay figures of the melodrama. The result is that it is the atmosphere of Benedick and Beatrice, not the atmosphere of Claudio and Hero, which is predominant in the play, and that the incidents of the melodrama are inevitably forced out of their own plane and into the plane of comedy. Now the plane of comedy— of ordinary straightforward Shakespearean comedy, I mean; not, of course, of fantastic comedy such as *A Midsummer Night's Dream* or *The Tempest*— is far nearer to real life than is the plane of melodrama. The triumph of comedy in *Much Ado About Nothing* means therefore that the things which happen between Claudio and Hero have to stand the test of a much closer comparison with the standard of reality than they were designed to bear. Words and deeds, which might have passed muster in their own surroundings, become impossible in the presence of Benedick and Beatrice. Before Beatrice's fiery-souled espousal of her cousin's cause, the conventions of melodrama crumble and Claudio stands revealed as the worm that he is, and that it should have been the dramatist's main business to prevent the audience from discovering him to be. The whole of the serious matter of the last act necessarily fails to convince. Don Pedro and Claudio could not, outside the plane of melodrama, have been guilty of the insult of staying on in Leonato's house and entering into recriminations with him. Claudio could not have complacently accepted the proposal to substitute a cousin for the bride he had wronged. Hero could not have been willing to be resumed by the man who had thrown her off on the unconfirmed suggestion of a fault. Such proceedings belong to the chiaroscuro of melodrama; in the honest daylight which Benedick and Beatrice bring with them, they are garish.

Against this devastation of the unity of *Much Ado About Nothing* by the fatal clashing of the plane of its comedy with the plane of its melodrama, there is but one advantage to be set; and that is in the completion and rounding-off of the character of Beatrice which is made possible by her intervention in her cousin's tragicomedy. High-spirited, witty, honest, shrewd of apprehension, capable of tenderness, all this we had seen or guessed her earlier in the play; but for the dialogue with Benedick in the church we should never have known how her inmost soul is wrought of forged steel and gold. This is all to our profit, and yet it must be borne in mind that the profit is only an episodic one, since, as the critic must never be weary of insisting, the object of a drama is not to depict character for its own sake, but always, by the help of depicted characters, to effect the transference from author to audience of emotions or of ideas.

HENRY the FIFTH

IF exception is made for *King John*, which stands alone and singular, and the belated *Henry the Eighth*, the 'Histories' of Heminges and Condell's classification fall naturally enough into two distinct groups or cycles of four plays apiece. There are the Plantagenet cycle containing *Richard the Second*, and the two Parts of *Henry the Fourth*, and *Henry the Fifth*, and the York and Lancaster cycle containing the three Parts of *Henry the Sixth* and *Richard the Third*. One may call them tetralogies, if it is kept clearly in mind that the parallelism with the Greek drama, which the term suggests, has its origin, not in a mere archæological fantasy of the Renascence, but in a real analogy between the solutions of analogous dramatic problems. It is improbable that Shakespeare had made his study of the methods of Æschylus; but it is certain that, when he began to replace by a structural unity the mere succession of events which had satisfied the compilers of the earlier chronicle plays, he had the same task before him which confronted Æschylus, when he undertook to weave into a beginning, middle, and end a series of dramatic narratives drawn from the legendaries of the house of Atreus or the house of Œdipus.

The earlier tetralogy is of course that of York

and Lancaster, which seems to date from about 1591 to 1594, when Shakespeare was as yet, so far at least as three of the four plays are concerned, little more than a furbisher up of other men's work. The later one, with which he occupied himself, perhaps, less continuously between 1594 and 1599, shows a considerable advance towards the goal of structural unity. Instead of the formal opposition of the two houses, which hardly serves to link the string of historic episodes from the siege of Rouen to Bosworth Field, there is a deliberate and effective contrast of types of character in the portraiture of the three successive kings, which forms the basis of a genuine dramatic study of kingship. The antithesis between Richard, the flowerlike king of pageantry and poetic speech, and the elder Henry, the strong resolute crown-grasper, is reconciled into unity, by a truly Hegelian process, in the figure of the younger Henry, which is the climax of the whole development. Like Richard, Henry is king by right divine, in virtue of his birth and parentage; like his father, he is king by virtue of his capacity for kingship and of the subtle something in his blood which makes it pulse in harmony with the blood of the people whom he leads. He has the external gifts and graces of Richard, without Richard's decadent soul; he has Bolingbroke's magnetic personality, without the stain of blood and usurpation which Bolingbroke could never wipe off. He is therefore the ideal king, the divinely chosen representative and embodiment of the spirit of England. Even formally, it will be observed, he holds the tetralogy together, from the first mention of his frolic boyhood at the end of *Richard the Second*, through the riot and the budding valours of *Henry the Fourth*, until he takes his kinghood on, and blazes forth, 'his vanities forespent,' in the glittering careers of Agincourt.

If, on the other hand, one changes the point of view, and regards dramatic handling, rather than dramatic structure, there is, of course, far less similarity between *Richard the Second*, *Henry the Fourth* and *Henry the Fifth*, than between *Henry the Sixth* and *Richard the Third*. The earlier series of plays has all the effect of a continuous composition, written in a common style, the characteristics of which only increase in intensity towards the close. The latter was evidently laid down and taken up at intervals during a considerable period, and bears the marks of various stages in the development of Shakespeare's literary manner. *Richard the Second* is the lyrical history, just as *Romeo and Juliet* is the lyrical tragedy and *A Midsummer Night's Dream* is the lyrical comedy. Its wealth of rhyme, highly wrought poetry, and insistent pathos belong to an experiment towards making drama more directly the expression of an emotional mood than it is by its nature very well fitted to be. Charles Kean caught the spirit of it when, as Pater says, the play became in his hands, 'like an exquisite performance upon the violin.' *Henry the*

Fourth is of a very different temper. The instinct of poetry has given way to the instinct of realistic observation, and the political theme, although by no means lost sight of, practically sinks into sub-ordination to those wonderful *genre* pictures of London life as it was lived in the highways and taverns of Eastcheap. In *Henry the Fifth* it is resumed. Falstaff, too dangerous a competitor for Henry with the suffrages of any audience, is remorselessly suppressed, and his ragged regiment in their turn serve but to furnish forth part of the background against which the heroic personality is relieved. *Henry the Fifth* is far more closely related to *Richard the Second* than is either of them to the mingled web of chronicle and comedy that has intervened. Yet the earlier manner is not wholly recaptured after the four or five years' interval. Both plays are primarily plays of emotion, but the emotion is of distinct types. In *Richard the Second* it is a lyric flood of pity which wells up around the slowly-gathering fate of the beautiful ineffective king; in *Henry the Fifth* the impulse is one of patriotic exaltation, a communal rather than a personal emotion, and one which touches the verse less with the lyric colour than with that of a vivid and sincere rhetoric.

Patriotism, indeed, is the keynote of the play. One may fairly regard it as the most complete expression of that heightened national self-con-sciousness, which is so characteristic a feature of the latter years of Elizabeth's chequered and anxious reign. It sums up, once and for all, the whole of that dramatic tendency, which took its origin in the enthusiasms of the Armada year and is responsible for the vogue and elaboration of the chronicle play. Ten years had elapsed since the Armada; and it is tempting to connect the immediate inspiration of *Henry the Fifth* with the renewed stimulus given to the patriotic order of ideas by the exploits of the Earl of Essex and his gallant company during the filibustering expedition to Cadiz in 1596 and the less successful island voyage to the Azores in 1597. Essex is of course the general of our gracious empress,' the hope of whose glorious return from Ireland—

> Bringing rebellion broached upon his sword,

gives occasion for one of Shakespeare's comparatively rare direct allusions to contemporary history in the prologue to the Fifth Act. I do not of course suggest, after the manner of too many critics, that the poet's Henry is in any way to be regarded as a 'portrait' of Essex, although it is certainly the case that a year or two after the play was written the Lord Chamberlain's company was employed in the interests of the earl, and on the very eve of his ill-starred enterprise of February, 1601, gave before his followers a performance of *Richard the Second*, which, justly or not, was interpreted at his trial as an attempt to arouse prejudice against the tyranny of Richard's successor, Elizabeth. At least there can be no doubt that from 1596 to 1599 Essex was the centre and focus of national

feeling, the darling hope of all those who looked
to see England a power upon the seas and the
champion of the Protestant cause in Europe. A
few months after *Henry the Fifth* was put upon the
stage, Essex had returned indeed from Ireland,
but not gloriously, and at his fall the star of
nationalism waned, hardly to lighten again through
the long days of James and his cloud of Spanish
intrigues. Drayton's fine ode of *Agincourt*, printed
not later than 1606, sounds already like a faint
and far-off echo of the forgotten Elizabethan
dream.

But the dream is still a reality in *Henry the Fifth*.
It is a pæan which Shakespeare comes singing, in
glorification of the dauntless spirit and invincible
endurance of Englishmen, of the folk at unity
with itself, among whom king and nobles, yeomen
and peasants, vie with one another to show the
mettle of their pasture. Even the arrogant French
cannot withhold their admiration from the 'nook-
shotten isle of Albion,' whose barley-broth can
decoct cold blood to such a heat. 'This island of
England,' says the Dauphin, 'breeds very valiant
creatures; their mastiffs are of unmatchable
courage.' And in the front of all is Henry himself,
'the mirror of all Christian kings,' one who goes
to battle as to a sacrament, and would rather be
on the weaker than the stronger side, for—

> If it be a sin to covet honour,
> I am the most offending soul alive.

Henry's secret is that he is so fully representative

of his fellow-countrymen. The Dauphin taunts
him with his wilder days—

> Not measuring what use we made of them.

But in reality his 'humorous youth' has been his
period of training for kingship. 'Unseen, yet
crescive in his faculty,' he has come, through close
contact with what is bad as well as what is good
among his kind, to exercise a sure empire over the
souls of men, and to be their true leader in the day
of stress. Even the incorrigible ruffian and cur,
Pistol, feels the finer influence, and cries amazed,
'I love the lovely bully!' and his mere presence
as he rides through the camp is sufficient to knit
men's sinews and steel their hearts—

> That every wretch, pining and pale before,
> Beholding him, plucks comfort from his looks.
> A largess universal like the sun
> His liberal eye doth give to every one,
> Thawing cold fear, that mean and gentle all
> Behold, as may unworthiness define,
> A little touch of Harry in the night.

Harry sets the spirit of the play; and this spirit is
pure English. As if with some deliberate intention
to make his picture representative, Shakespeare
has filled the canvas with figures which typify every
element in the mixed blood of the race. Fluellen
the Welshman, Macmorris the Irishman, and
Jamy the Scots captain jostle in the field of valour
with honest Saxon Williams. And with the virtues
of nationalism go its defects. To our modern
thinking the lust of conquest is at once base and

terrible. A spirited foreign policy has its reaction
in the ineradicable tendency to regard mere matters
of domestic concern as not worth taking thought
for. The king tells the French ambassador how—

We never valued this poor seat of England,

and one recognizes the prototype of the blatant
modern imperialist, with his insolent talk of
'little England.' Henry himself can do a cruel
thing in the pursuit of his high purpose. One
cannot quite forget poor Jack Falstaff, whose heart
was fracted and corroborate, before he died, by
the bad humours which had been run upon him;
and the treatment of Jack Falstaff remains a stain
even upon 'the mirror of all Christian kings.' One
need not suppose that Shakespeare was blind to
all this, or regarded his ideal king as a being
necessarily exempt from all criticism. Certainly
he is by no means unaware of the dark shadows
that edge what a later poet has called 'the sound
and splendour of England's war,' of—

The widows' tears, the orphans' cries,
The dead men's blood, the pining maidens' groans;

and of the desolation of a land wherein—

All her husbandry doth lie on heaps,
Corrupting in its own fertility.
Her vine, the merry cheerer of the heart,
Unpruned dies; her hedges even-pleach'd,
Like prisoners wildly overgrown with hair,
Put forth disordered twigs; her fallow leas
The darnel, hemlock and rank fumitory
Doth root upon, while that the coulter rusts
That should deracinate such savagery.

> The even mead, that erst brought sweetly forth
> The freckled cowslip, burnet and green clover,
> Wanting the scythe, all uncorrected, rank,
> Conceives by idleness and nothing teems
> But hateful docks, rough thistles, keckses, burs,
> Losing both beauty and utility.

Obviously, too, a dramatist who can include Pistol, Nym, and Bardolph in the same army with a Henry and a Williams has not failed to look upon the seamy side of imperialism.

Such a theme as that of *Henry the Fifth*, when put upon the stage, naturally calls for some elaboration of scenic setting. Patriotism loves the blare of trumpets and drums, glittering coats and the pomp and circumstance of alarums and excursions. It is always interesting when Shakespeare becomes his own critic, and the choruses to *Henry the Fifth* betray him as preoccupied with the inadequacy of his limited methods of production to answer to the stage-manager's ideal—

> Pardon, gentles all,
> The flat unraised spirits that hath dared
> On this unworthy scaffold to bring forth
> So great an object! Can this cockpit hold
> The vasty fields of France? Or may we cram
> Within this wooden O the very casques
> That did affright the air at Agincourt?

Or again—

> And so our scene must to the battle fly;
> Where—O for pity!—we shall much disgrace
> With four or five most vile and ragged foils,
> Right ill disposed in brawl ridiculous,
> The name of Agincourt.

So Shakespeare provides the refutation of those who deny the propriety of calling in the stage-carpenter and costume-designer to do their share, in such a degree as discretion and a sense of proportion may suggest, in the presentation of his plays. It was his poverty and not his will that consented to the primitive arrangements which an archæological fantasy of our day has elevated into an artistic gospel. He disposes you his ragged foils with an apology. But it is the art of the dramatist to sting the imagination of his audience into supplying for itself what may be lacking in the visual illusion. Hence the martial ring and hard brilliance of so much of the verse of the play, in which Shakespeare's style reaches its zenith of objectivity and rhetoric. Hence the unfailing imagery, the abundant eloquence, the swelling phrase. Hence, above all, the choruses themselves, which endeavour by strenuous description to add what the action must needs omit, and through which the total impression left upon the spectator has something of an epic, rather than of a strictly dramatic character. Within its limits all is magnificent; but the limits are unmistakable. Here you have a Shakespeare playing on the surface of life, much occupied with externalities and the idols of the forum. And with the exception of a few unconsidered words that fall from the mouth of a woman of no reputation, there is nothing that is intimate, nothing that touches the depths.

JULIUS CÆSAR

JULIUS CÆSAR, which most recent scholars—betrayed, perhaps, by the notion of a 'tragic period' in Shakespeare's development beginning only after the last of the 'joyous comedies' had been completed—have agreed to date in 1601, is found, upon a closer re-reading of the facts of literary history, to belong rather to 1599. The point is not wholly unimportant, and is at least interesting as a refutation of that extreme school of philosophical and æsthetic criticism, which too often affects to dismiss the nice investigation of dates and occasions of production as no more than a profitless pedantry. In itself the establishment of the chronological order of the plays matters but little; it becomes of significance when it helps to determine the relations in which those plays stand to each other, and to fix the stations by which the poet's unresting thought moved in its progress across the vast issues of time and eternity. In the interpretation of *Julius Cæsar* it is of the first moment to realize that it was probably written immediately after *Henry the Fifth*, and that its speculative outlook upon life begins precisely where that of *Henry the Fifth* leaves off. The similarity of the two plays, both in theme and in manner, only needs to be stated in order to carry conviction. There is the same preoccupation with a political problem in the relations of leader and

mob, and the same flow of inexhaustible eloquence
in which, as at no other period of Shakespeare's
career, speech is aptly and lucidly fitted to the
precise ideas which it undertakes to convey. This
is wholly true of *Henry the Fifth*, and it is true of
the greater part of *Julius Cæsar*, although here
there is already from time to time some foretaste
of the more troubled expression of later plays, in
which the pink and white of perfect rhetoric is
sicklied o'er with the pale cast of thought. But
this slight divergence of style is only symptomatic
of a far more deep-seated opposition of temper,
which may be briefly but accurately summed up
in the formula that *Henry the Fifth* and *Julius Cæsar*
treat the same subject-matter, the one as an
heroic play, the other as a tragedy. *Henry the Fifth*
is a pæan of the superman in the guise of the
popular hero. Its emotional basis is triumphant
nationalism, the exultation of a folk in the 'efficient'
champion, who incarnates their dreams of military
glory none the less surely that in the glamour the
strains of hardness which enable him to rise by
trampling upon the hearts of his friends pass
unperceived.

It is the superman, again, who is dealt with in
Julius Cæsar, in a very different mood indeed
from that of Agincourt, but with no less unhesitating recognition of his efficiency and his inevitable-
ness. The Cæsar of Shakespeare is the Cæsar of
Mommsen, 'the born ruler, who governs the
minds of men as the wind drives the clouds.' He

stands alone and unparalleled. His bodily infirmities, the falling-sickness and the fever, only
serve to throw into stronger relief the powers of
will and personal magnetism whereby he gets the
start of the majestic world and bears the palm alone.
For the dramatic value of this effect, Shakespeare
departs from Plutarch and falsifies history, representing the competent athlete, who in fact saved
his own life by swimming in the harbour of
Alexandria, as indebted to Cassius for bearing
him, spent and wearied, out of the torrent of
Tiber. It is noteworthy in the play that the impression which it yields of Cæsar's greatness is
largely afforded by his own self-conscious utterances. He speaks of himself more than once with
a touch of awe in the third person, and is ready to
dwell upon his own steadfastness of soul and withdrawal from the weaknesses of his fellows—

> I am constant as the northern star;

and—

> Be not fond,
> To think that Cæsar bears such rebel blood,
> That will be thawed from the true quality
> With that which melteth fools;

and—

> Danger knows full well
> That Cæsar is more dangerous than he.
> We are two lions littered in one day,
> And I the elder and more terrible.

This self-laudation, which is not perhaps wholly
inconsistent with the view of Decius Brutus that
Cæsar is 'then most flattered,' when he is told

that he hates flatterers, serves in its turn Shakespeare's dramatic purpose. It creates an atmosphere of ὕβρις, of greatness becoming over-ripe and toppling to its fall, which hangs the earlier scenes of the play about with dramatic irony. And none the less it carries conviction, as an estimate, not merely of what Cæsar would be taken to be, but of what he is. It is reinforced by that finer, if only because less self-conscious, saying upon which the whole fate of the conspiracy against Cæsar turns—

> What touches us ourself shall be last served;

and by the independent testimony of two such wholly different personalities as Antony and Brutus. It is to himself, and not as a lure to the conspirators or a goad to the populace, that Antony murmurs before Cæsar's corpse—

> Thou art the ruins of the noblest man
> That ever lived in the tide of times.

Even in the glow of moral indignation against tyranny, Brutus acknowledges—

> I have not known when his affections swayed
> More than his reason;

and long after, he reminds Cassius of the obligation to high ideals imposed upon those—

> That struck the foremost man of all this world.

The superman falls in Cæsar, but supermanity does not fall with him, for Antony is at once ready to step into the vacant place, and to become the heir of Cæsar, just as Cæsar himself had been the heir of 'great Pompey.' In Antony you have a second type of the 'efficient' man, none the less complete and dangerous because he hides his efficiency under a Bacchic mask and a wreath of flowers. Antony is 'gamesome'; he has a 'quick spirit' which 'loves plays'; he—

> Is given
> To sports, to wildness, and much company.

This deceives Brutus, but it does not deceive Shakespeare, or the audience who have already, with Shakespeare, watched the emergence of a Henry the Fifth from a wanton and roistering youth. Antony teaches Octavius to ride Lepidus as a horse—

> It is a creature that I teach to fight,
> To wind, to stop, to run directly on,
> His corporal motion governed by my spirit;

and the amazing scene in the market-place, in which under the very menace of death he makes himself instant master of the situation, winds the conspirators, themselves 'the choice and master-spirits of this age,' round his little finger, and seizes the one opportunity afforded to turn the passions of the mob irrevocably against them, shows clearly enough that his power over his fellow-men is by no means confined to such slight unmeritable creatures as Lepidus. One may stop to point out the delight which, here as elsewhere, and notably in certain scenes of *Richard the Third*, Shakespeare takes in painting from inside the processes of the born actor and the musician-touches with which he plays upon hearts.

But if *Henry the Fifth* and *Julius Cæsar* have it in common that they are dominated by the conception of the superman, they differ most profoundly in the sentiments and emotions which the spectacle of the superman is used to evoke. In *Henry the Fifth* your sympathy is claimed from beginning to end for the hero; the play is a glorification of leadership, a dramatized epic. *Julius Cæsar* reverses this point of view; the superman still triumphs, but your sympathy is to be transferred from him to the idealist who makes head against him, and who is doomed in the end to go down before the Durandal of his efficiency. Not exultation, but pity and awe, are the burden of the event. It was perhaps natural that Cæsar should provide a title, as he had done for so many earlier dramas of the Renascence, including that in which Polonius played the title-rôle and was killed like a calf in the university of Wittenberg; but it is in Brutus rather than either in Cæsar or in Antony that the centre of emotional interest is to be found. And so the last note on which you leave the theatre is a memory, from the mouth of Antony, not of Cæsar, but of Brutus—

This was the noblest Roman of them all.

Brutus, murdering from philosophy, stands for the revulsion of humanity against the superman, who, when you get him out of the circumstance of war into that of peace, and out of the mediæval atmosphere into that of a free community, becomes revealed for nothing else than what he is—plain tyrant. The stand of freedom against tyranny is elementary righteousness, and in Brutus the conscience of freedom is personified. Antony, posing as Chorus, admits that his action was taken 'in a general honest thought and common good to all.' When the call came to him, he was 'with himself at war.' The tradition of his house, the established reputation of one who for his virtue 'sat high in all the people's hearts,' formed claims which could not be set aside without disloyalty to an exalted sense of honour. He had no personal cause to spurn at Cæsar, whom he loved and admired; nor was there anything congenial to him in conspiracy with the 'dangerous brow.' His resolution was determined by nothing meaner than—

> The sufferance of our souls, the time's abuse.

To such idealism a foil is provided by the less reputable motives of some at least of the other conspirators, who—

> Did that they did in envy of great Cæsar.

Cassius is not without sparks of greatness in him, but Cassius himself would have been a superman if fate had willed it so. What irks him is not so much that the old civic ideals of freedom and equality should be set at nought, as that he personally should be an underling, and live in awe of such a thing as he himself. This is not to say that he is all hypocrite. A completer analysis might disentangle strains of sincerity and of self-seeking curiously interwoven in his composition. But when he puts the antique Roman on and voices his formulas of liberty to conspirator after conspirator, one has an uneasy feeling that the toga does not wholly fit him, and it is not altogether a surprise when it comes to be whispered amongst his colleagues that Cassius has an itching palm. And here comes in the irony of the play, that after all it is Cassius, and not the idealist Brutus, who might, if the opportunity had been his, have brought to the conspiracy just that element of efficiency which was needed to turn it into a triumphant revolution. Moral enthusiasms have not blinded his eyes to plain facts and their consequences—

> He is a great observer, and he looks
> Quite through the deeds of men.

Cæsar is no mean judge of a man, and had the name of Cæsar been liable to fear, it is the spare, seldom-smiling Cassius that he would have held dangerous. But efficiency is only as dust in the balance when weighed against character; the conspirators are hopelessly under the spell of Brutus, Cassius himself no less than the rest, as it is the dramatic function of the famous, although perhaps somewhat disproportionate, quarrel-scene to show; and once again lofty ethical ideals are allowed to wreak their full havoc in the world. Three several times Cassius urges the course of practical wisdom, and the headstrong and optimistic sentiment of

Brutus decides against him with fatal results. He would have Antony fall with Cæsar, and the idealist, who has no conception of the hidden Antony, replies—

> Let us be sacrificers, but not butchers, Caius.

He would intervene again to keep Antony out of the pulpit in the market-place, but Brutus, bent on doing the generous thing, will not heed the twitch at his elbow, and Antony gets the ear of the people, which is all he needs for his ποῦ στῶ. Finally, after the quarrel, he is overruled by the fatalistic desire of Brutus to take the tide of fortune at its flood, and meet the enemy at Philippi, although he is indeed the better soldier, and knows that the wiser policy would be to keep the hills and upper regions.

It is to a despondent view of life, then, that Shakespeare has passed from the light-hearted and complacent heroics of *Henry the Fifth*. Between this Brutus and this Antony a plain issue is set. It is righteousness matched against efficiency and showing itself clearly impotent in the unequal contest. Had we only to do with the fate of individuals, it might pass. But the selection of the artist makes his puppets more than individuals. They stand for spiritual forces, and in the spiritual order the triumph of efficiency over righteousness is tragic stuff.

AS YOU LIKE IT

BEFORE *As You Like It* Zoilus is disarmed. The temper of the play is so perfect, its poetry so mellow and so golden, that the critic would fain hold his hand in fear that, when all has been said, he shall but seem in his curiosity to have rubbed off the marvellous dust from the wings of a butterfly. Here you have a Shakespeare, the conscious lord of his art, launched triumphantly once for all upon the high tide of romance. He has come to the plenitude of his powers. He has found his characteristic formula; and we have nothing to do but to listen to the bugles blown as he hunts the quarry of his theme through the intricate glades and tangles of his bosky imagination. *As You Like It* is romance incarnate. All the wonderful elements of the secular tradition are gathered together there in its light-hearted compass. There is the romance of friendship in Rosalind and Celia, 'like Juno's swans, still coupled and inseparable'; the romance of Adam's loyalty, 'the constant service of the antique world'; the romance of love at first sight, acknowledged in words by the smitten Phebe's quotation of dead Marlowe's saw, and acknowledged as the mainspring of the whole plot when young Orlando wrestled and overthrew more than his enemies, and witty Rosalind, for all her cousin's warning, fell deeper in love than with safety of a pure blush she might in honour come off again. Then you have Orlando as the typical lover of romance, the love-shaked sonnetteer, hanging his odes upon hawthorns and his elegies upon brambles, and abusing the young plants with carving 'Rosalind' upon their barks. You have the conventional issues of romance in the wind-up of the story; the sudden changes of fortune which betray a beneficent disposer of events, the repentance of Oliver and the conversion of Frederick to a religious life, whereby the banished duke returns from exile and Orlando wins his father's inheritance, and earthly things made even atone together beneath the blessing of Hymen. Above all, you have the romantic spirit of adventure with which the play is filled; and never more high-spirited and picturesque company of knight-errant and squire and dwarf set out on their enterprise in *Palmerin of England* and *Amadis of Gaul*, than this of Rosalind with curtle-axe upon her thigh, and Celia smirched with umber, and the roynish clown. *As You Like It* is one of the plays, so numerous above all at the midmost stage of Shakespeare's development, which are dominated by their women; and if one polled the company of readers for their choice of a heroine, although some would swear fealty to Imogen's endurance or Beatrice's ardent soul, and I myself make my reserve of devotion to Portia, yet it can hardly be doubted that the majority of suffrages would be Rosalind's. Witty and brave, audacious and tender, with a grace that her doublet and hose cannot pervert, and a womanhood that they cannot conceal, it is indeed she that gives the piece its special human charm, its note of sane and joyous vitality.

And yet, splendid as is Rosalind's, there is an even greater part in *As You Like It*. And that is the part of the Forest of Arden. Commentators dispute whether Arden is a duchy on the confines of France and Germany, or whether it lies north of the Avon in Warwickshire, just as they dispute whether the island of *The Tempest* is this or that little nook of land in the Mediterranean. Actually, of course, it too is the essential forest of romance, with its strange fauna and flora, its possibilities of a lioness beneath every bush, its olive-trees and its osiers, its palms and its oaks growing together. It is here that men live like the old Robin Hood of England, fleeting the time carelessly as they did in the golden world. We have travelled through it already, in *The Two Gentlemen of Verona*. Then it stood between Milan and Mantua, and the out-laws swore in it 'by the bare scalp of Robin Hood's fat friar.' In its purlieus lie the pleasant pastoral lands which Theocritus invented, and after him Virgil and Mantuan sang of, where peaceful shepherds feed their flocks, careless of the court, and vexed only by the pains of love and the cruelty of a disdainful mistress. We are always conscious of the forest in *As You Like It*. It is something more than a mere scenic background; a spiritual force, bringing medicine to the hurt souls of men. The banished duke has the sentiment of it—

> Hath not old custom made this life more sweet
> Than that of painted pomp? Are not these woods
> More free from peril than the envious court?

Thus *As You Like It* does for the Elizabethan drama what the long string of pastoral poets, Spenser and Sidney, Lodge and Greene, Drayton and Browne, and the rest, had already done, or were still to do, for Elizabethan lyric. The temper of it is not strictly the temper of the actual country-dweller as that has filled our later literature for the last century. It is rather the temper of urban disillusion, the instinctive craving of the man who has been long in cities pent for green fields and quiet nights. And no doubt it yields rather a mirage of the country than a sober and realistic vision of the country as it really is. Yet it is a temper to be accounted with, and insistent upon its expression. There are those who speak of pastoral as if it were only a fashion of writing, a literary convention which filtered from the classics through the Italians to the literatures of the west. There is an element of truth in this, of course, but upon the whole it is more false than true. It is parallel to the misreading of Shakespeare's *Sonnets* which sees in them merely an exercise in the manner of Petrarch. Poets are not really so inhuman as all that; and why does a literary fashion have its vogue at a given moment in a people's history, if not because, just then and there, it answers to

158

some natural necessity in the hearts of men? The pastoral impulse of the end of the sixteenth century in England means that at the end of the sixteenth century Englishmen were learning to feel the oppression of cities. And we know that, during the later years of Elizabeth and the early years of James, statesmen were beginning to be preoccupied with the growth of London; that the builders were pushing out along Holborn and the Strand; that the fields were receding farther and farther into the distance; and that the problems of overcrowding were becoming known. The monstrous nightmare of the modern city had not yet made its appearance; but there was already reason enough, especially in days when court intrigue was merciless and none too savoury, for the finer souls to dream their dreams of Arcady or of Arden.

And if Shakespeare dreamed, one is tempted to ask whether he dreamed for others only, or for himself as well. Does *As You Like It* disclose the first stirrings of an impulse back to the land, which may be held to account for his ultimate return to Stratford in 1611 while he was still but a man of middle age and in the full enjoyment of fame and fortune? Did Arden mean for him the woods and parks in which he had wandered as a boy and taken his share, if tradition errs not, in goring the round haunches of the poor dappled fools? Such questions can hardly be answered. One likes to think that Shakespeare never became at heart a Londoner. But all that is certain is that he never wholly cut himself adrift from Stratford interests, since two or three years before he wrote *As You Like It* he had already bought the fine house there in which he was to end his days; and that in *As You Like It* itself there breathes more of the country than in any other play between *A Midsummer Night's Dream* and the group which immediately preceded his retirement.

The fact that its theme is inspired by the reaction against urban life naturally makes *As You Like It* a comedy as well as a romance. Its criticism is not only implied but direct. Consider the proceedings of Touchstone. Touchstone has been a courtier; he has proof indisputable of it. 'I have trod a measure; I have flattered a lady; I have been politic with my friend, smooth with mine enemy; I have undone three tailors; I have had four quarrels, and like to have fought one.' He gives himself airs accordingly; but, when he finds himself amongst the shepherds and shepherdesses, like the most capricious poet, honest Ovid, among the Goths, he certainly does not commend the court by the good sense or the decency of his love-making. He behaves, indeed, much like 'Arry in Epping. It is, however, to Jaques, rather than to Touchstone, that the function of voicing the satire of the play upon contemporary civilization chiefly belongs. Jaques is the professional cynic, always ready to rail against all the first-born of Egypt and to pierce with his invective the body of the country, city, court. It is, however, fair to note that the utterances of Jaques must not be taken as summing up the meaning of the play. Jaques is jaundiced, a *poseur*; he has the traveller's melancholy, which consists in disabling all the benefits of his own country. To the wholesome natures of Rosalind and Orlando he is plainly antipathetic. The duke, who finds entertainment in his humours, declines to take him seriously, and tells him to his face that his cynicism is but the reaction of his own evil life—

> For thou thyself hast been a libertine,
> As sensual as the brutish sting itself;
> And all the embossed sores and headed evils,
> That thou with licence of free foot hast caught,
> Wouldst thou disgorge into the general world.

Shakespeare's judgment of life is, indeed, too sane to let him even maintain the pretence that the perfection which is lacking at court will be found in the forest. Herein is the significance of the episode of the shepherdess Phebe, for Phebe is as vain and disdainful and wanton, and as remorseless in the prosecution of her selfish intrigues, as the finest lady of them all. She, no less than Oliver and Frederick, must learn her lesson.

And so we come to the point that the satire of the play is, after all, as much against as for the romantic ideals that the play sets out to expound; which is as much as to say, that the satire is converted into essential humour. Does Orlando stand for the romantic love of the sonnetteers? By the end of his encounters with the wicked wit of Rosalind, he is as dry-beaten with pure scoff as ever was

Berowne at the hands of Rosaline; and even the
faithful Celia must complain that her cousin has
simply misused their sex in her love-prate. Once
more an investigation of Touchstone is illuminating as to the intention of the dramatist. Touchstone, the court fool, is the first example of that
dramatic type which was afterwards to yield the
Feste of *Twelfth Night*, the Lavache of *All's Well
that Ends Well*, and the nameless fool of *King Lear*.
Mr Fleay ingeniously suggests that the court fool
succeeded the clown when Robert Armin took
the place of William Kempe as the leading
comedian of the Lord Chamberlain's company.
Be this as it may, it has often been observed that
the fools of Shakespeare's plays have a sort of
choric function. They are commentators rather
than actors, and if you read them aright, you may
catch in their fantastic utterance some reflection
of the maker's own judgment upon his puppets.
Herein Shakespeare is but true to an historic model.
In mediæval courts, where, as in all courts, the
serious man must needs dissemble, it was always
the privilege of those that wore the motley to speak
a shrewd word in jest, to use their folly like a
stalking-horse and under the presentation of that
to shoot their wit. Touchstone, however, must,
I think, be regarded as something of a variation
upon the type. He embodies Shakespeare's comment upon romance, but it is rather by what he is,
than by anything that he consciously says. For
how can romance more readily be made ridiculous

than by the disconcerting contact of the natural
gross man, who blurts out in every crisis precisely
those undesirable facts which it is the whole
object of romance to refine away? Adventure
brings us to Arden, and it is left for the fool to
realize that when he was at home he was in a better
place; nor can the literary graces of love at first
sight hold their own against Touchstone's ready
offer to 'rime you so, eight years together, dinners
and suppers and sleeping hours excepted.' It is
doubtless only an accident of chronology, that
Touchstone performs exactly the same office of
disillusion to the knight-errantry of Rosalind and
Orlando, as is performed by Sancho Panza to that
of the almost precisely contemporary Don Quixote
de la Mancha.

The MERRY WIVES of WINDSOR

ONE of the rare bits of gossip about Shakespeare's literary career, which have floated down the stream of time, clings to the side of *The Merry Wives of Windsor*. A legend, not indeed traceable before the opening years of the eighteenth century, has it that the play was written at the express bidding of Queen Elizabeth, who was so delighted with the character of Sir John Falstaff that she commanded the author to continue the story for one play more, and above all things to present the gross knight in love. 'She was so eager to see it acted,' writes John Dennis, who in 1702 'improved' *The Merry Wives* into *The Comical Gallant, or The Amours of Sir John Falstaff*, 'that she commanded it to be finished in fourteen days; and was afterwards, as tradition tells us, very well pleased with the representation.' Falstaff, by the way, had already appeared in what he, and perhaps also Queen Bess, would have called 'love,' in the scene of *Henry the Fourth* in which he takes leave of Doll Tearsheet before proceeding to levy troops for the king's wars. Doubtless the episode had tickled the robust fancy of the Tudor lady. At any rate, in spite of the late emergence of Dennis' anecdote, which is repeated by Rowe and others, there is no reason to doubt its substantial truth. In the epilogue to *Henry the Fourth* Shakespeare had promised to 'continue the story with Sir John in it,' and to let the popular hero 'die of a sweat.' In *Henry the Fifth* this undertaking was hardly fulfilled, for Sir John did not appear in person, although his latter end was depicted, with unexpected and immortal pathos, through the mouth of Mistress Quickly; and there is no inherent improbability in the notion that Elizabeth, in whom the sense of humour was doubtless stronger than that of pathos, may have imposed upon the peccant author the task of repairing his omission. Possibly the play was performed at Windsor, and, if so, the singing-children of St George's Chapel, who in earlier days had rivalled their better known fellows of the Chapel Royal in the acting of court plays, may have supplied the ouphes and meadow-fairies of the last scene. In the same scene is to be found an elaborate, and one may well think topical, compliment to the Garter and its motto, when Mrs Quickly instructs her troop—

> And nightly, meadow-fairies, look you sing,
> Like to the Garter's compass, in a ring.
> The expressure that it bears, green let it be,
> More fertile-fresh than all the field to see;
> And *Honi soit qui mal y pense* write
> In emerald tufts, flowers purple, blue, and white,
> Like sapphire, pearl, and rich embroidery,
> Buckled below fair knighthood's bending knee.
> Fairies use flowers for their charactery.

In an earlier passage occurs an allusion, which was expunged from the Folio version of the play, to 'cosen Garmombles,' by whom is apparently meant a certain Duke of Würtemburg and Count of Mümpellgart, whose persistent efforts during the latter part of Elizabeth's reign to obtain the insignia of the Garter, to which he had been elected in 1597, must have formed a standing joke among the members of the Order.

Elizabeth's whimsy has exposed her to the censure of critics, whose own qualities do not, perhaps, err on the side of excessive humour. 'That Queen Bess should have desired to see Falstaff making love,' writes Hartley Coleridge, 'proves her to have been, as she was, a gross-minded old baggage.' This proposition, as has already been suggested, one is certainly not called upon to dispute. But the critics go on, with a remarkable unanimity, to point out that Shakespeare's own dramatic ideals were far subtler than those of his mistress; that he only made a show, with his tongue in his cheek, of yielding to the royal demand; and that Falstaff, the misused gull of *The Merry Wives*, is in reality another personality altogether from the old Falstaff of infinite jest and triumphant mendacity, who 'coruscates the facts of life away' in *Henry the Fourth*. Professor Dowden, for example, tells us that Shakespeare deliberately wrote down to the occasion, and that *The Merry Wives* is 'a play written expressly for the barbarian aristocrats with their hatred of ideas, their insensibility to beauty, their hard efficient manners, and their demand for impropriety.' The phrases, by the way, smack perhaps a little more of the nineteenth-century than of the sixteenth-century way of looking at things. There were limits, however, says Professor Dowden, beyond which Shakespeare declined to go in the interests of his 'barbarian' entertainment.

Falstaff he was not prepared to recall from heaven or from hell. He dressed up a fat rogue, brought forward for the occasion from the back premises of the poet's imagination, in Falstaff's clothes; and the Queen and her court laughed as the buck-basket was emptied into the ditch, no more suspecting that its gross lading was not the incomparable jester of Eastcheap than Ford suspected the woman with a great beard to be other than the veritable Dame Pratt.

Obviously one can conceive no more congenial and delightful an employment for an 'æsthetic' critic, than this of discussing the psychological identity, or want of identity, of two of the figments of Shakespeare's airy brain. But it may be wholesome to recall the fact that Shakespeare was not only a poet and analyst, but also, and primarily, a practical playwright, and to express a doubt whether these speculations do not err in assigning to him a more deliberate and punctilious literary conscience than he really displayed. Certainly one can imagine the gust of laughter, 'broad as ten thousand beeves at pasture,' with which he would have greeted the statement, culled from the writings of yet another modern commentator, that the Falstaff of *The Merry Wives* is his 'literary crime.' After all, is there anything in this theory of a true Falstaff of *Henry the Fourth* and a mock Falstaff of

The Merry Wives beyond an ingenious paradox, born of that super-subtlety which is the special bane of those who are called, at this late hour, to add yet another stone to the monumental cairn of Shakespearean analysis—Gigadibses, compelled eternally to—

> Believe they see two points in Hamlet's soul
> Unseized by the Germans yet?

Allowance must be made, no doubt, for the fact that the humour of any comic creation is apt to wear a little thin by the third time of asking, especially when called upon at only a fortnight's notice; but when the allowance has been made, is not the Falstaff type as recognizable and consistent throughout the plays as could reasonably be expected? One might wager that so it appeared at the time, not to Queen Bess and her bevy of maids of honour alone, but also to those more notable critics, the gentlemen understanders of the pit. It is true that, in the wit-encounters of Eastcheap, Falstaff always came out on top, with the laugh on his side; and that at Windsor the laugh, from start to finish, goes woefully against him. But the difference in the conditions must be taken into account. We have seen Falstaff triumph over a careless prince, who after all was only biding his time, and over the riffraff of the Boar's Head tavern; never before have we seen him at odds with the impenetrable chastity and practical wit of the English middle classes. Neither effrontery nor humour shall save him here, for what avails the power to 'coruscate the facts of life away' as a weapon against Mrs Page and Mrs Ford and their buck-basket?

Any stick is, of course, good enough, in days of Catholic revival, to beat Queen Elizabeth with. There is certainly no reason to suppose that she was readily touched to the finer literary issues. But if the tradition of Dennis that she applauded *The Merry Wives of Windsor* is an authentic one, it cannot be denied that she had sound justification. The play is a good one, even more so on the stage than in the closet; and, after all, Shakespeare wrote for the stage, which gave him bread and butter and New Place at Stratford. In particular, it is markedly better than either part of *Henry the Fourth*, wherein, indeed, Shakespeare probably reaches his low-water mark as a dramatic artist. There is insufficient motive to fill the great space of blank canvas that stretches between *Richard the Second* and *Henry the Fifth*; and even the Falstaff scenes, amazing revelation of Elizabethan London though they are, can hardly galvanize the tedious Lancastrian chronicle into life. *The Merry Wives*, on the other hand, is admirably constructed, and moves, given competent interpreters, with astonishing vitality and go. On the modern stage it is apt to be overweighted by elaborate setting, which retards the rapidity of development essentially characteristic of a farce. But obviously Shakespeare cannot be held responsible for this, and the two central scenes, wherein the buck-basket plays its immortal part, fully attain that vivacity of action which so much of Elizabethan comedy, depending as it is apt to do upon fashions of verbal fence, unfortunately misses. Its complexities of domestic intrigue almost make the piece a farce in the modern sense; but it answers more precisely to the older conception of the form which prevailed in fifteenth-century France. Such farce you may define, if you will, as acted *fabliau*. And of acted *fabliau*, *The Merry Wives* is the best English specimen, just as Chaucer's *Miller's Tale* and *Reeve's Tale* are the best English specimens of *fabliau* in narrative. It has all the well-known characteristics of the *genre*; the realistic portraiture of contemporary types; the frankness, not to say coarseness, of manners; the light esteem for the marriage-tie; the love of 'scoring off' someone, and by preference in a matter of venery. The fact that the someone is the man of rather better birth can only give an added spice to so *bourgeois* a literary type as the *fabliau* has always been. Nor was the victory of the 'wives' over the gentlemen a subject in any way likely to offend the susceptibilities of Elizabeth and the company at the Garter feast. The great nobles who filled the stalls of St George's Chapel were not likely to trouble themselves about the dignity of a Sir John Falstaff or a Justice Shallow. They could look on in complacency while a mere knight or 'armigero,' from the social aspirations of whose class they had not improbably suffered, was made ridiculous by persons only a degree further removed from themselves in rank.

And for Shakespeare himself, the irrepressible poet, there is the wonderful forest scene at the end, with its delightful contrast to the bustling realism which fills the rest of the play. Out of the busy Windsor streets, with their eating and mirth and laughter, he steps into the dewy glades where the shadows of legendary oaks lie black across the white moonlight. A gross form wearing the horns and clanking the chains of Herne the Hunter lies prostrate in a ditch, while light-footed children flit amongst the trees with torches that glimmer like fireflies. And for a moment the mockery and the malice give way to romance, as sweet Anne Page, eluding alike him who would take her in white and him who would take her in green, trips disguised in red to where the priest awaits her with young Master Fenton, who has kept company, it is whispered, with the wild prince and Poins, but is an honest lad for all that—'he capers, he dances, he has eyes of youth, he writes verses, he speaks holiday, he smells April and May.' This sudden shifting of the mood, even if it war against a formal unity, is not the least of Shakespeare's irregular and poignant charm.

TWELFTH NIGHT

FROM beginning to end of his play-writing, the comic perception is rarely for long absent from Shakespeare's vision of things. He may hang his stage, as his shifting temper and the humour of his public move him, with the purple of heroic chronicle, the rose-pink of tragi-comedy, or the sables of tragedy; but from whatever heights or depths he readily passes back to that mood of triumphant common-sense which is the ultimate wisdom of life, and from which his 'conquering smile' looks out upon the follies and vanities of the world, and wins it through the wholesome ways of laughter to sanity and sincerity. Yet he, through whom the comic spirit found so characteristic an utterance, but rarely wrote a sheer comedy; preferring rather to let the lucid shafts of his criticism play, as it were incidentally, in the interspaces of emotional drama, so that Falstaff is outlined against the bustle and tramplings of civil war, and the babble of Juliet's nurse only dies away to give place to the disquieting passions of Juliet's fatal couch. Even of the plays which can properly be classed as sheer comedies there are some which fail to answer to the fullest conception of the kind. *A Midsummer Night's Dream* is a symbolical and mask-like comedy; *The Comedy of Errors, The Taming of the Shrew, The Merry*

Wives of Windsor, are in their various ways farcical comedies. And the appeal of symbolism or farce to the complicated state of mind of the theatrical spectator, although in each case real enough, contains elements whereby it differs in quality from the intellectual claim of true comedy upon the clear and unclouded reason. George Meredith, perhaps with some excess of subtlety, regards intellectual comedy as active only upon and in a polite and leisured society, whose women move upon an equal level with its men, while both are quick to recognize the authority of a criticism delicately malign to all that offends against an ideal of honesty and shapeliness by showing itself 'out of proportion, overblown, affected, pretentious, bombastical, hypocritical, pedantic, fantastically delicate.' So limited, intellectual comedy finds representation, other than episodic, in Shakespeare's work, chiefly through the early and not wholly fortunate experiment of *Love's Labour's Lost*, and through the little group of plays which make as it were a spiritual resting-place between the patriotic interpretation of history in the chronicles and the storm and stress of the great tragedies. Even of these the incongruous strain of melodrama in *Much Ado About Nothing* deflects it from the perfect type; while the later members of the group are already so vexed with satire and a preoccupation with the seamy side of existence, as themselves to lose that balance of utter sanity wherein the strength of comedy consists. Thus we

are left with the exquisite pendants of *As You Like
It* and *Twelfth Night*, two plays whose common
serenity of golden temper is indeed only a reflex
of their single intention. The parallels between
them are easy to draw. The ordered gardens of
the Boccaccio-like villa in Illyria and the pastoral
glades of the forest of Arden serve equally well
for images of that civilized and sheltered society
wherein alone, according to Meredith, comedy
obtains its real scope; and each lends an appropriate
setting to those wilful departures from the way of
right reason which it is the proper and special
mission of comedy to correct. The plays are as
physicians set to heal kindred ailments of an idle
brain; the affectations of the fields here and there
of the town. *As You Like It* is the comedy of the
romantics, of the imagination which runs away
with the facts of life and frames impossible ideals
on the extravagant assumption that human nature
in a forest is something wholly different from human
nature in a court. *Twelfth Night* in its turn is the
comedy of the sentimentalists, of the tendency of
minds pent in the artificial atmosphere of cities to
a spiritual self-deception, whereby they indulge
in the expression of emotions not because they
really have them, but because they have come to
be regarded by themselves or others as modish or
delightful emotions to have.

Thus Orsino, like the young Romeo before the
crisis of his fate, is a thistle-down amorist. He is
in love, not with Olivia, but with being in love

with Olivia. He deliberately cultivates his sentiment, stimulating it with music and flowers and
poses of languishment. He pleases himself with the
pomp and circumstance of courtship, sends em-
bassies of love to a cruel mistress, and is rightly
punished by the irony which makes his mistress
promptly fall in love with the ambassador. But he
has not really staked his heart, and is ready enough,
when his first devotion has been finally flouted, to
take a more accommodating lady for his 'fancy's
queen.' Olivia, in her turn, has adopted the pose
of the inconsolable sister. She will be a cloistress
and abjure the sight and company of men for full
seven years, in order to keep a brother's dead love
fresh and lasting in her sad remembrance. Yet
the fortress yields with unexpected celerity at the
first thrill of a passionate intonation, and the retired Olivia becomes an on-coming wooer, only
to find herself tangled in the net of an impossible
misconception.

Orsino and Olivia are self-deceivers, the dupes
of their own sentimentalisms. And the play touches
them with such delicate irony of criticism that its
sting might fail to reach the bosoms of an audience
not exceptionally tickle o' the sere. But Shakespeare's dramaturgy is ready with a device to
meet the contingency. He will illustrate and interpret the subtler situation by the juxtaposition of
others like in kind, but grosser and more obvious
of purport. Beside his principal characters, who
befool themselves, he places subordinate per-

sonages, who are befooled by others; and thus he succeeds in evoking an atmosphere of malicious chicanery and deception, which attunes the spectator to his main intention. The play, indeed, is full of gulls; and one at least, who spends the best part of his sober hours in laying schemes to abuse others, is himself most notoriously abused. This is the arch-plotter, Sir Toby Belch. At the beginning of the play he is living on the foolish knight, Sir Andrew Aguecheek, whom he has beguiled into paying heavily for their joint entertainment, on pretence of introducing him into his niece's house in the impossible quality of her suitor. This is for gain; he has been dear to his manakin, some two thousand strong or so, and makes no secret of it among his familiars. But it is through sheer devilry that he tricks Sir Andrew and the supposed Cesario into the duel which each, at any loss to dignity, would avoid; while revenge is the motive which leads him to conspire with Maria for the undoing of Malvolio. And in the end his rogueries recoil upon him. Not only does he take Sebastian for Cesario, and get his head broken accordingly, but he is so fascinated with the incomparable capacity for intrigue displayed by 'the youngest wren of nine' that when things are cleared up he finds his head in the ultimate noose of marriage with a waiting-maid. If Sir Toby is the arch-plotter of the piece, Malvolio may claim to be its arch-victim. 'Alas! poor fool, how have they baffled thee?' says Olivia. Yet, hard as is his fate, it cannot be denied that it serves admirably to vindicate comic justice. Like Orsino and like Olivia he is a notable self-deceiver. 'O! you are sick of self-love, Malvolio, and taste with a distempered appetite.' He has the austerity of a puritan and the insolence of a jack-in-office; and how should a free-thinking, free-living Elizabethan playhouse not split its sides in exultant hilarity at his downfall?

Like all Shakespeare's comedies, *Twelfth Night* is desultory in texture, and contains various threads of interest besides the central comic idea on which its dramatic unity depends. This comic idea must not be pressed too far as regards details. There is much excellent and irresponsible fooling for its own sake, and the charming songs assigned to Feste the jester have no particular relation to the principal theme. After all, a comedy must entertain. The sort of criticism which endeavours to trace and interpret topical allusions in Shakespeare's plays can easily be overdone, and has, as a matter of fact, in recent years been overdone. An Elizabethan dramatist was not likely to take the love-affairs of the queen, or the fortunes of the house of Stuart or the house of Devereux, as the deliberate groundwork of his plot. It is not to be supposed that the censorship is so modern an institution as that kind of theory implies. But in all ages the drama has been ready to glance, as occasion allowed, at events of public interest and at personages much in the public eye; nor is it probable that the

Elizabethan age, which was by no means averse to gossip, afforded any exception to the rule. A touch of courtly compliment or a discreet allusion to the latest jest or scandal of the backstairs would be a palatable spice to the comedy destined to furnish forth the Christmas merriment of Hampton Court or Whitehall. And it is tempting to illustrate the scene, in which the virtuous Malvolio rebukes the 'uncivil rule' by night of Maria and her disreputable consorts and is bidden in return by Sir Toby to go rub his chain with crumbs, by an amusing incident which a seventeenth century anecdotist relates of Sir William Knollys, the Comptroller of the Royal Household:—

> The Lord Knollys in Queen Elizabeth's time had his lodging at Court, where some of the Ladyes and Maydes of Honour used to friske and hey about in the next room, to his extreame disquiet a nights though he often warned them of it; at last he getts one to bolt their own backe doore when they were all in one night at their revells, stripps off his shirt, and so with a payre of spectacles on his nose and Aretine in his hand, comes marching in at a posterne doore of his owne chamber, reading very gravely, full upon the faces of them. Now let the reader judge what a sadd spectacle and pitiful fright these poor creatures endured, for he faced them and often traversed the roome in this posture above an hour.

Sir William Knollys, as we know from letters of his which are preserved at Arbury, although an elderly and a married man, had amorous relations with one of the Maids of Honour, the audacious and frail Mary Fitton, who apparently deceived him with promises to marry him after his wife's death, while she carried on the intrigue, which had so disastrous an ending, with the Earl of Pembroke. I like to think that the pompous and besotted old Comptroller gave Shakespeare his hint for Malvolio; and that Mary Fitton, whom some have vainly tried to identify with the dark woman of the *Sonnets*, does after all make her appearance in the plays as none other than the pert and ingenious hussy, Maria.

The weakness of comedy generally lies in the difficulty of finding any device whereby to keep the wheels of the plot moving onwards. This is met in *Twelfth Night* by the introduction of the romantic story of Sebastian and Viola, their lamentable separation and joyous reunion. This motive, which Shakespeare had taken from the *Menaechmi* of Plautus and handled even more elaborately in *The Comedy of Errors*, is neatly woven into the fortunes of Olivia and Orsino; but it is kept in proper subordination, since it is no part of the dramatist's intention to turn the play into a melodrama. An interesting contribution to the total dramatic effect is made by the character of Viola, which in its naturalness and transparent honesty seems designed to heighten and set off by deliberate contrast the insincerities which it is the purpose of the comic muse to correct. Into the perfumed chamber of Olivia's sentimentality Viola comes like a breath of spring air, with her grave and contemptuous rebukes of the fine lady's poses—

> I see you what you are; you are too proud.
> But, if you were the devil, you are fair.
> My lord and master loves you. O! such love
> Could be but recompensed, though you were crowned
> The nonpareil of beauty.

With Orsino's dangling she has as little patience.
Were she refused a suit, she would not sit at home
and refine on love-philosophy; and when Olivia
asks her what she would do, she replies—

> Make me a willow cabin at your gate,
> And call upon my soul within the house;
> Write loyal cantons of contemned love,
> And sing them loud even in the dead of night;
> Halloo your name to the reverberate hills,
> And make the babbling gossip of the air
> Cry out 'Olivia!' O! you should not rest
> Between the elements of air and earth,
> But you should pity me.

And when love, a love that must be hidden, grows
like a flower in her own soul, she bears herself with
a gallant and sensitive pathos that informs the
scenes in which she appears with touches of
exquisite poetry. Surely it is Viola, not Olivia, of
whom it should have been written—

> Methought she purged the air of pestilence.

With the specific of simple truth she purges the
pestilence of artifice and rhetoric.

HAMLET

AN interrogation of the critical utterances that have accumulated during a century of eager Shakesperean study would doubtless place *Hamlet* upon a pinnacle as the extreme and most characteristic expression of the poet's tragic mood. One need not be concerned to challenge the judgment, although it probably owes something to the consonance of the subject-matter of the play with the intellectual history of the century itself; its spiritual upheaval, the paralysis of will that for a time inevitably proceeded from its blurred and uncertain vision of the ultimate tendency of things. It is not without consequence that the modern world has read Shakespeare through the spectacles of Coleridge. But, while criticism has lost its interest in the allocation of superlatives, it cannot allow *Hamlet* to be summed up as 'characteristic' of Shakespearean tragedy without a distinction. *Hamlet* belongs to the first book of Shakespeare's tragic reading of life, the psychological book in which he seeks to penetrate to the emotional springs of pity and awe through an analysis of the mental and moral nature of man, and to bring into relief at once the splendid potentialities of that nature, and the causes, rooted in itself, whereby a piece of work—'how noble in reason! how infinite in faculty! in form and moving how express and admirable! in action how like an angel! in apprehension how like a god!'—is foredoomed to sterility and failure. It is of this type of tragedy that *Hamlet* is characteristic; and it must not be forgotten that Shakespeare subsequently wrote his second book of cosmic tragedies, in which the tragic issue is sought, not so much in the faulty composition of man, as in the forces beyond and above man which are dimly discerned as making for his temporary exaltation and his eternal undoing. Of cosmic tragedy *Macbeth* and *King Lear* are characteristic, not *Hamlet*, wherein the cosmic themes are at the most fore-shadowed, in the questioning soliloquies of Hamlet himself, which, inconclusive as they are, begin to suggest some essential antinomy between the Christianity that serves as the official philosophy of the play and the tangle beyond all ravelling of the things that pass on earth. None the less the tragedy of *Hamlet* lies, if one may put it so, not in the content of the soliloquies, but in the fact that the soliloquies come to be uttered. It is the tragedy of the *intellectuel*, of the impotence of the over-cultivated imagination and the over-subtilized reasoning powers to meet the call of everyday life for practical efficiency. Thus it is an exact pendant to *Julius Cæsar*, in which the tragedy is that of the impotence in its turn of the most genuine and self-sacrificing moral idealism when brought face to face with precisely the same practical ordeal. And one must note the element of irony which hangs about all

tragedy. Hamlet does not fail because the problems
of practical life are not subtle; and Brutus does not
fail because there is no room in practical life for
self-sacrifice. Tragedy comes because the subtle-
ties are so many and the occasions for self-sacrifice
so obvious, that only the stupid brain or the blunt
moral sense is able to disregard them, and reach
the goal.

In his way, Shakespeare has imposed his
psychology, apparently by means of more than
one recension, upon an existing theme of popular
tragedy, the features of which he has, after all, not
wholly eliminated. There was certainly an earlier
Hamlet, probably by another hand, which one may
think of as a sufficiently crude piece, pulsating
with blood and revenge, in the manner of *The
Spanish Tragedy* and *Titus Andronicus*. Into the
midst of such a story the dramatist has deliberately
set his modern born out of due time, the high-
strung dreamer who moves through it to the
disaster of its hurried close. He is the academic
man, the philosopher, brought suddenly into the
world of strenuous action, and proving himself
but the clay pot there. The fatal habit of speculation, fatal at Elsinore, however proper and desirable
at Wittenberg, is his undoing. Cursed with the—

> Craven scruple
> Of thinking too precisely on the event,

he is predestined to a failure in the hour of trial
from which no truth and intensity of feeling, no
delicacy of moral fibre, no compass and profundity

of intellectual judgment, can save him. *Hamlet* is presented as no ordinary prince. His spirit has been touched to fine issues; his wit is keen-edged and dipped in irony; his ethical outlook is unusual among the ruder Danes. He is not a mere boy when the play opens, but up to that moment his life has been serene and undisturbed. The unexpected death of his father has called him back from the University of Wittenberg, where his time has been spent in an atmosphere of studious calm and philosophic speculation. His tastes are those of the scholar; he loves to read for hours together, and, like most literary men, he takes great delight in the stage, with whose theory and practice he is familiar. He is no recluse; he has the genius for friendship and for love; when at Elsinore he has been conspicuous in the gallant exercises of the age. He is the darling of the court and beloved by the people. But his real interest is all in speculation, in the play of mind around a subject, in the contemplation of it on all sides and from every point of view. Such a training has not fitted him to act a kingly part in stirring times; the intellectual element in him has come to outweigh the practical; the vivid consciousness of many possible courses of conduct deters him from the strenuous pursuit of one; so that he has lost the power of deliberate purposeful action, and, by a strange paradox, if this thoughtful man acts at all, it must be from impulse.

Quite suddenly the dreamer finds himself face

to face with a thing to be done. According to the ethics of the age it becomes his imperative duty to revenge his father's murder; a difficult task, and one whose success might well seem doubtful. But Hamlet does not shrink at first from recognizing the obligation; it is 'cursed spite' that the burden of setting the world straight should have fallen upon him, but he will not refuse to shoulder it. Only the habits of a lifetime are not to be thrown off so easily. As the excitement of the ghost's revelation passes away, the laws of character begin to reassert themselves. The necessity of 'thinking it over' is potent with Hamlet. Instead of revealing all to his friends and enlisting their assistance, he binds them to secrecy and forms the plan of pretending madness that he may gain time to consider his position.

Criticism of the play is apt to centre round the question, 'Was Hamlet, at any time and in any sense, really mad?' Admittedly he set out to put an antic disposition on; but it has been held, sometimes with much learning of the alienist, that in course of time, under the strain of the situation, the pretence adopted as a mask passed into a reality. I do not think that the text, fairly read, supports this theory, and in the abstract it is surely untenable. Psychology, indeed, is hard put to it to establish a rigid dividing-line between the sane and the insane. The pathologist may distinguish certain abnormal conditions of brain-areas and call them diseased; or the lawyer may apply working tests to determine the point at which restraint of the individual liberty becomes necessary in the public interest. But beyond that you cannot go. No one, from any wider point of view, can lay his finger upon one manifestation here or there of the infinite variety of human character, and say with assurance, 'This way madness lies.' Only of one thing we may be sure. Shakespeare did not mean Hamlet to be mad in any sense which would put his actions in a quite different category from those of other men. How could it be so, since the responsibility of the free agent is of the essence of psychological tragedy, and to have eliminated Hamlet's responsibility would have been to divest his story of humanity and leave it meaningless?

Consideration, however, cannot make Hamlet's position other than a disconcerting one. In the first place, he is absolutely alone. The court at Elsinore is filled with quite ordinary people, none of whom can understand him, to none of whom he can look for help. This note of contrast between Hamlet and his surroundings is struck again and again. They are of another world than his, limited, commonplace, incapable of ideals. His motives and feelings, his scruples and hesitations, are hopelessly beyond their comprehension. And therefore—this is the irony of it—most of them are far more fitted to deal with a practical crisis in life than this cultured idealist of a prince. There are 'the good king and queen'; Claudius, shrewd and ready for an emergency, one who has set foot in the paths of villainy and will not turn back, for all the dim visitings of momentary remorse; Gertrude, a slave to the stronger nature, living in the present, unable to realize her own moral degradation. There is Horatio, a straightforward upright soldier, one whom Hamlet intensely respects, comes even to envy, but who is not subtle enough to be of much use to him. There is Polonius, a played-out state official, vain and slow-witted, pattering words of wisdom which he does not understand and cannot put into practice. There are his son and daughter, Laertes and Ophelia; Laertes, a shallow, vigorous young noble, quick with a word, and quick with a blow, but of less than average temper in brain and ethics; Ophelia, a timid conventional girl, too fragile a reed for a man to lean upon. Hamlet loves her, and she loves Hamlet, but it is not a love that will bear him through the deep waters of affliction. The rest of the court are typified by Osric the waterfly, and by Guildenstern and Rosencrantz, of whom if you say Rosencrantz and Guildenstern it makes no difference; echoes, nonentities. With Hamlet on one side and these on the other, the elements of a tragedy are complete; the problem can work out to no satisfactory conclusion.

Once Hamlet has shrunk from immediate action, the possibilities of delay exercise an irresistible fascination over him. The ingenuity of his intellect exhausts itself in the discovery of obstacles; he takes every turn and twist to avoid the fatal necessity for action. At first he looks to

Ophelia, the well-beloved. She will give him strength to accomplish his mission; but the scene in her closet, and still more the lie which she tells when her father is behind the arras, confess her weakness and compel him to renunciation. In the meantime he continues the assumption of madness. It serves a double purpose; he is free from the intolerable burden of keeping on good terms with Claudius and the rest; he can fight out the battle with himself in peace, while he mocks them with the ironies congenial to his mood. And what is more, he can let himself go; the strain of his overwrought mind relieves itself in bursts of an extravagance only half affected. He plays the madman to prevent himself from becoming one. But all the while he is no nearer the end. He has turned the whole matter over and cannot decide. His thoughts slip away from the plain issue and lose themselves in a bitter criticism of all created things. In this the speculative temper infallibly betrays itself; the interest of the universal, not of the particular, is always dominant with Hamlet; not his mother's sin, but the frailty of women, is his natural theme. And so it is with a pang that he constantly recalls himself to the insistent actual life, from the world in which he is a past-master to that wherein he gropes ineffectively. Of course he is fully aware of his own weakness; a deficiency of self-analysis is not likely to be one of his failings; but this does not give him power to throw it off, or help him from his maze of recurring dilemmas.

More than once he is on the point of cutting the knot by death, but even for that he has not sufficient conviction.

At last the crisis comes. Hamlet has resolved that the play-scene shall decide once for all the question of the king's guilt. That guilt is made most manifest, and the opportunity for revenge is offered him. He does not take it. Covering his weakness with unreal reasons, he passes into the queen's chamber. After that it is too late. The impetuous murder of Polonius is the first link in a chain of calamities. Moreover it gives Claudius his chance. The king has never been wholly deceived by Hamlet's madness; he is sent to England, and only escapes that trap to fall into another. True, in the end the king dies by one impulsive stroke; but that cannot repair the ruin which Hamlet's want of purpose has caused. The infinitely sad fate of Ophelia; the deaths of Polonius, Laertes, Gertrude, Rosencrantz, Guildenstern; for all their faults, all these are a sacrifice on the altar of his infirmity. Only for Hamlet himself is the fatal blow, opening to him the doors of forgotten felicity, 'a consummation devoutly to be wished.'

The tragic ineffectiveness of the speculative intellect in a world of action, that is the keynote of the play. In Hamlet, as in Brutus, the idealist gets the worst of it, and we are left to wonder at the irony of things by which it is so. And just as the figure of Brutus is set between the two triumphant Philistines, Cæsar and Antony, so Shakespeare is careful to provide a similar contrast for Hamlet. Partly this is to be found in Horatio, 'the man who is not passion's slave,' but still more in the stranger from Norway, Fortinbras. The very existence of Fortinbras and the danger with which he threatens the state show the need for an iron hand in Denmark; Hamlet's reflections on his meeting with the Norwegian soldiers emphasize the same point; and the final appearance of Fortinbras on the weltering stage and his selection by Hamlet in his last will and testament as the true saviour of society are fully significant. It is the lesson of *Henry the Fifth*, the lesson of the 'still strong man in a blatant land.' Only in *Hamlet* it is the other side of the shield that Shakespeare approaches. The heroic play comes singing the pæan and blowing the trumpets of triumphant efficiency; the tragedy looks deeper, to shed its unavailing tear over—

> All the world's coarse thumb
> And finger failed to plumb;
> So passed in making up the main account;

and the blare of the trumpets ceases, as the poor heap of ineffectual ideals and fantastic loyalties is borne away upon the bier. 'The rest is silence.'

TROILUS and CRESSIDA

COMEDY, in *Troilus and Cressida*, becomes critical, and Shakespeare goes tilting at illusions. Naturally, they are illusions which he has himself shared, for these are always the worst enemies of the speculative intellect. When he was hardly out of his apprenticeship to the stage, he had found the fullest and most perfect expression for the lyric imagination of youth in the great romantic tragedy of *Romeo and Juliet*. Herewith he added one to the small number of the world's immortal love-stories, and at the same time uttered a faith that was in him. The exaltation of the passion of sex into a spiritual ideal is unhesitating. Love is shown to be stronger than hate, stronger than death itself; and the common way of a man with a maid blossoms forth into the central mystery of things. A few years later he wound up his series of studies in the psychology of kingship with the splendid portrait of Henry the Fifth, and sang the typical hero, the leader of men, the knight who gathers into his own chivalric personality all the magnificent qualities which bring liberty and domination to a warlike race. This is another ideal, no longer that of dreamy and emotional youth, but that of effective and vigorous manhood. *Romeo and Juliet* and *Henry the Fifth* mark each a stage in Shakespeare's spiritual development; in each he affirms a conviction, waves a banner.

It may be taken as established that, within a year or two after *Henry the Fifth*, a singular change had come about in Shakespeare's disposition, which reflects itself clearly both in the themes and in the temper of his plays. The note of tragedy struck in *Julius Cæsar*, which already gives a very different presentation of the hero to that of its predecessor, is repeated and intensified in *Hamlet*; and with *Hamlet* begins a period in which the dramatist consistently sees things black instead of rose-coloured, a period of ever-deepening tragedy, and of embittered comedy, from which all that is gay and genial in the comic perception of life has been omitted. It is easier to recognize this change than to account for it. An earlier school of criticism found in it the echo of those disappointments in love and friendship of which the shadowy and enigmatic chronicle is in the *Sonnets*. But it is no longer possible to maintain a date for the writing of the greater number of the *Sonnets* which can in any way be made to bear out such a theory. Whatever may be the experience which they reveal or refuse to reveal, it was long ago buried with Shakespeare's youth; and all the light-heartedness of *As You Like It* and its fellows had intervened before *Hamlet* came to be written. It is more plausible to trace some connection between Shakespeare's world-sickness and the dashing of the hopes for England which many, and perhaps he too, had founded upon the career of the Earl of Essex. But such conjectures are apt to prove will o' the wisps, and the pursuit of them to lead into bogs of controversy where the sure foothold of ascertained fact is altogether lacking.

In *Troilus and Cressida* a disillusioned Shakespeare turns back upon his own former ideals and the world's ancient ideals of heroism and romance, and questions them. Love of woman and honour of man; do they really exist, or are they but the thin veils which poetic sentiment has chosen to throw over the grinning realities of wantonness and egoism? The comedy sets the issues with a grave irony which alone differentiates it from a tragedy. The choice of its theme is determined by the audacity of genius. The idealists are challenged upon their own ground. The tale of Troy had had a unique literary history. In its turn it had served as the supreme expression, first of epic and then of romance. Upon Homer's great narrative of the ten years' struggle between Greece and Ilium and of the chivalric heroisms of Hector and Achilles, Chaucer had raised a superstructure in which the relations of Troilus and Cressida were decked out with the last dying splendours of mediæval amorous romance. It would be the triumph of disillusion to bring the battering-rams of analysis to bear upon this unassailable story, until Achilles shall be displayed as no better than a poltroon and Cressida as the merest light o' love.

The thing is written as a comedy, and the

intention does not at once declare itself. But for the doubtful talk of and about Helen and the significant presence of Pandar the early scenes in Troy might be the introduction to an ordinary love plot. Troilus is an honest boy enough—

> As true as truth's simplicity,
> And simpler than the infancy of truth;

and although one could wish that Cressida's resentment at her uncle's intervention were more thorough-going, her oncomings and her shrinkings do not differ much, save perhaps for a touch of hotter blood, from those of Rosalind in *As You Like It*. Nor does Shakespeare, to heighten his contrast, spare an expense of poetry in the delineation of the raptures and the vows of the lovers. The illusion must convince before it is pricked and shown to be a bubble. Troilus finds great words with which to sign away his soul for an eternity—

> True swains in love shall in the world to come
> Approve their truth by Troilus. When their rhymes,
> Full of protest, of oath, and big compare,
> Want similes, truth tired with iteration,
> 'As true as steel, as plantage to the moon,
> As sun to day, as turtle to her mate,
> As iron to adamant, as earth to the centre,'
> Yet after all comparisons of truth,
> As truth's authentic author to be cited,
> 'As true as Troilus' shall crown up the verse
> And sanctify the numbers.

And the shallowness of Cressida's little nature is hidden when she lifts her eyes to reply—

> If I be false, or swerve a hair from truth,
> When time is old and hath forgot itself,
> When waterdrops have worn the stones of Troy,
> And blind oblivion swallowed cities up,
> And mighty states characterless are grated
> To dusty nothing; yet let memory,
> From false to false, among false maids in love,
> Upbraid my falsehood!

It is a delicate love-scene too in the cool dawn before the fateful knocking of Æneas comes upon the door of Pandar's house; and the lark which gives warning that brief night is past can hardly fail to suggest a deliberate reminiscence of the corresponding episode in *Romeo and Juliet*. Then comes the parting, and a reluctant Cressida must to the Grecian camp. The lyric note is sustained to the end, and the vague doubts that already begin to haunt the soul of Troilus lend pathos to his hurried leavetaking—

> Injurious Time now, with a robber's haste,
> Crams his rich thievery up, he knows not how.
> As many farewells as be stars in heaven,
> With distinct breath and consigned kisses to them,
> He fumbles up into a loose adieu;
> And scants us with a single famished kiss,
> Distasted with the salt of broken tears.

Cressida is beheld only twice again; firstly when the cool self-possession which she shows at her somewhat disconcerting reception in the Grecian camp leads Ulysses, who knows the hearts of men and women, to set her down at first sight as a sluttish spoil of opportunity and daughter of the

game; and lastly in the midnight scene before the
tent of Calchas, where all her coquetries are be-
stowed upon Diomede before the revolting eyes
of Troilus, and the lad's young edifice of faiths
and loyalties comes crumbling about his feet. The
disillusionment of Troilus is our disillusionment,
and to Pandar, with his insolent leer at the 'brethren
and sisters of the hold-door trade' whom he
professes to find in the audience, is committed
the epilogue of the play. Troilus will not have us
'square the general sex by Cressid's rule'; but
indeed it is to be surmised that Shakespeare meant
little else. The soul of Cressida is strange to the
loyalties of a Juliet before her or an Imogen after
her. Her nearest sister is perhaps the pitiful and
frail Ophelia. But she is not a psychological
monstrosity like her uncle. To set her down as a
professional wanton who deliberately angles for
the soul of her lover, were to mistake the play. It
is in her humanity that the bitterness of it lies.
She was not made of the stuff of heroines, but her
vows and protestations were real enough when
they were uttered. She was but a light woman.
And when Shakespeare wrote her story he was in
a mood to say, 'She was but a woman.'

The scenes dealing with the fortunes of the war
contain much, in the disquisitions of Ulysses and
the heart-searchings of Hector and his brothers
with regard to the obligations of honour imposed
upon them by the rape of Helen, in which a
satirical intention is not obvious; and they lend

some colour to the theory that Shakespeare was utilizing material originally composed in a different vein. One fancies that, as the play was first conceived, Ulysses was intended to occupy a more significant part in it, and that it may have been designed as a sort of pendant to *Julius Cæsar*, which should analyse the respective contributions to efficiency made by the tall man of his hands on the one side, and on the other by the strategic brain with its bedwork, mappery and closet-war. The last act, again, shows Shakespeare carried away to some extent by the glamour of the old epic narrative, and writing with gusto of the dreadful Sagittary, and of Margarelon standing colossus-wise, waving his beam, upon the pashed corpses of the kings. It is, of course, in the figure of Achilles that the critical purpose is concentrated. In Achilles the hero is set before us as a brawny and brainless swashbuckler, a kind of guardsman, as guardsmen were conceived of in early Victorian fiction, sulking in his tent out of a childish arrogance, and incapable of any lofty vision or of sacrifice for any cause other than his own reputation. He is lazy as well as stupid; lolls on a day-bed with Patroclus, and amuses himself, so far as he understands them, with the ineffable jests of Thersites, whose foul tongue and all-pervading cynicism serve as a constant chorus to this side of the play. The meanest motives alone determine Achilles for and against participation in the war; he will fight, out of jealousy against Ajax and

197

because he is stung with the taunts of Hector; he will not fight, because so to do would interrupt an idle amour with Polyxena. Finally, when he is roused by the death of Patroclus and the havoc wrought among his Myrmidons, he vanquishes Hector, not in single combat, but by a treacherous plot in which he directs the swords of others against an unarmed man. So he triumphs over the corpse, and the Greeks vaunt a hero from whose composition courage and chivalry are alike omitted. Thersites here, as there Pandar, is justified of his creed.

Ajax, for the purposes of the play, is an echo of Achilles; but it is just possible that he also serves an object of literary controversy. The Cambridge play of *The Return from Parnassus* puts into the mouth of the actor Kempe an allusion to a certain 'purge' administered by 'our fellow, Shakespeare,' to put down that redoubtable champion Ben Jonson. If this 'purge' is to be looked for in Shakespeare's plays as they have come down to us, it is to be found more probably than elsewhere in the description of Ajax which Alexander gives to Cressida in the second scene of the first act.

This man, lady, hath robbed many beasts of their particular additions; he is as valiant as the lion, churlish as the bear, slow as the elephant; a man into whom nature hath so crowded humours that his valour is crushed into folly, his folly sauced with discretion. There is no man hath a virtue that he hath not a glimpse of, nor any man an attaint but he carries some stain of it. He is melancholy without cause, and merry against the hair. He hath the joints of every thing, but every thing so out of joint, that he is a gouty Briareus, many hands and no use; or purblind Argus, all eyes and no sight.

This, with its reference to humours, may pass for a caricature of Ben Jonson, and has no special bearing upon the actual personality of the beef-witted Ajax, as he is represented later in the play. Perhaps the actor who represented Ajax gave point to the jest by making up so as to imitate Ben Jonson's rough-hewn features. There are indications in the epistle to the play that it had never been represented on the ordinary London stage. On the other hand, it had certainly been acted somewhere before 1603. One wonders whether it had been produced, like *The Return from Parnassus* itself, at Cambridge. *Hamlet* is shown by the title-page of the First Quarto to have been performed there; and the classical subject would have its appropriateness before an academic audience.

ALL'S WELL that ENDS WELL

A RATHER fantastic desire to identify *All's Well that Ends Well* with the *Love's Labour's Won* mentioned by Francis Meres is mainly responsible for the persistent attempt of many scholars to trace in its occasional rhymed passages the survivals of an earlier and discarded version of the play. But Shakespeare's use of rhyme, after he had given it up as a normal vehicle of dialogue, is apt to be deliberate, serving to indicate a heightening of the dramatic mood or to fulfil some other quite definite purpose; and it becomes in consequence a very untrustworthy guide in determining questions of chronology. There is no reason to suppose that *All's Well that Ends Well* affords an exception; and in any case, even if an earlier draft lie concealed, there can be little doubt that the whole structure and handling of the play in its present form belong to the same and to a fairly advanced date in Shakespeare's development. It groups itself undeniably with *Troilus and Cressida* and *Measure for Measure*, as one of the bitter comedies; for it is a comedy from which all laughter has evaporated, save the grim laughter which follows the dubious sallies of Monsieur Lavache and the contemptuous laughter which presides over the plucking bare of the ineffable Parolles. The spiritual affinities of Helena's

200

story are indeed far less with the radiant humour of *Twelfth Night* and *As You Like It* than with the analytic psychology of the great advance-guard of tragedy, *Julius Cæsar* and *Hamlet*, which was almost contemporary with these. Of *Hamlet* in particular, one is again and again reminded. The advice of the Countess to Bertram in the opening scene curiously re-echoes that of Polonius to Bertram's counterpart, Laertes; and what is Parolles but the more elaborate portrait of the same type of human vanity which is represented by the thumb-nail sketch of Osric the water-fly? The analogy to be traced, however, goes far deeper than this. In Brutus and in Hamlet, Shakespeare had set side by side two tragic studies of greatness failing to be greatness through the excess or defect of certain qualities whose perfect balance is necessary to efficiency. It is precisely such another study that the fortunes of Helena, if rightly read, reveal.

Like all the difficult plays, *All's Well that Ends Well* was bound to mislead the more superficial commentators. Over Helena sentiment has run riot. Hear how Mrs Jameson gushes—

There never was, perhaps, a more beautiful picture of a woman's love, cherished in secret, not self-consuming in silent languishment—not pining in thought—not passive and 'desponding over its idol'—but patient and hopeful, strong in its own intensity, and sustained by its own fond faith....The mere pride of rank and birth is a prejudice of which she cannot comprehend the force, because her mind towers so immeasurably above it; and, compared to the infinite love which swells within her own bosom, it sinks into nothing. She cannot conceive that he to whom she has devoted her heart and truth, her soul, her life, her services, must not one day love her in return; and once her own beyond the reach of fate, that her cares, her caresses, her unwearied, patient tenderness, will not at last 'win her lord to look upon her'....It is this fond faith which, hoping all things, enables her to endure all things; which hallows and dignifies the surrender of her woman's pride, making it a sacrifice on which virtue and love throw a mingled incense.

One would hardly gather from this rhapsody the simple truth that the play is drenched in irony; and that what in virtue of her 'fond faith' and her 'unwearied, patient tenderness' Helena really effects is, firstly, to drive a man, who not merely does not love her but loves someone else, into a forced marriage by a trick, and then by another trick to substitute herself in her husband's bed for the mistress whom he wishes to seduce, and so to obtain the consummation which his not un-natural coldness would otherwise have denied her. Surely this unsavoury adventure, for the sake of a not very desirable prize, is inadequately described as 'the surrender of her woman's pride.'

Obviously, I think, the issue of the thing is not Helena's triumph but Helena's degradation. I conceive Shakespeare's design to have been some-thing like this. He has shown noble manhood made ineffective as a practical instrument for life, in Hamlet by very intellect, and in Brutus by very idealism. He will now show noble womanhood made equally ineffective by the highest quality of womanhood itself, which is love; by the imperious instinct of sex, which drives Helena through unworthy paths to a profitless goal, and turns man's tender helpmate, like Mr Bernard Shaw's Anne Whitefield, into the keen and unswerving huntress of man. Thus indeed is she Dian's maid. The play will bear closer analysis from this point of view. Certainly Helena is a nobly planned woman. Her level brain, her depth of feeling, her easy mastery of every situation in which she finds herself, place her of all Shakespeare's heroines nearest to the Portia of *The Merchant of Venice*. Thus she impresses everyone with whom she comes into contact and who is competent to judge. She is the worthy child of a worthy father. 'She derives her honesty and achieves her goodness.' To the gracious old Countess she is dear as a daughter. 'She may lawfully make title to as much love as she finds; there is more owing her than is paid, and more shall be paid her than she'll demand.' To Lafeu, experienced and sane in judgment, for all his light deliverance, she is—

> One, that in her sex, her years, profession,
> Wisdom and constancy, hath amazed me more
> Than I dare blame my weakness.

To the dying king, after his first conversation with her, it seems that—

> All that life can rate
> Worth name of life, in thee hath estimate,
> Youth, beauty, wisdom, courage, all
> That happiness and prime can happy call.

Only Parolles the witless and Bertram the unseeing fail to recognize the charm and the strength that are in her. Even beyond Portia she is dowered with an indomitable will, a will that exactly measures its means to its ends and regards no obstacles in its direct advance to the achievement it has set itself. In the very first scene her judgment of character is shown by her treatment of Parolles, with whose equivocal conversation she plays as if he were a child, while her mind is set on other things. She has no doubt whatever about him, knows him a notorious liar, thinks him a great way fool, solely a coward. But Bertram she loves, and cannot judge him at all. This unequalled virgin has fallen in love with a good-looking boy, as any other woman might. Her passion lingers on his arched brows, his hawking eye, his curls. She has come to think him desirable, and herself unworthy of him. She has forgot her father—

> My imagination
> Carries no favour in it but Bertram's.
> I am undone; there is no living, none,
> If Bertram be away. It were all one
> That I should love a bright particular star,
> And think to wed it, he is so above me.

As a matter of fact, of course, Bertram is a young ass, and has shown no touch of any quality worthy to mate with Helena's save the spirit which makes him unwilling to stay at court while others go to the wars—

> Creaking his shoes on the plain masonry,
> Till honour be bought up, and no sword worn
> But one to dance with!

The weakness of his nature is apparent in the influence won over him by Parolles, an empty-headed and boastful fool, with just enough intelligence to make his profit out of the novice to whom he has attached himself. Parolles chooses to treat Helena as a waiting-maid, and his pupil is not likely to lay aside the insolence of birth and to recognize how far a poor physician's daughter has the advantage of him in all the gifts of head and heart. He does not improve by acquaintance. The wisdom of the king in desiring to keep him from following the wars soon becomes apparent when he reaches Florence. He does honourable service in the field, but he has no power of self-restraint, and under the apt guidance of his ring-carrier he shows himself a dangerous and lascivious boy, and a whale to virginity. Ultimately he proves even worse than this, and in the last ordeal, when he is confronted with Diana and the rings, stands confessed a cur and a liar.

It is not for long that Helena continues in the mood of self-depreciation which leads her to think Bertram out of her sphere. Even while she is talking to Parolles she realizes the strength of her own love and of her own will, and before the end of the scene her resolution is taken. Henceforward she dominates the play, and passes from dishonour to dishonour on the path to her final victory—

> Our remedies oft in ourselves do lie
> Which we ascribe to heaven. The fated sky
> Gives us free scope; only doth backward pull
> Our slow designs when we ourselves are dull.

The first remedy is clearly to follow Bertram to Paris, and so she lies glibly and with an air of extreme candour to the Countess, and leaves behind her the impression that the only motive of her journey is the hope of curing the king. The king is cured, and Helena, who has been careful to secure the promise of her reward beforehand, claims Bertram's hand. There is a pretty air of modest deference about her—

> I dare not say I take you; but I give
> Me and my service, ever whilst I live,
> Into your guiding power.

Nevertheless she does take him, standing by cool and self-possessed, while the grateful king forces her hand upon a most reluctant husband. Even young asses have their rights, and one cannot but feel some sympathy with Bertram, who, as it appears afterwards, has already cast his eyes on Maudlin Lafeu, when he bursts out with his—

> O my Parolles, they have married me!

After the ceremony he dismisses Helena briefly enough. She is reduced to beg a kiss, which is denied her; and with this humiliation makes her way to Roussillon. Here she learns that it is his intention never to bed her, and at the thought of him in the wars her first instinct is to relent and set him free. But will is elastic and reasserts itself. She lies again to the Countess in the letter which expresses her intention to go upon a pilgrimage, so that Bertram may return; for, although she does put on the palmer's garb, it is only to pursue

her husband to Florence. Here occurs the substitution incident which, in this play as in *Measure
for Measure*, proves a difficult morsel for the
sentimental reader. Mrs Jameson faces the
problem by saying that 'the circumstances and
details with which Helena is surrounded are
shocking to our feelings and wounding to our
delicacy; and yet the beauty of the character is
made to triumph over all.' Of course that is not
really so. The meanness of the device to which
Helena stoops in order to secure a nominal posses-
sion of her husband is a measure of the spiritual
straits to which the instinct of sex has reduced the
noblest of women. Then come more lies, growing
easier and easier each time, until she can shepherd
Bertram with the report of her death back to
Marseilles, and there claim him in the presence of
the king by a proof of the literal fulfilment of the
conditions he had laid down.

In the end Bertram is reconciled. He has already
outgrown the 'snipped-taffeta fellow' and 'red-
tailed humble-bee' Parolles, and perhaps Helena
may succeed in making a man of him some day.
But after all it is a poor prize for which she has
trailed her honour in the dust; and comedy has
made strange progress with Shakespeare since he
shook our sides at the gross roguery of Falstaff, or
even the befooling of the poor coxcomb Malvolio.
Behind comedy so unsmiling as this some pertur-
bation of the once sunny spirit must needs lie.

MEASURE for MEASURE

MANY honest readers of Shakespeare quite frankly resent the very existence of *Measure for Measure*. They have formed a conception of the poet as the great idealist; as one who, although he has indeed sounded the heights and depths of experience, has yet kept unspotted his romantic soul; as one with whom they may be sure of breathing the ampler ether and diviner air, and who, through whatever searchings of heart he may lead them, may always be trusted in the long run to present and vindicate the eternal laws of righteousness. There are plays of Shakespeare, written in the healthy optimism of his youth or in the golden serenity of his waning years, which fit in well enough with this temper. There are others upon the purport of which it is able to put a subtle misconstruction. But *Measure for Measure* falls within neither of these categories. It just perplexes and offends, with its deliberate painting of the seamy side of things, through which intolerable personages pass to an end that is certainly determined by no principles of poetic justice. We are in unwholesome company, with Mistress Overdone the bawd and Pompey the pander. Claudio, who would sacrifice his sister's honour to save his life, is allowed to keep both his life and his Juliet. Even the hypocrite Angelo

has no worse fate than quiet days of oblivion with
Mariana in his garden circummured with brick.
There is no clear issue here, and to no profit of
righteousness has Isabella's white soul been
dragged through the mire. So the play is condemned, and all its beauties cannot save it; not
the sleepy music of the moated grange, nor the
marvellous psychology of the scenes between
Isabella and Angelo in the second Act and between
Isabella and Claudio in the third, nor the haunting
phrases that constantly startle the imagination at
turn after turn in the murky way. In vain Isabella
tells us in her passion of devotion—

> The impression of keen whips I'ld wear as rubies;

in vain is the deep maxim of the Duke—

> Spirits are not finely touched
> But to fine issues;

in vain the splendid flicker of poor weak Claudio's
soul, when he thinks for a moment that he is going
to be a hero—

> If I must die,
> I will encounter darkness as a bride,
> And hug it in my arms.

Measure for Measure is an unpleasant play, and
there is an end of it, for the sentimentalist.

Fortunately the critic has long ago made up his
account with sentimentalism, and has come to the
firm conviction that his business is with the
understanding, stage by stage, of Shakespeare's
spiritual development, rather than with the wish,
certainly idle and probably insolent, that this

development had been otherwise. He, therefore, without reference to any *a priori* conception, may take *Measure for Measure* for what it is, as forming, together with the group of plays to which it belongs and which includes also *All's Well that Ends Well* and *Troilus and Cressida*, the singularly interesting record of a particular phase in the poet's shifting outlook upon humanity and upon the universe to which humanity is bound. They are all unpleasant plays, the utterances of a puzzled and disturbed spirit, full of questionings, sceptical of its own ideals, looking with new misgiving into the ambiguous shadows of a world over which a cloud has passed and made a goblin of the sun. It is perhaps hardly worth while to speculate what causes, within or without, may have precipitated a mood so alien to that in which, quite recently, such light-hearted comedies as *As You Like It*, *Much Ado About Nothing*, and *Twelfth Night* had been written. To seek them in the misadventure of the *Sonnets*, or in the disconcerting politics of the Essex rebellion, is less to employ evidence than to indulge in the pleasant sport of biographical conjecture. Whatever the explanation, the fact remains that for a period in Shakespeare's history near the beginning of the seventeenth century the rose-red vision gave place to the grey, and that, if he still wrote as an idealist, it was as an idealist into whose imagination had passed the ferment of doubt and the bitterness of disillusion. And so *Measure for Measure* wears the rue of comedy with a difference.

Lucio is of the tribe of Mercutio, just without Mercutio's saving grace of the readiness to throw away his life for the sake of the game. The *milieu* of Mistress Overdone is the *milieu* of Mistress Quickly, and you may catch a veritable echo of the talk of mine hostess of Eastcheap in Pompey's description of the stewed prunes, 'which at that very distant time stood, as it were, in a fruit-dish, a dish of some threepence. Your honours have seen such dishes; they are not China dishes, but very good dishes.' The change is not in the puppets, but in their observer and interpreter. Sin, which was human, has become devilish. Here are the forms of comedy, the by-play of jest and the ending of reconciliation. But the limits of comedy, which may be serious but must be suave, are sorely strained. There is a cruel hint in the laughter, and the engineer of the reconciliation is surely a cynic.

It is perhaps characteristic of the state of mind out of which *Measure for Measure* came, that it is not only a painful, but also an extremely difficult play. As in certain modern plays, to which its affinities are perhaps closer than to anything in its own age, while the general critical intention is evident, it succeeds in evading rigid analysis. The intelligence of the spectator is stimulated, rather than satisfied. And in fact it may be doubted whether Shakespeare wrote it with any very clear scheme before him. It suggests rather the random and tentative exercise, in various directions at once, of a mordant analysis, resulting in a some-

what intricate design of unresolved and interwoven
themes. It is the work of a man searching somewhat vaguely for truth in unfamiliar paths. Some
threads of these cross-purposes may perhaps be
disentangled. There is one which resumes the
earlier criticism levelled in *Love's Labour's Lost*
at the life against nature. The philosophers of
Navarre shut their ears to the voice of nature's
most imperious instinct, until that instinct takes
its rapid and disconcerting revenge. More tragically disastrous is the issue of the less playful
attempt of the ruler of Vienna to shut out the
wantonness of the flesh. Claudio has hardly sinned.
'He hath but as offended in a dream,' says the
Provost. But the too hasty revival of the forgotten
edict shatters his youth and Juliet's, and hurries
him to a fiery ordeal which his frail soul proves
ill-fitted to endure. So is the idle way of a man with
a maid turned to tragedy. To Lucio's satire of the
man 'whose blood is very snow-broth,' in whose
house-eaves 'sparrows must not build, because
they are lecherous,' one need not attach too much
weight; for Lucio, in spite of his honest reverence
for the 'enskied and sainted' Isabella, speaks with
the voice of unregenerate Vienna. Yet there is
practical wisdom, did the Duke but know it, in
the worldling's warning that the nature of the
vice is such that 'it is impossible to extirp it quite,
friar, till eating and drinking be put down.' It is
Angelo's own case, however, which affords the
most complete refutation of the folly of endeavouring

to bind human nature in too strait bonds of discipline, in the picture of the austere man tripped by the very fault he most condemns, and driven through hypocrisy into the darkest ways of tyranny, violation, and judicial murder.

Another very obvious element in *Measure for Measure* is the remorseless analysis which probes the inmost being of man and strips him naked before the spectators while he—

> Plays such fantastic tricks before high heaven
> As makes the angels weep.

It is the temper of the inquisitor; and you can but shudder as a soul is brought into the torture-chamber and shrivels into nothingness before some sharp test of circumstance. The slow degradation and exposure of the 'prenzy' Angelo is a case in point; and still more the pitiful failure of the lad Claudio when called upon unawares to make his choice between death and disloyalty. It is a terrible scene, led up to with grave irony by the Duke's philosophical disquisition upon the vanity of life and of man, who is merely 'death's fool.' Claudio, indeed, is resigned to death, when a door to life, even though a dishonoured life, suddenly swings open before him. At first—for he is an honest boy—he rejects the thought. And then his imagination begins to work and to terrify itself with the details of mortality. Isabella knows her brother, and her spirit girds itself for quick battle with his weakness.

> *Claudio.*   Death is a fearful thing!
> *Isabella.*   And shamed life a hateful!
> *Claudio.*   Ay, but to die, and go we know not where;
> To lie in cold obstruction, and to rot;
> This sensible warm motion to become
> A kneaded clod; and the delighted spirit
> To bathe in fiery floods, or to reside
> In thrilling region of thick-ribbed ice;
> To be imprisoned in the viewless winds,
> And blown with restless violence round about
> The pendent world; or to be worse than worst
> Of those that lawless and incertain thought
> Imagine howling—'t is too horrible!
> The weariest and most loathed worldly life
> That age, ache, penury, and imprisonment
> Can lay on nature is a paradise
> To what we fear of death.

Claudio has undergone his ordeal, and has failed. It is but a step now to the unmanned cry of 'Sweet sister, let me live,' and to the pitiful contemplation of the ruins of a human soul. Is it the corroding atmosphere of moral suspicion which hangs about the play that leaves one not absolutely certain whether Isabella too has not had her ordeal and in her turn failed? She is a saint, of course; even Lucio feels that; and perhaps it comes quite naturally to a saint to say, 'More than our brother is our chastity.' Shakespeare does not suggest an alternative; but is it not legitimate to think that the question whether Isabella was wholly justified in the eyes of her creator is one of the enigmas of this most enigmatic play? In any case I am quite sure that the actual issue which is found in the pretended submission of Isabella and the device of the substituted Mariana, commonplace of romance as the latter may be, does not commend itself to the modern conscience. It is, however, perhaps a shade less displeasing than the inversion of the same situation in *All's Well that Ends Well*.

But is the criticism of *Measure for Measure* confined to humanity, or is Shakespeare already, as in some of his later plays, unable to exclude man's maker from his indictment of man? The 'old fantastical duke of dark corners,' from whose absence Angelo's brief authority springs, who amicably assists the development of the plot, and finally returns to reward the evil-doers and to abash Lucio, is a somewhat mysterious personage. It is not quite clear what is the dramatic purpose of Lucio's scandal about him, or how far he has judged the character of Angelo, of whose relations with Mariana he is aware, before the beginning of the action. His part in the story is a version of the familiar Haroun-al-raschid theme; and he must, I think, be held in a play dealing seriously with the problems of life to symbolize the workings of Providence. But then surely the treatment of Providence is ironical. Just as in the almost contemporary *Troilus and Cressida* Shakespeare is almost certainly turning to ridicule the traditional ideals of heroic romance, so here the duke can be nothing but a travesty of a Haroun-al-raschid. Theoretically it is his function to resolve all the

complications of the plot, and to re-establish the
shaken foundations of eternal justice by punishing
the wrong-doers and rewarding the innocent. In
effect, after prying about in disguise and preaching
sermons throughout the greater part of the play,
he is unable to perform his simple task without a
wholly unnecessary structure of superfluous mysti-
fication and intrigue. Why does he conceal from
Isabella, in her grief, the knowledge that her
brother yet lives? To what purpose is the further
prolongation of her agony, after his return, by the
pretended disbelief of her story and the suspicion
cast upon the friar, in whose person he has coun-
selled her? These are the antics of a cat with a
mouse, rather than the dispositions of a wise and
beneficent ruler; and it is difficult to see anything
in the grave elaboration of them, except a satirical
intention of Shakespeare towards theories about
the moral government of the universe which, for
the time being at least, he does not share. As yet,
indeed, his nascent pessimism has only advanced
to the point of finding ineffectiveness and not
deliberate ill-will in the ordering of things.
The thorough-going denunciations of *King Lear*
are still to come. But a narrower spiritual
gulf divides *Measure for Measure* from the tragedy
of *King Lear* than from the comedy of *As You
Like It*.

I do not suppose that everyone will read the
play exactly as I read it. Like all works of art that
spring out of a vexed, and not out of a limpid

mood, it lends itself to many and diverse interpretations. It must be confessed that it is broken music, and that broken music is not the highest form of composition; but at least it takes on new interest when the harp from which it is struck is the heart of a Shakespeare.

OTHELLO

Of all the great and moving Shakespearean plays, *Othello* is that in which the fullest expression is given to that particular quality of sentiment or emotion, to which belongs the name of pathos. One may perhaps define pathos as tragic pity. It is the welling up of human sympathy at the sight of something beautiful and frail in the grip of forces utterly beyond its own control, at the fate of the windlestraw in the floods. Tragedy, as Aristotle hinted long ago, arises out of the contemplation of the clash of forces and the triumph of the greater force, and its result in the human soul is to awake the feelings of pity and of awe. And pity or awe predominates according to the extent of the disproportion between the strength of the triumphant force and that which is defeated. It is awful when the Titans make head against the Gods, even though the ultimate issue can be in no way doubtful; it is pitiful when the chariot-wheels of destiny roll over and crush a human flower. The one spectacle yields tragedy in the fullest sense; the other pathos. This distinction corresponds closely to that between the effect upon the spectator of *Othello* and the effect of the two other tragedies which, both in time and in temper, stand nearest to it, *Macbeth* and *King Lear*. In *Macbeth* the pathetic hardly finds any expression; in *King Lear* it attaches itself mainly to the subordinate character of the helpless Cordelia, and if to Lear at all, not to him who wrangles with the elements upon the blasted heath, but to the ruined piece of nature who wanders, mad as the vexed sea, and crowned with rank fumitory and furrow weeds, through the acres of the sustaining corn. Lear and the Macbeths are of the race of Titans, and when they go under, the heavens may vaunt themselves to have conquered those who, for a moment at least, were in some sort their equals. About Othello and Desdemona there is nothing of the Titanic. They are noble, of course, and gracious in their lives; otherwise their fate would have altogether lacked that exalted interest which is essential even to pathetic tragedy. But nevertheless, when the push comes, the simple open-hearted soldier and the tender woman who loves him prove to have nothing to oppose to the forces that beset them. They are easy victims, and it is with the sense of springing tears rather than with the thrill of lost battle that we watch them to the hopeless end.

In other respects, the grouping of *Othello* with *Macbeth* and *King Lear* is complete. Already the subtle change has come over Shakespeare's attitude towards the problems of existence whereby cosmic tragedy has replaced the earlier psychological tragedy of *Julius Cæsar* and of *Hamlet*. The issue has shifted from the relations of man and man to the relations of man and his creator. The sceptical ironies of the bitter comedies begin to take shape as a definite arraignment of the scheme of things. Failure is presented as a resultant no longer of character but of destiny; and the fall of Othello is not merely the fall of a good man, but the purposed and inevitable defeat of goodness itself. The play is a duel, in which goodness as such is pitted against evil as such, and to represent evil Shakespeare has recourse to the revival of a type of character which finds its analogues in some of his earliest plays and still more in plays not his. In Iago he returns, with a more definite philosophic purpose as well as with a far greater subtlety of delineation, to the model which he had taken from Marlowe's Barabbas and used, with an imperfect comprehension of its real dramatic significance, in Aaron the Moor and in Richard Crookback. Once more, and now to be treated as what he is, a symbol, not as what he is not, a human being, there comes upon the stage the terrible man according to Machiavelli, with his deliberate and self-conscious choice of evil to be his good, and his superhuman resource and efficiency in shaping all events towards the realization of his diabolical end. Iago, playing upon the souls of all the other personages in the drama like puppets, and manipulating them this way and that as the intricacies of his plot for their common destruction require, is obviously enough the efficient cause of the whole tragic working of *Othello*. His essential inhumanity is no less apparent. He has the outward form and members of a man, but his dramatic function is

that of the incarnation of the forces of evil, of the
devil himself.

> I look down towards his feet; but that's a fable,

says the disillusioned Othello, when the whole
map of Iago's villainy is suddenly unrolled, an
hour too late, before him. Iago is clear enough
about himself and his calling—

> Divinity of hell!
> When devils will the blackest sins put on,
> They do suggest at first with heavenly shows,
> As I do now.

In the sinister soliloquies with which, at every
pause in the action, he delights to take the stage
and let the audience into his secrets, he reveals
the clearest intellectual appreciation of the good
points, which are for him the weak points, of his
opponents; and it is precisely upon these, upon
the unquestioning confidence of Othello and upon
the generous impulses of Desdemona's translucent
soul, that he fastens most securely the web of the
intrigue that is to be their ruin. Those Mephisto-
phelean confidences give an added horror to the
scenes in which the other personages reappear
and Iago composes the sneer upon his countenance
to assume once more the profitable *rôle* of the disinterested follower or the sympathetic friend. And
so, at the height of his villainy, his unsuspecting
victim sings his praises—

> This fellow's of exceeding honesty,
> And knows all qualities, with a learned spirit,
> Of human dealings.

Honest Iago! That virtue should bestow this epithet upon vice is a measure of the defenceless-ness of virtue in the eternal conflict. It has been doubted whether Shakespeare did not intend to qualify the abstract devilry of Iago by assigning for his hatred of Othello certain motives not altogether inhuman. He represents himself to Roderigo as bearing the grudge of a soldier who has been passed over for one less worthy. It is not perhaps necessary to believe everything he says to Roderigo, although he is elsewhere not too careful to conceal his real self before so incon-siderable a hearer. Roderigo is not a fish that requires much playing. But it is in the more intimate revelation of his soliloquies that he pro-fesses a suspicion that the Moor has played him false with Emilia and a desire to be evened with him, wife for wife. It is hardly to be supposed that this suspicion is meant to have any foundation. Othello's behaviour to Emilia certainly lends it no credence, and it is clear that for Iago himself it is an occasion rather than a motive for treachery—

> I know not if it be true;
> But I, for mere suspicion in that kind,
> Will do as if for surety.

What is illustrated is the willingness of evil to be convinced of evil, in contrast to the reluctance with which a similar suspicion is entertained and the profound upheaval which it causes in Othello's noble soul.

The type of Iago fitted in with something

profound in Shakespeare's tragical apprehension of the world. It is resumed, not in the main plot but in the sub-plot of *King Lear*, where the melodramatic Edmund has precisely Iago's trick of analysing his own infamy in cynical comment before the audience. And it recurs for the last time, with a significant difference, in the Iachimo of *Cymbeline*. One may almost take *Cymbeline* as the palinode to *Othello*, and the comparison between Iago and Iachimo serves well to measure the gulf that lies between the perturbed Shakespeare of the great tragedies and Shakespeare in the golden mood of recovered optimism which inspires the last romances. The function of the character is the same; it is the relation of that function to the general drift and ultimate outcome of the drama which is altered. Iachimo is not, indeed, so self-conscious a Machiavellian as Iago; he does not stop in the course of his intrigues to hug himself on his villainy, or to give expression to the diabolical faith that is in him. Yet on any other hypothesis than that of sheer devilry his actions are unintelligible. The mere desire to win his wager with Posthumus is too clearly an inadequate inducement to the undertaking of a toilsome journey and a desperate enterprise. It is as the incarnate spirit of evil that he comes, first to tempt Imogen, and when that fails, to ensnare her and Posthumus in the folds of a plot closely parallel to that which Iago weaves for the undoing of Othello and Desdemona. Like Iago he is a disintegrating force,

223

and out of the innocence and confidence of his victims he fashions the weapons which are to be used for their destruction. Only in the long run the power which Iago represents and symbolizes proves greater than innocence, and the same power as represented and symbolized by Iachimo proves less than innocence. And of course this, from the point of view of philosophy, and from that of drama as a reflection and material expression of philosophy, is a very fundamental difference indeed. The darkness which settles upon *Othello* is lit by no gleam of hope at the close; but the sunshine breaks into the last scene of *Cymbeline*, and it becomes apparent that not only has evil proved impotent to wreck the faith and happiness of Imogen, but also evil has ultimately ceased to be dominant even in the black soul of Iachimo itself. By Imogen the very devil is taught—

> The wide difference
> 'Twixt amorous and villainous.

Othello, no less than Iago, would seem at first sight to be paralleled in the later plays, to some degree by Posthumus, and to a greater by the Leontes of *The Winter's Tale*. But the resemblance is too superficial a one to bear much analysis. On this there is perhaps little to be added to one of the finest passages in Coleridge's unequal Shakespearean comment.

Jealousy does not strike me as the point in Othello's passion; I take it to be rather an agony that the creature, whom he had believed angelic, with whom he had garnered up his heart, and whom he could not help still loving, should be proved impure and worthless. It was the struggle *not* to love her. It was a moral indignation and regret that virtue should so fall:—'But yet the *pity* of it, Iago!—O Iago! the *pity* of it, Iago!'

Clearly, if Othello had been a Leontes, he would have been unfitted for the part he has to play in the drama. Shakespeare's scheme entails an opposition between black and white, and jealousy in the meaner sense would have lost Othello the sympathies which he is bound to maintain in order that tragic pity may be evoked. By his simplicity he falls, but his nobility of soul must remain unstained. It is not so with Posthumus or Leontes, for it is not Posthumus but Imogen, and it is not Leontes but Hermione, upon whom the dramatist depends to hold the sympathies of the audience and to carry them on through the changing fortunes to the ultimate triumph. The jealous husbands of *Cymbeline* and *The Winter's Tale* are only instruments of the emotional history; and their own personalities may remain unsympathetic until the time comes when their repentance is needed to contribute to the general reconciliation. But Othello must never be unsympathetic. From the beginning he is a gracious and doomed creature, a child in spirit, walking on the abyss; and the tragic pity slowly gathers as he moves on with honest eyes to the sudden disaster which Iago has prepared.

MACBETH

POPULAR tragedy demands its obvious and acknowledged villain, a visible and as it were professional worker of iniquity, whose deeds of blood and ravishment may bring the authentic thrill of horror to gross nerves and imaginations far from tickle o' the sere. As soon as psychology meddles in the matter and spectators with cultivated faculties begin to ask that drama shall, at any rate in some degree, answer to the average experience of life, this puppet ceases to appeal. For the actual organization of society, however far from perfect, is at least so far advanced as to leave little room for the obvious villain, whose undramatic fate it usually is to be discovered at an early stage, and treated, according to circumstances, as a criminal or as a lunatic; in either event, gagged and rendered harmless. The exceptions are so rare as hardly to interest the typical spectator, or rather the typical crowd of spectators, whose measure of psychology compasses mainly the normal. Moreover, it readily becomes apparent that the obvious villain is by no means an essential factor in the production of tragedy. By expelling the monstrous incarnation of evil you certainly do not expel evil itself; and, when once the primitive level of intelligence has been passed, the clash of the forces that make for and against righteousness in the various heart of man yields the tragic thrill none the less because the showman has left off painting in the old primary colours—

> In tragic life, God wot,
> No villain need be! Passions spin the plot:
> We are betrayed by what is false within.

Thus, in the ordinary course of literary evolution, external tragedy gives way to psychological tragedy. But there is a third grade, to which only the gods or titans of literature successfully attain. This is cosmic tragedy. From the contemplation of good and evil in the individual soul, the philosophic mind passes to the contemplation of good and evil in the totality of things, or more precisely, in that tangled web of individual souls acting under material conditions, which is all of the totality of things whereto the limitations of the human spirit permit access; and on this basis forms its conceptions of the intention and working of the non-human forces, perhaps imaginary, which it assumes to ply behind the veil. In the course of this process are in fact generated, however questionable they may be metaphysically, those habitual attitudes or tempers in the face of the ultimate interrogations of things which we know as optimism and pessimism; and of pessimism an ancient and characteristic utterance is to be found in cosmic tragedy. Raised to this plane, tragedy ceases to be a mere record of the pity and terror of the facts of human nature, and takes shape as an arraignment of heaven, a grave and unflinching exposure of eternal laws which make of man nothing more than an outraged toy, a self-conscious windlestraw upon the remorseless floods of fate. The corollaries perhaps follow, that cosmic tragedy must necessarily be pagan in sentiment, since the Christian scheme of things, except in a morbid perversion of it, formally excludes pessimism; and that for a Christian writer tragedy is therefore confined to the failures of the individual soul in the frail and blundering exercise of its free-will. Humanity he is free to probe, but the stars do not abide his question.

External tragedy, psychological tragedy, cosmic tragedy; the tragedy of villainy, the tragedy of character, the tragedy of fate; all three types find their occasional and tentative expression among the earlier plays of Shakespeare. Nothing, indeed, is more remarkable in his genius than the triumphant ease which he shows in combining the devices of the popular entertainer with the interests of the freely moving thinker and artist. In *Titus Andronicus* he handled, or perhaps only rehandled, a representative theme, dripping with blood and revenge, of the school of Kyd; and personages of the Aaron tradition may be traced through to the Iago of *Othello* and the Iachimo of *Cymbeline*, although a comparison of Aaron and Iago will show the difference between the villain who is the efficient cause and the villain who is merely the instrument of tragedy. *Richard the Second* is definitely psychological tragedy, in its deduction of failure in kingship as the natural result of the absence of kingly qualities in a king. *Romeo and Juliet*, on the other hand, lays the burden on fate. The lovers are star-crossed from the beginning; their splendid passion only comes into existence to be the victim of an inexorable and malignant destiny. Even in *Romeo and Juliet*, however, pessimism is not beyond question; and tragedy of any kind is the rarer mood during the first half of Shakespeare's dramatic career, throughout which the riot of farce and the graver mirth of comedy are dominant. About 1601, the biographers agree in detecting a change of temper. The poet lost his faith in the world. The light-heartedness of his earlier manner vanished; the laughter died away upon his lips; and the note of criticism came to be more plainly heard, swelling at last to the bitter and comprehensive denunciations of Lear and Timon. Various attempts, more or less fantastic, have been made to connect this phase of spiritual development with external events; with personal losses by death; with some of the love-troubles suggested by the *Sonnets*; with the political disappointments of the close of Elizabeth's reign, and, in particular, with the shock given to English patriotism by the ruin of the hopes that had been staked upon the Earl of Essex. These are regions of shadowy conjecture, which it is safer to leave untrod. The clear fact remains that for eight or nine years Shakespeare devoted himself to the analysis of victorious evil, setting forth in strong relief the failures, the disillusions, the ineffectiveness of humanity. Temperament at war with circumstances; the brute in man trampling upon the god; these are the themes he is impelled to illustrate. To this period, so far as one can be sure about dates, belong all the greater tragedies with the exception of *Romeo and Juliet*, together with the three 'bitter' comedies, *Troilus and Cressida*, *All's Well that Ends Well*, and *Measure for Measure*, in some respects more sad than the tragedies themselves. The pessimistic attitude to life was not, indeed, final for Shakespeare. For awhile—to borrow Professor Dowden's happy phrases—he was 'in the depths,' but he rose to walk 'the heights'; his last words proclaim the ultimate triumph of good in the serene optimism of *Cymbeline*, *The Winter's Tale*, and *The Tempest*. But, so long as it endured, as Swinburne pointed out in the case of *Othello*, his pessimism was yet deeper and more unchequered than that of Æschylus; there is not even, as in the *Oresteia*, the purification of Apollo shining in the distance.

Pessimism, in the quasi-philosophical sense, does not, of course, become articulate in every play of the group. The antithesis, already indicated, between psychological tragedy and cosmic tragedy holds good, although, like every such distinction, it must not be applied with rigidity to individual cases. If this caution is borne in mind, it is perhaps safe to select *Julius Cæsar*, *Antony and Cleopatra*, and *Hamlet* as typical tragedies of the psychological order, which deal primarily with problems of human will and conduct, and *King Lear* and *Macbeth* as typical tragedies of the cosmic order, in which the speculation of the dramatist is primarily directed to the working of powers which are conceived of as transcending the purely human. Thus *Julius Cæsar* is the tragedy of the failure of the idealist in conflict with the 'efficient' man; *Hamlet* the parallel tragedy of the failure of the speculative man in the face of a claim for unreflecting strenuous action; *Antony and Cleopatra* the converse tragedy of the dissolution of 'efficiency' before the spells of wantonness. In the two cosmic tragedies, on the other hand, human personalities do but struggle helplessly in the net of the superhuman. The affections of *King Lear* shatter themselves against the will of gods that know no love; while *Macbeth* presents the whole mystery of temptation and retribution, of man driven from sin to sin and on to sin's undoing by resistless forces beyond his own control.

The hand of time has not been tender with *Macbeth*. An interpolator has contaminated the witch-scenes with singularly inappropriate prettinesses; while a drastic process of shortening, apparently in the interests of an acting-version, has wrought havoc with the rhythm and occasionally left even the dramatic intention obscure. Yet the disrespect done to the text cannot avail to conceal the great lines of the planning; and it is even possible that the excision of some of the side-issues with which, in the true romantic manner, most of

Shakespeare's plays abound, may have served to throw into stronger relief the vastness and terror of the central theme. Certain it is that nowhere else has Shakespeare so nearly escaped the pitfalls of romanticism, or approached so closely to the simplicity, the large sweep, of Æschylus. From beginning to end the action is tense and concentrated; and the subtlest use is made of tragic irony and of every other rhetorical device to create an enveloping atmosphere of moral and spiritual gloom. One may mark some of the innumerable delicate touches which gradually lead the spectator on towards the full horror of that unspeakable midnight murder of the guest and king. First comes the scene in which Duncan, after dismissing the treachery of the fallen Cawdor with the comment that—

> There's no art
> To find the mind's construction in the face,

turns to place himself with absolute trust in the hands of his 'worthiest cousin' and 'peerless kinsman' Macbeth; then Lady Macbeth's receipt of her husband's letter and immediate irrevocable resolve; then the grim dialogue in which the tempted pair first envisage their crime face to face. 'Duncan goes hence tomorrow—as he purposes,' says Macbeth; and she, with the same half hesitation on words of double meaning that rise unbidden to the tongue, 'He that's coming must be—provided for.' Duncan comes and an awful chill falls upon the house, as he walks slowly to the gate of

the trap where Lady Macbeth waits to welcome him.
How Æschylean the irony of his commendations!—

> This castle hath a pleasant seat; the air
> Nimbly and sweetly recommends itself
> Unto our gentle senses.

And there is the confiding bird, 'this guest of
summer, the temple-haunting martlet,' nesting
on the hospitable wall. Night falls, a night fit for
the deed to be done. 'There's husbandry in
heaven; their candles are all out.' Evil influences
are abroad—

> The night has been unruly; where we lay
> Our chimneys were blown down, and, as they say,
> Lamentings heard in the air, strange screams of death,
> And prophesying with accents terrible
> Of dire combustion and confused events
> New hatched to the woeful time. The obscure bird
> Clamoured the livelong night. Some say, the earth
> Was feverous and did shake.

As the guilty hosts start about the preparations for
their sin, the vaulted hall is lit by lightning and
re-echoes with thunder. In the intervals of silence
we hear with them 'the owl shriek and the cricket
cry.' Innocent men are visited by strange thoughts
and dreams—

> There's one did laugh in his sleep, and one cried 'Murder!'
> That they did wake each other. I stood and heard them;
> But they did say their prayers, and addressed them
> Again to sleep.

Even such a nobly-strung soul as Banquo's is
smitten with a strange sense of moral weakness
and shrinking from the battle with temptation—

> A heavy summons lies like lead upon me,
> And yet I would not sleep. Merciful powers,
> Restrain in me the cursed thoughts that nature
> Gives way to in repose!

The most awful touch of all is that knocking of some unknown comer at the gate, which calls our minds, strained by the intensity of the situation almost into sympathy with the crime, back to the frightful realities of fact; and this effect is grimly enhanced by the drunken porter, whose fumbling for his keys and swearing at the disturbers of his rest delays for some moments the imminent discovery. By such delicate workmanship of detail Shakespeare contrives to produce an impression of weirdness, of something uncanny, which signalizes the play throughout and harmonizes with its cosmic theme.

A cosmic tragedy is primarily philosophical and not psychological; but the philosophical interest transcends rather than excludes a psychological interest, since after all it is through and not apart from human character that external forces are conceived as acting upon and disposing of human destinies. The psychological interest of *Macbeth* lies in the study of the contrasted effects of sin and the results of sin upon two characters of different mould and fibre—one that of a man, the other of a woman; one realizing itself in action, the other in thought and will. When first Macbeth comes before us it is as a mighty warrior—he is spoken of as 'valour's minion,' 'Bellona's bridegroom,

234

lapped in proof'; by performing prodigies of personal valour he has saved the country on one day from a civil and an alien foe. This is the noble side of him. Away from the battle-field his greatness is gone, he sinks to the level of quite common men. Lady Macbeth herself expresses this in a passage which has been misunderstood—

> Yet do I fear thy nature;
> It is too full of the milk of human kindness
> To catch the nearest way.

'The milk of human kindness'—that is clearly not 'a tender nature,' of which Macbeth never shows a trace, but rather 'the commonplace ordinary qualities and tendencies of humankind.' As for Lady Macbeth, it is not easy to accept the traditional stage view of her, originated probably by the actress Mrs Pritchard, as a sheer human monster, and the evil genius of her husband's soul. Hers is both a subtler and a nobler nature than his. Living a woman's solitary life, she has turned her thoughts inward; she, too, is a conqueror and has won her triumphs, not in war, but in the training of her intellect and the subjugation of her will. And withal, she is a very woman still—

> I have given suck, and know
> How tender 'tis to love the babe that milks me;

and—

> Had he not resembled
> My father as he slept, I had done it;

and that despairing cry of horror, 'Yet who would have thought the old man to have had so much

blood in him.' Macbeth addresses her in language
of love, and she in her turn has the instincts of the
tiger's mate. Her immediate impulse to crime is
ambition for her husband rather than herself, and
in the banquet scene she puts the sternest control
upon her nerves to save him from blunders.

Thus the antithesis between the two is that
between the practical life and the intellectual,
and the effects of this difference are everywhere
apparent. Macbeth is bold and resolute in the
moment of action; he can kill a king, and he has
a curious gift of ready speech throughout, which
avails him to answer unwelcome questions. But
when there is nothing to be actually done he is
devoid of self-control; he cannot wait nor stand
still; he becomes a prey to countless terrible
imaginings; he is wildly superstitious. Of all this
Lady Macbeth is the exact converse; she has
banished superstition from her soul; she is strong
enough of will to quell her husband's cowardly
fears; she can scheme and plot, but she cannot act;
she must leave the actual doing of the deadly deed
to Macbeth; at the moment of discovery she
faints. The emotional effects of their crime are
totally different on the pair. In Macbeth it is
purely fear; there is no word of sorrow or sense of
sin, only a base dread lest he should be found out
and lose what he played for; if the fatal blow—

>Might be the be-all and the end-all here,
>But here upon this bank and shoal of time,

he is willing to 'jump the life to come.' In time

this fear assumes terrible proportions; it drives him to new murders; he slaughters Banquo, he slaughters the family of Macduff; finally he becomes a craven and bloody tyrant; even his old love for his wife is swallowed up in selfishness; when her death is told him he cannot stay to mourn. 'She should have died hereafter.' Only in the last hour of battle does he for one moment recover something of his old brave spirit. With Lady Macbeth the curse works itself out, not in fear but remorse. It impels her husband to fresh deeds of blood; she has no hand in any murder but the first. But her sin is ever present to her; awake or dreaming she can think of nothing but that awful night and the stain upon her hand and soul. At last her overtasked brain breaks down; we witness her mental agony in the sleep-walking scene. 'Here's the smell of the blood still. All the perfumes of Arabia will not sweeten this little hand. Oh! oh! oh!' And then she dies, a voluntary and most wretched death.

The psychological analysis assumes the facts of sin and retribution. Temptation begets crime, and crime yet further crimes, and these again punishment sure and inexorable. Once the murder of Duncan has been committed, the possibility of regress disappears; the chain of cause and consequence unfolds with remorseless fatality, until the end is ruin of the moral sense or even reason itself, so that death comes almost as a relief, although it be a miserable death, without hope of repentance. But from the cosmic point of view, it is precisely these facts of sin and retribution that are the springs of tragedy. For the philosophic mind cannot but challenge them, with the enquiry why these things should be so. Is man's free-will purely illusory, and if not why should it be determined by suggestions which he does not initiate to ends which he certainly does not desire? Directly the matter is so stated, forces external to man are brought into question, and a cosmic issue arises between the limited and baffled but still self-conscious and struggling free-will of man and a power, not himself, which does not make for righteousness. And such an issue is a tragic one, provided indeed that the characters at stake have enough of greatness of some kind or another in their composition to sustain a conflict without too obvious a disproportion. For while the clash of the great with the great yields the thrill of tragedy, the clash of the puny with the great yields only that of pathos. And in Macbeth and Lady Macbeth greatness is not wanting. Their temptation comes to them in the guise of ambition, the subtlest form in which it can approach high souls. Their end is terrible, and in Macbeth's case at least, not without sublimity. 'At least we'll die with harness on our back!' They throw their all on a great hope, and fail greatly.

But the gravamen is against the first cause. Here Shakespeare acknowledges a mystery, and, as it would seem, an unholy mystery. As is his custom he indicates mystery by way of symbolism. His witches are not literal, but they are real enough. They stand for the non-human agents of the whole cosmic drama. Their first appearance synchronizes with the welling-up of temptation in Macbeth's secret heart; their second with that of the false security which lures him on the slippery path to retribution. Nor do I think that the symbolical use of the supernatural in the play is exhausted in the witches. The ghost, indeed, unlike the ghost in *Hamlet*, is subjective; nobody sees it except Macbeth himself. But are we not to find a supernatural agent in that third murderer who silently joins the two commissioned to undertake the way-laying of Banquo? Some have thought that this third is none other than Macbeth, who mistrusts the swords of others, and determines to take his own part in the action. But the scene is a critical one for the evolution of the plot, since the escape of Fleance forms, as it were, a turning-point in Macbeth's fortunes. And Fleance escapes, because one of the murderers knocks out the light. Is it pushing the bounds of conjecture too far, to see in this the swift momentary interposition of the hand of inscrutable Providence? One does not, of course, suppose that Shakespeare set his spectators conundrums to guess; but the scene is not very clearly intelligible unless some interpretation or other is read into it, and it may be that the rash hand of a stage-manager has suppressed just what was intended to give the requisite clue.

KING LEAR

AMONG the tragedies of Shakespeare, *King Lear* stands out as, in the Aristotelian sense of the word, the most tragic. It is the most tremendous in design, brings into play the most elemental forces, makes the most irresistible demand upon those emotions of pity and of awe, the purification of which is the function and deliberate end of tragedy. I say purification, not purgation, since, whatever may be the metaphorical sense which philologists find in κάθαρσις as it is used elsewhere than in the treatise *On Poetry*, experience must needs bear it out that the actual effect of tragedy is not to purge away or eliminate pity and awe from the soul of the spectator, and is to purify and ennoble those emotions, by calling them from the personal to the universal and fixing them upon just those elements in the totality of things which, essentially and in themselves, are the most pitiful and the most awful. This ideal of tragedy is realized in *King Lear*, as it has only been realized some dozen times in the history of literature, largely by virtue of the cosmic scope of the play. Like the *Oresteia*, like *Tess of the D'Urbervilles*, it is a philosophical drama; the aim which it sets before itself is nothing less than 'to grasp this sorry scheme of things entire.' Here indeed the quotation must stop. It does not go on to 'remould it nearer to the heart's desire.' It is analytic, not constructive; contents itself with an understanding of things, and offers no remedy to make these odds all even. But, for the philosopher, to understand is already to have half the remedy.

King Lear belongs to the later manner of Shakespearean tragedy. All tragedy, of course, depends upon the interplay of two factors; on the one hand human character in its unequal and faulty composition, on the other the environment of conditions within which character moves, and by its reaction upon which it is determined to success or failure. When Shakespeare first began seriously to consider life from a tragic point of view, it was the element of character that claimed his interest and stung his imagination. *Julius Cæsar* and *Hamlet*, like *Antony and Cleopatra* afterwards, are essentially psychological tragedies. The failure which each of them studies is traced directly to some point of weakness, some vulnerable heel of Achilles, in an otherwise finely-wrought and admirable personality. The general drift of their themes may be illustrated by an incidental phrase from one of them—

> The fault, dear Brutus, is not in our stars,
> But in ourselves, that we are underlings.

In a second group of tragedies, however, Shakespeare's speculation seems to shift from the nature of man to the nature of what is around and above man, and to seek the primary causes of tragic disaster, less in the imperfect mettle of a hero, although that indeed must still contribute, than in external forces which are conceived of, if not as making directly for evil rather than for righteousness, at least as unmoral and blind in their working. Thus in *Macbeth* sin and the retribution of sin are represented as the two closely related parts of a mysterious curse imposed upon the sinner from without, and the symbolism of the witches is used, in characteristic fashion, to indicate its superhuman origin. It is only natural that this change in the dramatist's attitude to tragedy should carry with it an ever-deepening pessimism, for while there is always hope that the frailties of humanity may find amelioration, it would be presumptuous to suppose that the external forces can ever be rendered other than what they are.

Of the second or cosmic kind of tragedy, *King Lear* is perhaps even a more typical example than *Macbeth*. Like the psychological *Hamlet*, it takes its starting-point from the family relations and the human emotions which are built up upon these. Of course it does not disregard psychology, merely because ultimately it is to transcend psychology. Lear himself, in particular, is a most subtle psychological study. He is a man of passionate fibre and unrestrained temper, wholly swayed in his old age by two imperious instincts, that of personal domination and that of natural affection for his daughters. As might be expected, his affection tends to manifest itself, not as self-renunciation, but as one among other forms of domination. His instincts possess him wholly. They warp his judgment of character and drive him to acts of which he has not the imagination to foresee the inevitable results. He abdicates out of an impulse to endear himself to his daughters by a liberal abandonment of everything, and thinks, sincerely enough for the moment, that he will be for ever content to set up his rest in their kind nursery. But it has never entered his head to conceive what abdication really means. His first act after surrendering his kingly prerogative is to exercise that prerogative by ordering Kent into banishment. The same temperament determines his behaviour to Cordelia. Absorbed, as a true egoist, in his own emotions, even when they are most generous, he has no eye for the fine shades of expression and conduct in others, and is thus led into the irony of rejecting the one daughter who would have comprehended and endured. Obviously, with such a father and with pelican children, the attempt to resign power and yet to keep the name and all the additions to a king is doomed to failure. He gives an easy handle to the malevolence of Goneril and of Regan. How should one adapt himself to an alien rule who cannot even bear to stay a jot for dinner when he returns from hunting? No doubt his 'retinue' is insolent and his fool is 'all-licensed.' His first word to Goneril, his daughter and his queen, is a reproof for being 'too much in the frown.' She

cannot but have an appearance of right on her
side when she declares—

> By day and night he wrongs me; every hour
> He flashes into one gross crime or other,
> That sets us all at odds. I'll not endure it.
> His knights grow riotous, and himself upbraids us
> On every trifle.

Of course it is really Lear who is wronged; but
Lear, by his own unbalanced act, is helpless.
Goneril and Regan outvie each other in their
merciless use of the advantage which his blind
impulse has given them.

The disillusion of the sentimental egoist leads
to a violent reaction. Outraged affection and outraged self-will find vent in unmeasured denunciations of those who have set the claims of fatherhood
at naught. Lear appeals from his daughters to the
heavens, to the heavens who surely love old men
and must give effect to 'the untented woundings
of a father's curse.' He is confident in the justice
of his cause. He need hardly formulate his plea,
but may leave the stored vengeances of heaven
to their inevitable working. They cannot fail him—

> I'll not chide thee.
> Let shame come when it will; I do not call it.
> I do not bid the Thunder-bearer shoot,
> Nor tell tales of thee to high-judging Jove.

And in this reliance he leaves the castle, on whose
unfilial queens he—

> Will do such things,
> What they are, yet I know not, but they shall be
> The terrors of the earth.

And now comes in the cosmic side of the tragedy; for once more the confident Lear has hopelessly misjudged the position with which he is confronted. The heavens prove as deaf to his call as either Goneril or Regan. They are not on the side of righteousness. The tempest which greets him upon the heath is symbolical; and here, in a scene which surely represents the extremest stretch of Shakespeare's titanic mood, we find him contending with the 'dreadful pudder' of the elements, now calling upon them to—

> Crack nature's moulds, all germens spill at once
> That makes ingrateful man,

and now upbraiding them for joining their high engendered battles with his pernicious daughters against so old and white a head. And in the end it is wind and rain, rather than unkindness, that beat him into submission, and force him to acknowledge what a 'poor, bare, forked animal' is 'unaccommodated man.' Then for symbol, once more, of his tragic defeat comes the crash and ruin of his wits, since madness, inadmissible as a motive of tragedy, is here in its right place as an acknowledgment of the culmination and catastrophe of a tragic issue.

It is worth observing with what care Shakespeare has arranged every detail of the play so as to give edge to his indictment of the forces that make sport of man's nothingness. The plot, which deliberately rejects the Christian interpretation of the universe, is set in a pagan environment. The heavens are invoked in a pagan terminology, as Nature, or under the names of the classic deities. Pains are taken, contrary to the usual disregard of anachronisms in the plays, to avoid the introduction of Christian language or Christian sentiments. Again, the story of Lear is not allowed to stand by itself, alone and individual. It is part of the intention that the theme of the play should be of universal significance. And therefore, side by side with the main plot, is set a sub-plot, in which the fortunes of the house of Lear are repeated in the fortunes of the house of Gloucester. The story is less tremendously urged, in order that the main interest of the spectators may not be diverted; but the parallel is complete. Gloucester, like Lear, judges falsely among his children; and like Lear is led by this initial error, heaven conspiring, to a ruin, which in his case includes dispossession, the blinding of his eyes, and the ultimate bursting of his flawed heart. In the sub-plot the agent of iniquity is a bastard; and this touch helps to carry out the universalizing purpose, since it suggests the activity of the principle of evil in households of every degree, legitimate and illegitimate alike.

The story of Gloucester is an addition made by Shakespeare to the plot of the old play, known as *The Tragical History of King Leir*, which was doubtless his principal source. Another modification which he introduced is even more significant. The old play was not a tragedy but a tragicomedy. In its conclusion a French invasion confounded the

evil-doers, vindicated Providence, reconciled Lear
to Cordelia, and restored him triumphantly to his
kingdom. But such an ending would not have
suited Shakespeare's design, because it would not
have borne the burden of the final victory of evil.
Therefore he remorselessly altered it. There are
forces of good, indeed, in the play—Cordelia and
Edgar, the faithful Kent, the generous France,
the reluctant Albany; but they are represented as
proving in the end quite ineffective agents for the
mastering of evil. Emphasis is laid upon this issue
by the temporary suggestion shortly after the
crisis of a contrary solution. During the Fourth
Act things look as if they were tending to a happy
close. The fever of Lear's distemper has abated.
He is no longer buffeted by the elements, but
wanders through the fields, still, no doubt, mad
as the vexed sea, but—

> Singing aloud,
> Crowned with rank fumitory and furrow weeds,
> With burdocks, hemlock, nettles, cuckoo-flowers,
> Darnel, and all the idle weeds that grow
> In our sustaining corn.

There is hope that repose and simples may yet
restore him to his senses. Gloucester has fallen in
with Edgar and has been saved from destruction
on the cliff. Both have made their way to Dover,
and at Dover Cordelia, the radiant white soul of
the play, awaits them. With her are the armies of
France, the righter of wrongs. All seems as if the
victims of filial treachery would have their own

again, and Goneril, Regan, and Edmund meet
with a richly-deserved Nemesis. Only, when it
comes to the point, the heavens refuse to have it
so. In the last Act, the hopes of tragicomedy are
ruthlessly brushed away. High-judging Jove
sends down his thunders and lightnings to the
end, no less than his rain, upon the just and upon
the unjust. There is Nemesis in plenty for the
wicked, who are taken in the web of their own
devising; but this carries with it no salvation for
Lear and for Cordelia. The final reversal of poetic
justice is complete. Cordelia and her army are
simply defeated. Then, through the ineffectiveness
of Albany, Cordelia is murdered, and the tale of
Lear's disasters is full. There is no more to be
said but—

> Vex not his ghost! Oh, let him pass! he hates him
> That would upon the rack of this tough world
> Stretch him out longer.

Here is the tragic awe in abundant measure. And
that the tragic pity may not be lacking also, the
fate of Cordelia gives the needful touch of pathos
in the story of Lear, just as the fate of Ophelia
gives it in the story of Hamlet.

ANTONY and CLEOPATRA

IN the course of his tragic analysis of man and of man's splendid impotence beneath the unpitying stars, Shakespeare reaches two plays, wherein he handles the great ideals which the incurable sentiment of the race is wont to set up as a screen between itself and its destiny, and shows that these also are but tragic stuff. It is honour of chivalry and love of woman, the twin beacons of romance throughout the ages, that must stand their arraignment in *Coriolanus* and in *Antony and Cleopatra*. One may turn back over the pages, and find in this later treatment something of deliberate palinode to the exaltation of triumphant honour in *Henry the Fifth* and of love as, even when vanquished, the blossom and fruitage of life in *Romeo and Juliet*. Already the ideals had been questioned in that comedy of disillusions, *Troilus and Cressida*, where Cressid's love is writ in water, and honour hardly holds up its head amongst the treachery and bickerings of the Greeks. And now, without any question at all, Shakespeare returns to the double theme, to strip the mask of worship from the spectre of egoism, and to indict passion as the ruin of greatness, magnificent and devastating as Attila and his Huns.

Antony is resumed, after a fashion not customary with Shakespeare, except in the historical plays

and in the doubtful case of the resurrected Falstaff
of *The Merry Wives of Windsor*, from *Julius Cæsar*.
Here, as against Brutus, he is the inheritor of the
tradition of victorious efficiency, which else would
have fallen with Cæsar himself. In *Antony and
Cleopatra* this function, which has become the
background rather than the motive of the play, is
transferred to the hard and passionless Octavius.
Antony, who even in *Julius Cæsar* had been 'gamesome' and 'loved plays,' is developed upon more
generous lines. The great composition of the man
finds room for the most diverse potentialities. He
rejects nothing and will drink to the full of every
cup that life proffers. He is a mighty warrior and
is able to inspire enthusiasms, not only in such
poor folk as Lepidus, for whom—

> His faults, in him, seem as the spots of heaven,

but also in his own followers and captains. He
outdoes his greatest rivals, alike in the nights of
revelry and on the field of battle. He drinks the
other triumvirs from the deck of Pompey's vessel.
At Philippi it was he who struck the lean and
wrinkled Cassius, while the boy Octavius kept
his sword e'en like a dancer. And so he has won
his way to be a triple pillar of the world, and may
speak of himself in his downfall as one—

> Which had superfluous kings for messengers
> Not many moons gone by.

His very capacity is his undoing. The exuberance
of his vitality overflows into sensuousness as well

as into resource and endurance. The palate that
at need—

> Did deign
> The roughest berry on the rudest hedge,

is not proof against the temptations of 'lascivious
wassails' or the stimulating excitements of a
'gaudy night.' And Antony would not be Antony
if, to whatever he gave himself, he did not give
himself wholly and without reserve. He, who—

> With half the bulk of the world played as I pleased,

is also 'the ne'er lust-wearied Antony.'

In an evil day Antony crosses the path of the
amorous Cleopatra, and is entangled in the strong
toils of a passion which for him at least, whatever
the dreams of the sentimentalists, makes no contribution towards a strenuous life. His captain's
heart reneges all temper, and alliances and empires
slip away while he becomes the bellows and the
fan to cool a gipsy's lust. There is a struggle, of
course. The instinct of domination and the instinct
of sex are at odds in him; and if he chooses the
worser course, it is not without clear consciousness
on his part of the issues at stake. He knows well
how Cleopatra is called in Rome, and that he must
break the strong Egyptian fetters, if he is ever to
recapture his proper place in the counsels of the
nations. Once, under the shock of Fulvia's sudden
death, he does break them; and his return to
activity disconcerts the calculations of Pompey,
and obliges even Octavius himself to play the

second fiddle. But Cleopatra nods him to her
again, and the crisis of Actium, determined by her
cowardice, leaves him little more than 'the noble
ruin of her magic.' Octavius may now affect to
speak of one who had quartered the world as no
more than an 'old ruffian' and a 'sworder'; and
the epitaph of the past he has squandered is in
his own mouth—

> We have kissed away
> Kingdoms and provinces.

It is to be observed that it is no part of Shakespeare's scheme to belittle passion. Tragedy lies
in the incompatibility and clash of greatnesses,
and love that is to be the scourge of the world,
even if it is rooted in sensuality, must possess the
attributes of majesty. And therefore Cleopatra is
so conceived that she is fit to mate with her lover.
Even in those, such as Enobarbus, who most
deplore her baleful influence, she awakes amazement—

> Age cannot wither her, nor custom stale
> Her infinite variety.

She is 'a wonderful piece of work,' one—

> Whom everything becomes, to chide, to laugh,
> To weep.

And thus her relations with Antony take on
something of the sublime. He is hardly alone in
thinking Rome well lost for her sake, and that
the nobleness of life is to be found in a kiss—

> When such a mutual pair
> And such a twain can do it, in which I bind,

> On pain of punishment, the world to weet,
> We stand up peerless.

And she is no Cressida. A marvellous psychology, wrought surely out of bitter experience, has gone to the making of this subtle princess. She is half a courtesan and half a *grande amoureuse*. Certainly she has at her command all the resources of that most ancient art of those who angle for the souls of men. She plays on Antony like an instrument, ever twitching the sentimental string, and knowing well how to renew her influence, just at the moment when it is upon the wane, with nicely simulated outbursts of pathos or upbraiding. And yet these are not all simulated. 'I have seen her die twenty times upon far poorer moment,' says Enobarbus; and when Antony judges that 'She is cunning past man's thought,' replies, 'Alack, sir, no! Her passions are made of nothing but the finest part of pure love.' Her art is indeed instinctive, and does but utilize the ebbs and flows of her own wayward and uncertain nature. She is at no time wholly mistress of herself, but lives in that unstable equilibrium of nerves and emotions which is the temperament of such a woman. Characteristically she drugs herself with mandragora and with music—

> Give me some music; music, moody food
> Of us that trade in love.

She has the courtesan's bitter resentment against the respectable members of her sex; against 'shrill-tongued' Fulvia, Fulvia 'the married woman,' and later against Octavia 'with her modest eyes and still conclusion.' Even in the unbalanced fury of the scene in which she receives the news of Antony's secret marriage, she recovers herself sufficiently for a quick appraisement of her own personality against that of her new rival; and the admission of the messenger that Octavia is low-voiced and less tall than Cleopatra is turned with naive spite into a conviction that she is 'dull of tongue and dwarfish.' Obviously Cleopatra has had lovers before Antony. She admits that she was a morsel for Cæsar in her salad days when she was green in judgment, and how great Pompey would stand and make his eyes grow in her brow. Since then the Roman world has rung with her gallant adventures. But, though Antony has come late into her life, he now possesses it wholly. She would but sleep out the great gap of time, when he is away. When they met—

Eternity was in our lips and eyes,

and the love that then came into being is to endure, through the wreck of empires, to the close of all time. She is at least as much hypnotized by Antony as he is by her, and the very intensity of this sentiment, baleful as it is, invests it with sufficient dignity to make it worthy of the tragedy.

And so, when Cleopatra has dragged the good name of Antony through the mire and has brought him by cowardice unworthy of a queen to the twin defeats of Actium and Alexandria, the play, which throughout has been written on Shakespeare's

254

highest level of pregnant metaphor and melodious phrase, swells into the organ-notes of a magnificent dirge. I do not know where to turn for anything to surpass the haunting splendour of the two great scenes in which it culminates. In the Fourth Act, Antony, beaten and disgraced, receives a lying message from Cleopatra, who fears the reaction of his mood, that she is dead. For him too it is time to make an end, and he calls upon his freedman to take off his armour with words of double meaning—

> Unarm, Eros! the long day's task is done,
> And we must sleep.

Cleopatra has gone before, and calls upon him to o'ertake her—

> Eros!—I come, my queen.—Eros!—Stay for me!
> Where souls do couch on flowers, we'll hand in hand,
> And with our sprightly port make the ghosts gaze.
> Dido and her Æneas shall want troops,
> And all the haunt be ours.

Presently, taught by Eros, he gives himself a mortal wound, and then learns that he has been misled and that Cleopatra yet lives and is in the monument. He is carried to the foot of it, and Cleopatra beholds what has occurred—

> *Cleopatra.*   O sun,
> Burn the great sphere thou movest in; darkling stand
> The varying shore of the world. O, Antony,
> Antony, Antony! Help, Charmian! help, Iras, help!
> Help, friends below!—let's draw him hither!
>
> *Antony.*   Peace!
> Not Cæsar's valour hath o'erthrown Antony,
> But Antony's hath triumphed on itself.

    Cleopatra. So it should be, that none but **Antony**
Should conquer Antony; but woe 't is so.
    Antony. I am dying, Egypt, dying; only
I here importune death awhile, until
Of many thousand kisses the poor last
I lay upon thy lips.

So he is drawn up, and dies; and Cleopatra says—
                   O, see, my women,
The crown of the earth doth melt. My lord! my lord!—
O, withered is the garland of the war;
The soldier's pole is fallen; young boys and girls
Are level now with men; the odds is gone,
And there is nothing left remarkable
Beneath the visiting moon.

And then—

Our lamp is spent; it's out.—Good sirs, take heart!
We'll bury him; and then, what's brave, what's noble,
Let's do it after the high Roman fashion,
And make death proud to take us.

In the Fifth Act, Cleopatra's own turn has come.
She has played through her interview with Cæsar,
but Cæsar's promises cannot stay her. Even the
wild bedfellows, her hand-maidens, Iras and
Charmian, rise to the height of the great argument.
It is Iras who says—

       Finish, good lady; the bright day is done,
       And we are for the dark.

The countryman with his figs is introduced and
wishes her joy o' the worm. Now she has immortal
longings in her, but Iras is the first to die. It is as
a rebuke to delay—

              This proves me base.
    If she first meet the curled Antony,

> He'll make demand of her, and spend that kiss
> Which is my heaven to have.

Then, as the eastern star breaks, the asps are applied, and Cleopatra's speech falters, and Charmian pronounces her elegy—

> Now boast thee, Death, in thy possession lies
> A lass unparalleled.

And the soldiers of Cæsar break in upon the silence with their question—

> What work is here? Charmian, is this well done?

And Charmian, before she too falls, makes reply—

> It is well done, and fitting for a princess
> Descended of so many royal kings.

The might of language can hardly go further than in such monumental phrases as these, which with their austere and lucid simplicity bring this most poignant tragedy to a close upon that note of awe and reverence which is the fitting accompaniment of the sublimest art. It is probable that *Antony and Cleopatra* was almost Shakespeare's final tragic utterance, before that mysterious change came over the spirit of his vision, and he entered those happy glades of Arcady in which his last romantic dreams were dreamed. If so, it is worth while to record that the tragic mood, however vexed and perturbed its course might sometimes be, was yet at the end able to face its mortal issues with a serenity hardly less absolute than that which could be attained by the optimistic faith of a Prospero in his overruling providence.

CORIOLANUS

FINELY critical ears may detect in *Coriolanus* the exhaustion of a mood. The tragedy claims admiration and respect for the dignity of its planning and the justice of its thought; but it lacks variety and decorative quality, and the inexhaustible buoyancy of its predecessors gives way to deliberate and purposed effort. For the first time since some of the painful humours and strained wit-combats of his early experiments, Shakespeare has become tedious. Perhaps that is why the schoolmasters are so fond of the play. It is intelligible enough, this slackening of the creative energies, when one reflects that *Coriolanus* came at the very end of the great tragic cycle, and may well have been the last gathering of that vintage of pessimistic speculation, which had already yielded alike the denunciations of *King Lear* and the intolerable pathos of *Othello*. And after it was written there came, quite suddenly, it would seem, a turning-point in Shakespeare's life. There was a crisis; whether determined by physical or by spiritual causes, or by the blending and interaction of the two, can be but dimly conjectured. And of this a fault or cleavage in both the content and the style of the plays is but the outward and visible sign. Shakespeare had no more tragedies to write.

What more he wrote was in the key of recovered

romance. With the return to the peaceful meadows of Stratford, if one divines rightly, a happier mood awoke. The burden of the city days fell off. The three closing dramas, *Cymbeline*, *The Winter's Tale*, *The Tempest*, are filled with a mellow philosophy and a deep-veined humanity; the poet's last words are of belief in an over-ruling power, that somewhere far-off faintly makes for good. But of this new spirit there is nothing yet in *Coriolanus*. The closest affinities of the play are with that which probably comes nearest to it in point of time, *Antony and Cleopatra*. In each is to be found the same readiness of bitter criticism, the same remorseless analysis, probing and dissecting, as with a cruel scalpel, the intimate weaknesses and basenesses of mankind. In each ideals are shattered, heroes are discrowned and stripped of their heroism, until it is with difficulty that the sympathies of the spectator, so essential to the sense of tragedy, are retained. It is the triumph of the dramatist that they are not wholly lost. Antony and Coriolanus, although we are made to see through and through them, yet grip us to the end, not through the character of their passions, but through their sheer intensity. In *Antony and Cleopatra* we have the tragedy of sensuality. The shattered ideal is that of love. Shakespeare sets before us a man who holds an empire in the hollow of his hand, but who comes to ruin through a passion that is all of the senses and the imagination, with nothing in it that is tonic, nothing bracing, nothing inspiring. The play is a pendant, or, if you will, a palinode, to that first young tragedy, of lives redeemed and ennobled by love, in *Romeo and Juliet*. In *Coriolanus* the shattered ideal is that of honour. Beneath the mask of honour there lurks the subtle sin of egoism, laid bare to us, as in the Sir Willoughby Patterne of later days, by the patient and pitiless insight of the philosopher. Here is the central idea which determines the structure and the issues of the play.

But in the first place it is necessary to remove a possible misconception. As in *Antony and Cleopatra*, the environment of the action is a political one; there, the pursuit of empire; here, the struggle for municipal power between nobles and people. But here, as there, the political interest is not the primary one; it is subordinate throughout to the study of the individual soul set in the midst of it. Purely political problems, indeed, have ceased to be absorbing to Shakespeare. He worked them out, once for all, in his English histories, and came to a final conclusion in his picture of the true king, the mirror of glittering efficiency, Henry the Fifth. Politics are but backgrounds to him now for the passions and idealisms of men. We need not suppose, then, that in delineating after Plutarch the contests of the patricians and the plebeians of republican Rome he is writing with any prophetic insight into the coming troubles of his own country. Indeed, the struggle for English liberties, as it slowly shaped itself in the earlier part of the seventeenth century, was not primarily a struggle of democratic and aristocratic elements in the state. It resulted, no doubt, in a certain widening of popular liberties, but in its origin it was less political than religious and ethical, the uprising of the wholesome English city and country life against a selfish king and a corrupt court. In judging Coriolanus, nevertheless, Shakespeare judges that familiar ideal of the 'person of honour' from which the Cavalier party was destined to derive so much of its support, an ideal based on no profound notion of honourable merit, but on exclusions and a false sentiment of refinement.

Rome then is split up into two opposed camps of patricians and plebeians. On the one side tradesmen and handicraftsmen, botchers and forset-sellers; on the other a society of nobles, wealthy and luxurious, enjoying all the privileges of a caste, occupied chiefly in war, and esteeming war the highest of all human employments. They are not altogether unworthy of their position, for they have fought for Rome, and have again and again led her forces to victory. But of late the plebeians, weary of dearth, forced wars, and usury, have rebelled against the old order of things, and have made good their claim to a share of political power. Certain magistrates, known as tribunes, are appointed to protect the popular rights. The majority of the patricians are willing, for the sake of peace, to accept the altered conditions and to make the best of them. They hope to surrender the appearance of power only and to keep the reality. But there is an irreconcilable minority to whom all concessions appear degrading and dishonourable. Of these the leader is Coriolanus.

Coriolanus is inheritor of the traditions of one of the proudest houses of Rome. He has been brought up by his mother to set all his ambitions upon the pursuit of honour; above all, the honour that is won on the field of battle. He is the flower of warriors. Since the expulsion of the Tarquins he has been the hope of Rome and the mainstay of her armies. When we first meet him he is the acknowledged leader of the city in battle, her protagonist, admirable for his valour and for his single-eyed pursuit of honour. Of the more petty self-seeking there is nothing in him. His disdain of plunder, or even of vulgar applause, is complete. And yet, as we study his character in the clear light of the Shakespearean analysis, we find that the very root of him is a thorough-going egoism. Honour is a fine thing, as the reward and the sign of services to one's country and deeds well done. But for Coriolanus, honour has come to be an end in itself. 'For my country' is on his lips, but at heart he thinks of his country's good only as the ladder of his own reputation. And as we shall see, it is this craving for honour, with the subtle egoism it implies, that leads to his tragedy. With such an ideal and of such a humour, Coriolanus is naturally a patrician of the patricians. He is a

Tory and a gentleman to the backbone. Courteous to those whom he accepts as, at least by convention, his equals, he has nothing but a curse and a sneer for any man of the people. A humane sympathy with humanity as such is no part of his nature or of his training. The tradesmen and toilers of Rome are to him but as a multiplying spawn, fashioned of another clay from those of his ordinance. Their cowardice in battle and their unwashed hands are equally distasteful to him. Their fickleness and instability in politics move his scorn and ire. For any natural rights of theirs he cares not a jot. He is a soldier, and his notion of government is discipline when he gives the word of command. And it should be observed that it is no part of Shakespeare's scheme to exalt the character of the plebeians at the expense of the patricians. He is no democratic sentimentalist. In this play he is painting in black throughout. The people are indeed dirty and greedy and changeable and cowardly and ungrateful. Their teachers, the tribunes, are envious and conceited and self-interested and treacherous. Nevertheless there are such things as the natural rights of citizens, even of unwashed citizens, and the political problem is not to be solved by disregarding them.

Coriolanus is the central point of the warring factions of Rome, and over against him stand the tribunes. He and they are the leaders of the opposed parties, and the hatred between them is

mutual. And round Coriolanus the other personages of the play group themselves. The dramatic
unity depends upon him, and with reference to
him they are all conceived. Cominius represents
the moderate men of the senate, the statesmen,
cautious or timid as you will, who would gladly
compromise with the spirit of democracy. In
closer personal relations with Coriolanus stand
Volumnia and Menenius. Volumnia is the Roman
matron of the stern antique type. She has brought
up Coriolanus, courageously indeed but unwisely,
and has lit and fostered in him that wayward ideal
of honour. Of sympathy or of any ethics save
those of the camp, she has taught him nothing.
Yet her own patriotism is more single-hearted
than his, and it is not until their wills come into
conflict that Coriolanus realizes how greatly she
dominates his spirit. She is the only one of the
women in the play who counts for anything.
Virgilia, the wife whom Coriolanus loves as well
as he can love anything besides himself, has for
her sole function to touch the tragedy here and
there with tears. Menenius, too, has had his share
in spoiling Coriolanus' character. He is a foolish,
witty old noble, fond of eating and drinking, and
fond of hearing himself talk, hail-fellow-well-met
with everybody, including the tribunes, and
pluming himself on a diplomacy which has no
existence. At bottom he shares all the aristocratic
prejudices, but his genial manners win him a
superficial popularity. His one serious emotion

is his love for Coriolanus; him he 'gods indeed' with foolish praise and still more foolish advice. The only other important element in Coriolanus' environment is his enemy, Aufidius the Volsce. In the heyday of Coriolanus' success his personal rivalry with Aufidius is a keener incentive to him than the cause of Rome. After his disgrace the brooding envy of the defeated antagonist contributes greatly to his final ruin.

Such are the *dramatis personæ*, and the course of the plot flows with remorseless necessity from their characters. It is essential to tragedy that interest should be in some sense secured for the tragic hero. Tragedy springs from that conflict and clash of forces which brings about the fracture of something great, with Shakespeare generally the ruin or failure of a great human character. In order then that the catastrophe of the play may affect the spectator tragically, he must first be impressed with the greatness involved. The First Act shows us Coriolanus, on the whole, great; a great warrior, undaunted in danger, removed high above the greed and poltroonery of common men. Flushed with victory he returns to Rome to win the applause of the whole city. Throughout the whole of this Act, the weaker and dangerous elements in his character, although hinted at from time to time, are kept in the background. But ere long they must be brought into prominence, in order that we may see how the doom of Coriolanus' career is rooted in them. The purpose of the Second

Act is to make clear his deficiencies—deficiency of sympathy and deficiency of self-control. These are shown in his maladroit candidature for and ultimate rejection from the consulship. He is now tangled in a web, woven more by the threads of his own nature than by the intrigues of his enemies. A crisis comes in the Third Act, with his banishment from Rome. During the last two Acts he has almost lost sympathy through his folly and insolence; but he bears himself with dignity in adversity, and thus sympathy is restored, in subtle preparation for the inevitable end. But the end is not quite yet. Baffled and disgraced in Rome, the poor remains of Coriolanus' imperfect patriotism rapidly vanish. His wrath is as much against the patricians who permitted his banishment as against the plebeians who clamoured for it. But 'there is a world elsewhere.' He will retrieve his fortunes and re-establish his ideal of himself on a new stage. He will again be 'a person of honour'—in Corioli. And so in the Fourth Act he appears among the Volsces, and casts his all upon the generosity of Aufidius. At first his design prospers; he sees his way clear to revenge upon Rome. But he has reckoned without the laws of human nature. The past cannot be so easily set aside, and his past is bound up with Aufidius and Volumnia. The smouldering envy of Aufidius is reinforced by new jealousy, and dogs Coriolanus' footsteps. And this prepares us for the catastrophe of the Fifth Act. In the great third scene the old influence of Volumnia resumes its sway over her son. His resolution is vanquished, and he returns to Corioli, knowing that it is to his death. It could only end so. Man has not two destinies; and the chance once thrown away is not offered again.

TIMON of ATHENS

CRITICS are agreed that there is something enigmatic about *Timon of Athens*, that its genesis and composition present a literary problem which cannot as yet be thought to have quite reached its solution. In many ways, of course, it is what the Germans call *echt Shakespearisch*. Its general conception is continuous with the development of pessimistic thought which is traceable along the whole line of the tragedies. The ruin and eclipse of Timon's soul in the discovery of human baseness is a vision which was assuredly not revealed to another than the delineator of Lear and of Othello. And from beginning to end of the play, especially where Timon himself is to the front, there are passages whose magnificent phrasing bears the indubitable craft-mark of the Shakespearean workshop. The opening scene takes up the tradition, with its—

> A most incomparable man, breathed, as it were,
> To an untirable and continuate goodness,

and hands it down to the last noble utterance which winds up all the whirling words—

> Come not to me again, but say to Athens,
> Timon hath made his everlasting mansion
> Upon the beached verge of the salt flood,
> Who once a day with his embossed froth
> The turbulent surge shall cover; thither come,
> And let my grave-stone be your oracle.

Nevertheless, the instinct is a right one which refuses to accept *Timon of Athens* as a complete and jointed Shakespearean whole. There are impossibilities in it. The moment the eye passes from the dominant figure of Timon himself, it falls upon scenes which appear to be in different planes from that of the main composition. What, for example, is the spiritual relation between Alcibiades and Timon? Is some effect of contrast intended, or is Alcibiades merely Timon over again, in a weaker and less clearly motived version of the disillusioned child of fortune? And what is the precise dramatic purpose served by the good steward Flavius and his sentimentalities, which seem to give the lie to Timon's wholesale condemnation of humanity, without any appreciable effect upon its direction or its force? These are structural incoherencies which it would have been more Shakespearean to have cleared away, or at least to have glossed over, so as to prevent their jarring, as they undeniably do jar, against the ready acceptance of the play. Alcibiades ought to mean something, and is introduced as though he were going to mean something; and the reader very naturally resents the discovery of how very little, if anything, he does in the end mean. Nor is it only a question of structure. There are certain scenes or parts of scenes, in which the expression is so halting, so lacking in the golden mastery of speech, as to raise a doubt whether they can be Shakespeare's. These passages are fairly well marked off from the rest. They include

269

a conversation between Timon, Apemantus, and
the Steward in the banquet scene of the First Act;
the three scenes in which Timon's servants endeavour to borrow money, the scene between the
Steward and the creditors, and the scene between
Alcibiades and the Senate, in the Third Act; the
Steward's resolve to follow Timon, and his subsequent dialogue with Timon, in the Fourth Act;
and Timon's interview with the Poet and the
Painter in the Fifth Act. They are all subordinate
passages; the great scenes of Timon's agonies and
denunciations, although the flow of their verse is
sometimes broken, give no such impression of
uncouthness and want of finish. And, as will be
observed, they are largely scenes in which Alcibiades and the Steward, the two personages who
have already been noted as imperfectly fused into
the plot, make their appearance. Certain other
scenes, mainly prose passages in which the cynical
philosopher Apemantus takes a principal part,
have also been questioned, but on less satisfactory
grounds. They are by no means of an un-Shakespearean type; and although they are certainly
not inspired, there is no reason why they should
not have been written by Shakespeare in the somewhat jaded mood of which at least one other play,
Coriolanus, closely contemporary with *Timon of
Athens*, shows decided signs. The nature of the
passages that remain under suspicion may be well
illustrated by the following lines, which are spoken
by the Steward—

O, the fierce wretchedness that glory brings us!
Who would not wish to be from wealth exempt,
Since riches point to misery and contempt?
Who would be so mocked with glory, or to live
But in a dream of friendship?
To have his pomp and all what state compounds,
But only painted, like his varnished friends?
Poor honest lord, brought low by his own heart,
Undone by goodness! Strange, unusual blood,
When man's worst sin is, he does too much good!
Who, then, dares to be half so kind again?
For bounty, that makes gods, does still mar men.
My dearest lord, blessed, to be most accurst,
Rich, only to be wretched, thy great fortunes
Are made thy chief afflictions. Alas, kind lord!
He's flung in rage from this ingrateful seat
Of monstrous friends; nor has he with him to
Supply his life, or that which can command it.
I'll follow and enquire him out.
I'll ever serve his mind with my best will;
Whilst I have gold, I'll be his steward still.

The peculiarities of rhythm which are to be noted here, and in especial the alternation of jolting rhymed couplets with lines in which the metre seems suddenly to come to an abrupt stop, are repeated in the other suspected passages, and differentiate them clearly enough from the undoubted Shakespearean matter.

The explanations of scholars, in other respects sufficiently divergent, generally assume the presence of a second hand in the play. There can hardly be any question of direct collaboration, such as we find somewhat later in *Henry the Eighth* and

The Two Noble Kinsmen, for the share to be assigned on this hypothesis to a collaborator would not have been worth dividing off. Nor is it a very plausible suggestion that Shakespeare was working on the text of an older play, and that the passages to be accounted for represent surviving fragments of that text. There is no evidence of the existence of any such older play, and nothing to show that, wherever Shakespeare may have gone for the plots of his plays, he ever, after the days of his apprenticeship, found any advantage in using the dialogue of a predecessor. Moreover, the theory does not really remove the difficulty which it professes to remove, since, even if there were an older play, it would still be necessary to ask why the process of adaptation was so incomplete, and why Shakespeare was willing to accept the sketchy characters and the halting lines bequeathed to him. One is thrown back on the alternative of a play unfinished by Shakespeare; and in fact most editors explain the origin of *Timon of Athens* as we now have it, by supposing that such a play was handed over to an inferior playwright and eked out by him with additional scenes, either for performance on the stage, or, according to a less plausible version of the hypothesis, to fill up blank pages in the First Folio. Some bold spirits have even gone further, and have attempted to find stylistic analogies to the suspected passages in the work of one or another contemporary writer, Tourneur, or Heywood, or Wilkins, or Chapman, whom they have then saddled with the responsibility of the patch-work.

I should be sorry to dismiss the second hand as altogether out of the question, but it does not seem to me that its presence is rigidly necessitated by the conditions of the problem. May not *Timon of Athens* have been left unfinished by Shakespeare, and be unfinished still? The soliloquy of the Steward quoted above gives me the impression of being not so much un-Shakespearean as incompletely Shakespearean. The themes, even the phrases—the 'dream of friendship' and the 'varnished friends'—might have found their place readily enough in a rhythmic and developed period from the master's hand. So it is with the other suspected passages. They might be rough notes, first drafts of scenes, jotted down in half prose or gnomic couplets, just as they came to the surface in the early stages of composition, to be taken up and worked over again during the process of revision. This is a very natural way of writing, and there is no reason why Shakespeare should not have practised it. The famous statement of the editors of the First Folio, that 'what he thought, he uttered with that easiness, that we have scarce received from him a blot in his papers,' is hardly convincing evidence that he never made a rough copy before he prepared his final manuscript for the actors. So far as the substance of the doubtful scenes is concerned, it is on the whole more likely that they were originally shaped by Shakespeare than that they were interpolated in his work by someone commissioned to complete a task which he had laid aside. They, or some scenes equivalent to them, are structurally necessary to the play. But for the scenes in which the lords refuse the applications of Timon's messengers for loans, there would surely be too hurried a passage from the first hint of Timon's bankruptcy to the full crisis of his disillusion. His disavowal of mankind would be unintelligible without some previous evidence of man's baseness. Alcibiades, again, could hardly have come marching to sack Athens in the Fourth Act, without some exposition in an earlier scene of the grievances against Athens which were his justification. And if the dramatic claim of the Steward to his place in the action is somewhat less clear, it must be remembered that without him the Fourth and Fifth Acts would have afforded even less variety of interest than they do at present, to break the long and even monotonous outpourings of Timon's invective. But none the less these are subordinate elements in the scheme of the play, and if the text which has reached us represents only a partial revision of the original draft, it is natural that such a revision should have been first directed to Timon himself and the central scenes in which he figures, and that Alcibiades and the Steward, who form the background, should have been left to wait to the last for the final touches which would have cleared away all ambiguities and given them their right dramatic value.

As to the reason why *Timon of Athens* should have remained unfinished at all, conjecture alone is possible. The metrical evidence forbids that it should be regarded as the last of Shakespeare's plays. But it might very well be the last of his tragedies, and it is in some sort the ultimate summing-up of that long and remorseless analysis of human nature and divine ordering of which the tragedies must be taken as the expression. Its immediate predecessors were most probably *Antony and Cleopatra* and *Coriolanus*. In the one of these the love of woman, in the other the honour of man, is put through the crucible, and reduced to ash and nothingness. And then Shakespeare seems to have gathered himself together for a last and bitterest effort, in which no longer one sex only, but the whole of humanity, was to receive its meed of utter and comprehensive scorn. Timon is no mere Apemantus, snarling at a world in which he sees nothing but the reflection of his own un-generous impulses. He is humanity suddenly become conscious of itself and realizing with horror that its women are but sluts with aprons mountant, and that the strain of its men is bred out into baboon and monkey. The noble disillusion of Timon bears some such relation to the railing of Apemantus as was traced by the fine judgment of Coleridge between the horn-mad jealousy of Leontes and the great despair of Othello at a ruined ideal of womanhood. Tragedy, in *Timon of Athens*, is not yet robbed of awe; but the finer ear may perhaps detect in the play a want of balance and of measure, a touch almost of hysteria in the vituperation, which suggests that the stress of pessimistic thought is becoming a little more than the imagination can endure, and that in the brain of Timon's creator some strange crisis is at hand. That the crisis took place is indisputable. With *Timon of Athens* pessimism ends abruptly. Between its temper and that of any of the work that followed it there is a spiritual gulf fixed. It is tempting to suppose that the deep waters closed over Shakespeare's head while he was still elaborating the play, and that when he faced the world once more in his new mood the inclination to finish the task had left him.

PERICLES

QUITE unmistakable is the cleavage in *Pericles, Prince of Tyre* between the work of Shakespeare and the work of another; nor is there any literary experience so immediate in its conviction of style, as that of passing from the tedious commonplace of the first two Acts to the magnificent opening of the third, with its storm of passion set in a storm of sea and sky—

> Thou god of this great vast, rebuke these surges,
> Which wash both heaven and hell; and thou, that hast
> Upon the winds command, bind them in brass,
> Having recalled them from the deep! O, still
> Thy deafening, dreadful thunders; gently quench
> Thy nimble, sulphurous flashes!—O, how, Lycorida,
> How does my queen?—Thou stormest venomously;
> Wilt thou spit all thyself? The seaman's whistle
> Is as a whisper in the ears of death,
> Unheard.—Lycorida!—Lucina, O
> Divinest patroness, and midwife gentle
> To those that cry by night, convey thy deity
> Aboard our dancing boat; make swift the pangs
> Of my queen's travails!

Henceforward to the end of the play, with the exception of the rather absurd speeches of the presenter, Gower, Shakespeare is revealed. I do not share the hesitation which some have felt in ascribing to him the scenes in which the lost Marina carries her chastity unspotted through

the dangers of a bawdy-house. The dialogue of
these scenes is in his manner, and the theory that
he would not sully his pen by writing of such a
subject can only be due to one of those waves of
sentimentalism which occasionally sweep from an
early Victorian drawing-room over Shakespearean
criticism. It cannot survive the recollection of
the Pandarus of *Troilus and Cressida* and the
Pompey of *Measure for Measure*; and still less
that of the 'sluts with aprons mountant,' whose
social influence, as of a devastating fire, becomes
almost a morbid obsession in the Fourth Act of
the play by which *Pericles* must have immediately
been preceded, *Timon of Athens*. It is true that
Pericles is cast in a very different vein from that of
Timon; but it is a characteristic of the group of
romances to which it belongs, not to ignore the
black possibilities of human nature, but rather to
acknowledge these, and to transcend them in the
strength of a boundless and confident optimism.
Cymbeline has its Cloten; *The Winter's Tale* its
horn-mad Leontes; *The Tempest* its profoundly
symbolic Caliban. On the other hand, I find it
difficult to trace in the first two Acts any touch
whatever of Shakespeare, beyond the single simile
which he must have inserted with a vagrant pen
in the first scene of all—

The blind mole casts
Copped hills towards heaven, to tell the earth is thronged
By man's oppression; and the poor worm doth die for it.

But even when Shakespeare's share in the play

has been satisfactorily marked off, the literary
problems which it suggests are far from done with.
Who was the author of the first two Acts, and how
did Shakespeare's work come to be associated at
all with such very inferior stuff? It would seem
that we have to recover facts which had already
passed out of cognizance by the Restoration.
Dryden appears to have thought the play a prentice-
work of Shakespeare. Writing in 1672 of the
'lameness' of many of the plots of Shakespeare
and Fletcher, 'especially those which they writ
first,' he says, 'I suppose I need not name Pericles
Prince of Tyre, nor the historical plays of Shakespeare.' In some verses of 1684 he is even more
explicit—

> Shakespeare's own Muse his Pericles first bore,
> The Prince of Tyre was elder than the Moor.

The fullest weight must of course be given to
anything that looks like a Shakespearean tradition
handed down by Dryden. But even with the
confirmation that, when *Pericles* was revived in
1631, Jonson called it a 'mouldy tale,' this is an
impossibility. The tone and temper of Shakespeare's contribution, no less than its rhythmical
qualities, are too obviously those of his latest and
not those of his earliest work. You cannot dis-
sociate the storm of Pericles from the storm of
The Tempest, or Cerimon from Prospero, or the
double recovery of Marina and Thaisa from the
double recovery of Perdita and Hermione; any
more than you can conceive the Shakespeare of

279

the historical plays penning the subtle harmonies
of such a speech as that of Pericles over Thaisa's
death-bed—

> A terrible childbed hast thou had, my dear;
> No light, no fire. The unfriendly elements
> Forgot thee utterly; nor have I time
> To give thee hallowed to thy grave, but straight
> Must cast thee, scarcely coffined, in the ooze;
> Where, for a monument upon thy bones
> And aye-remaining lamps, the belching whale
> And humming water must o'erwhelm thy corpse,
> Lying with simple shells.

It would be tempting to take *Pericles* as an early
work of Shakespeare, partly rewritten by him in
1608, as I suspect that an early play of his on
Henry the Eighth was more completely rewritten
by him and Fletcher in 1613. But this again is
an hypothesis which will not for a moment bear
comparison with the facts. The rhythm of the
first two Acts, with their frequent double endings
and curiously interspersed rhymes, is no more like
Shakespeare's early rhythm than it is like his
rhythm in 1608. It is not like anything which he
ever wrote at any time in his life. It is a little
more difficult to say to what undistinguished
writer it should be credited. A recent critic has
argued for Thomas Heywood, but it is extremely
improbable that Heywood, who was an actor in
the Queen's company from 1603 to 1619, and
regularly wrote for his own fellows, would once
and once only have contributed to the repertory
of their principal rivals. I see no reason to differ

from the common conclusion that on the whole
the probabilities are in favour of the authorship
of George Wilkins, who is known to have been
employed upon other work for the King's men
about the date of *Pericles*, and who published a
prose story with the title of *The Painful Adventures
of Pericles, Prince of Tyre* in 1608. This is admittedly
based upon the play, and in many places adopts
its very phrasing. It may be incidentally observed
that in one place it yields material for the restoration of Shakespeare's original text. Thus, in the
story, Pericles addresses his sea-born babe: 'Poore
inch of Nature (quoth he) thou arte as rudely
welcome to the worlde, as euer Princesse Babe
was, and hast as chiding a natiuitie, as fire, ayre,
earth, and water can affoord thee.' There are
variations here from the passage in the first scene
of the Third Act of the play which may be due to
Wilkins; but it would be odd if 'Poore inch of
Nature,' which is not in the play as we have it,
were by another than Shakespeare. There is not
much dramatic work by Wilkins upon which to
base a comparison, but such as there is does not
discredit the hypothesis that the first two Acts of
Pericles may be his.

Still the question recurs, How is it that Shakespeare, who did not ordinarily follow the practice,
usual enough among other contemporary dramatists, of collaboration, came for once to collaborate
with so arrant a literary hack as Wilkins? Various
speculations have been hazarded on this point,

and those who are most agreed upon finding Wilkins in the play differ widely when it comes to explaining how he got there. The first solution that offered itself was that Wilkins was the sole author of an original *Pericles*, and that the extant text represents a revision undertaken by Shakespeare. But there are many considerations upon which this breaks down. Wilkins is not known as a dramatist before 1607, and it seems hardly likely that he can have written a play early enough for it to require revision by 1608. Again, if the last three Acts of the original were anything like the first two of the present text, why should Shakespeare have taken the trouble to revise them at all, instead of spending his time, with no less ease and surely to greater profit, in writing a wholly new play? It would be a curious process of revision, moreover, which took the form of entirely rewriting the last three Acts and leaving the first two, rubbish as they are, practically untouched. A far more ingenious theory is that which supposes that the last three Acts were originally written by Shakespeare as the substance of a complete play, that they were laid aside as too short, and that they were afterwards handed over to Wilkins, who eked them out by prefixing additional matter drawn from the same familiar narrative, although irrelevant enough to the dramatic purpose of Shakespeare's fragment. This explanation has the advantage of recognizing the singular incoherence between the two parts of the play; its weakness lies in the not very probable initial mis-calculation which it ascribes to an experienced and practical dramatist.

Clearly, we are upon a ground where, at the best, nothing but a more or less plausible con-jecture is attainable. But I do not think that it is possible to advance even upon the lines of conjec-ture, without taking into account, in addition to the presence of two hands in *Pericles* itself, two other considerations. One is the unfinished state of its immediate predecessor, *Timon of Athens*; the other is the complete contradiction which these two fragments present to each other, when con-sidered in the light of the spiritual tempers which they reveal and the judgments of life which they convey. *Timon of Athens* is the last word in that pessimistic analysis of man and man's place in eternity which is the underlying motive of all the long range of Shakespearean tragedies. It is little more than the literary expression of a settled hate and loathing which, inch by inch, the poet and idealist has come to bear to humanity. And it is an expression which so directly reflects the workings of the tortured brain behind it, as almost to pass the limits of intelligible speech. Compared to *Timon of Athens*, the Shakespearean part of *Pericles*, with its touches of exquisite poetry, and its happy dreams of purity that triumphs over sin and of wrongs that all come to be righted in the process of time, is like the first fresh outlook of a sick man, as the besetting fancies drop away from him, upon

283

the green fields of his convalescence. Within the bounds of permissible conjecture, I find it hard not to believe that the metaphor comes very near to being a statement of literal fact. The change from the Shakespeare of the last tragedies to the Shakespeare of the romances is so fundamental and above all so sudden, as to need some exceptional and drastic explanation. It is not a mere transition, such as took place when Shakespeare gradually laid aside the unreflecting optimism of his high-hearted comedies and entered upon the tragic view of things. It is rather a conversion, a complete reversal of standards and values, which at once betrays itself through the whole man, in his sense of rhythm no less than in his spiritual outlook. Something happened when he laid aside *Timon of Athens,* some crisis of overwrought brain and nerve; and when he recovered, lying there, let us hope, in the great chamber of New Place in Stratford, it was no longer the Shakespeare of *Timon* who regarded a new-washed world. And when he came back to work, he took up the silly piece which George Wilkins had been allowed to begin for the King's men in his absence, and put in the latter end of it the beautiful idyll which centres round the figure of the good physician Cerimon, with his noble exposition of the ideals of a calling which his learning and his charity alike illustrate and adorn—

> I hold it ever,
> Virtue and cunning were endowments greater
> Than nobleness and riches. Careless heirs

May the two latter darken and expend;
But immortality attends the former,
Making a man a god. 'Tis known, I ever
Have studied physic, through which secret art,
By turning o'er authorities, I have,
Together with my practice, made familiar
To me and to my aid the blessed infusions
That dwell in vegetives, in metals, stones;
And I can speak of the disturbances
That nature works, and of her cures, which doth give me
A more content in course of true delight
Than to be thirsty after tottering honour,
Or tie my treasure up in silken bags,
To please the fool and death.

So at least I read the story of the making of *Pericles*, and perhaps it may pass for a conjecture as well as another. I do not think that I am the first who has liked to trace in the lineaments of Cerimon some likeness of the Stratford physician, John Hall, who married Shakespeare's daughter Susanna in the very year 1607, and who, if Shakespeare was indeed ill at Stratford that year, most certainly tended him. And one remembers, not altogether inconsequently, how another poet, Robert Louis Stevenson, dedicated his *Underwoods* to eleven members of the profession which, for him too, represented 'the flower of our civilization.'

CYMBELINE

RECOGNITION has long been given to the fact that the three last plays completed by Shakespeare, *Cymbeline*, *The Winter's Tale*, and *The Tempest*, together with *Pericles*, for which he can only in part be responsible, form a distinct group among his works, and are marked by certain qualities of temper and outlook upon life which differentiate them rather sharply from their immediate predecessors. It is a far cry indeed from the later tragedies, with their remorseless analysis of human frailties and their sombre interrogation of human destiny, to the serene optimism which slowly directs the travail of a Hermione or an Imogen to its golden close, or to the solemn vindication of an overruling Providence through the symbolism of Prospero's triumphant magic. Hardly less is the gulf between the imperishable phrasing, cast in monumental bronze, of *Antony and Cleopatra*, and the facile and disordered prettinesses, which hang about the relaxed and structureless periods of the later plays. A recent thesis, supported by a fund of learning and a gift of critical perception that command all respect, endeavours to trace this fundamental change in Shakespeare's dramatic methods to the growing reputation of Beaumont and Fletcher, and to the fresh stimulus afforded to the imagination of the older poet by the need of catching the trick of romantic writing which his younger rivals had brought into vogue. In particular it is suggested that *Cymbeline* owes its inspiration to *Philaster*, the elements of whose plot it reproduces in a new and ingenious combination, while the slandered and disguised Imogen has her double prototype in the slandered Arethusa and the disguised Bellario.

It would be easier to determine the question of priority if there were less uncertainty as to the chronology of the plays produced by the King's men during the first Jacobean decade; in the present state of the evidence upon that subject, it is hardly possible to go beyond guess-work. There is nothing, for example, to show whether, as a matter of fact, *Philaster* preceded or followed *Cymbeline*; and therefore, so far as there is anything in the nature of direct imitation between the two plays, it may have been either on the one side or on the other. I am not myself impressed, in actually reading the two plays, by a sense of direct imitation to anything like the extent which a formal comparative analysis of their motives suggests. Apart from any such issue, it may freely be admitted that the general scope of the later tragicomedies of Shakespeare and that of the early tragicomedies of Beaumont and Fletcher is much the same. They have many devices of construction and many types of character in common. Wickedness triumphs for a time, but never in the end. Truth and chastity pass through the furnace and come out unstained. Any lie, however improbable, finds temporary acceptance. The happiness of lovers is broken by intrigues and misunderstandings, and restored by fortunate discoveries. Heroines conceal themselves in the garb of pages and endure moving accidents by flood and field. Children are lost and found again. Ancient feuds and shattered friendships come to reconciliation in the fullness of time. The woods prove less savage than the court, and the pomp of kings is contrasted to its disadvantage with pastoral content. The tyrannical father, the cruel step-mother, the devoted wife, the credulous lover, the loutish rival, the wanton maid of honour, the faithful servant, all play their parts. The salad is variously compounded and flavoured, but the ingredients are always the same. They belong to the formulæ, not of life, but of romance. The opportunities which they afford for dramatic situations and for sentimental embroidery seem to have made them especially dear to Jacobean audiences. But obviously they are neither the invention of Shakespeare nor of Beaumont and Fletcher. They had long been common form in the narrative romances both of the middle ages and of the Renascence; and the earlier dramatists themselves, even if less continuously and with less abundance of rhetoric and pathos, had freely exploited them. So far as Shakespeare is concerned, many of the individual incidents and motives of *Cymbeline* can readily be paralleled from former plays; what is new is the emphasis with which they are selected and arranged.

In adopting tragicomedy as, for him, the final dramatic expression of life, Shakespeare was, in a sense, returning to a way of dramatic writing which he had first experimentally essayed in *The Two Gentlemen of Verona* and *The Merchant of Venice*, had then used to provide an emotional background to the comedy of *As You Like It* and *Twelfth Night*, had allowed to become conspicuous and questionable in *Much Ado About Nothing*, and had finally rejected with the unsmiling satire of *Measure for Measure* and *All's Well that Ends Well*. In the storm and stress of the great tragedies there is naturally no room left for the happy ending. The new tragicomedy succeeds in steering clear of certain technical faults upon which the old was apt to be wrecked. So conventional a representation of life can only maintain itself by being consistent. If it is brought into contact with the touchstone of real humanity, it ceases to persuade. This is an artistic principle which Shakespeare had not always grasped. In *The Two Gentlemen of Verona*, the reality of Proteus, imaging in the play the poet's own unstable friend, puts to shame the hollow artifices of the concluding scene. Still more, in *Much Ado About Nothing*, does the melodrama of Claudio and Hero pale into unconvincingness beside the exuberant vitality of Beatrice and her Benedick. There is no such mistake in *Cymbeline*. This is to be a symbolical and idealized

289

rendering of life, and there must be no such clashing of dramatic planes as would result from the intrusion of an actual transcript taken from the book of life itself. Shakespeare works with puppets throughout; and the puppet Imogen, set between the puppet Cloten and the puppet Posthumus, may pass for perfection, so long as the danger of comparison with the flesh and blood of a Cleopatra or even of a Cressida is scrupulously avoided.

The chief difficulty in the theory, which traces the characteristics of Shakespeare's last dramatic manner to the imitation of Beaumont and Fletcher, seems to me to lie in its failure to account for the profound change of spiritual mood which underlies the transition from tragedy to romance. For years the soul of Shakespeare had trodden the abyss of vexed and gloomy speculation. From the questionings of *Macbeth* he had passed to the denials of *King Lear*, and had seen love of woman as the scourge of the world in *Antony and Cleopatra*, and honour of man as the mask of the egoist in *Coriolanus*. The last echo of the Titanic denunciation is in the half incoherent mutterings of *Timon of Athens*; and then, tentatively at first in *Pericles*, but fully and without hesitation in *Cymbeline*, comes this entirely new utterance, the expression of a mind at peace with itself and ready to accept the ordering of things with the contented optimism of an unembarrassed faith. *Cymbeline* is, as it were, a palinode to *King Lear*. The radiant whiteness of Cordelia, impotent of old to make head against the forces of evil, revisits earth again in Imogen, and broods like a dove over a *dénouement* in which unspotted purity and simple honesty come in the ultimate issue, after much vexation, to their own. The unanswered cosmic problems are laid aside, or take on new colours in the light of a regained faith. Life, which the purged eye once scanned with a splendid despair, is now seen only through a golden haze of sentiment. The broken harmonies are resolved before the close. A great and gracious peace descends upon the autumn of thought—

> Fear no more the heat of the sun,
>   Nor the furious winter's rages;
> Thou thy worldly task hast done,
>   Home art gone and ta'en thy wages.

What is remarkable is not, of course, that the tragic mood should come to an end, and the perturbed spirit find rest at last; but rather that the change should come so suddenly, presenting itself as a breach of continuity instead of as the natural term of a logical process of mental growth. Up to this point Shakespeare's development has been intelligible enough. Play has led on to play by sensible and regular gradations. The blossoming and fruitage of his art, however astonishing, have none the less formed an organic whole. And now the links are broken. Something inexplicable has intervened, and without hint or warning the whole outlook of the poet has changed. He accepts where he denied; blesses where he banned. The universe, which but a moment ago he reviewed and judged to be chaos, now spreads itself out before his eyes as the ordered and sunlit garden of God. I hope to give all credit to the critical principle which bids us remember that Shakespeare, in addition to being a great poet, was also an expert and adroit stage-manager. But I do not find it possible to ascribe so fundamental a metamorphosis to a mere desire to rival others in exploiting a dramatic convention, which had proved congenial to the easy temper of Anne of Denmark or the chivalrous instincts of the young Prince Henry. Surely to adopt such a theory would be to refuse a spiritual content alike to the tragedies and to the romances, and to see nothing either in *Hamlet* or in *The Tempest* but the product of an inventive brain intent on penny-knaves' delight. There must be more in it than this. The profound cleavage in Shakespeare's mental history about 1607–1608 must have been due to some spiritual crisis the nature of which it is only possible dimly to conjecture; some such process as that which in the psychology of religion bears the name of conversion; or perhaps some sickness of the brain which left him an old man, freed at last from the fever of speculation and well disposed to spend the afternoon of life in unexacting and agreeable dreams. This latter hypothesis would help also to explain the marked change of style which accompanies the change of dramatic purpose in the romances. In these complicated and incoherent periods, in these softened and un-accentuated rhythms, in these tender and evanescent beauties, I find less a deliberate attempt to reduce the declamation of the stage to the colloquial dialogue of daily life, than the natural outcome of relaxed mental energies, shrinking from the effort after the wrought and nervous rhythms of the past.

Whatever it was that happened to Shakespeare, one may suspect that it profoundly affected his way of life no less than his way of thought. Characteristic of all the romances is that tendency to the idyll, which it is difficult not to connect with his apparent withdrawal, at an earlier age than one would have looked for, from the town to the country, from London and its stage to Stratford and its meadows. This element has also been attributed to the influence of Beaumont and Fletcher, and in particular the Welsh scenes in *Cymbeline* have been regarded as an amplification of the fine aspiration after the forest life in the Fourth Act of *Philaster*—

Oh, that I had been nourished in these woods
With milk of goats and acorns, and not known
The right of crowns, nor the dissembling trains
Of women's looks; but digged myself a cave,
Where I, my fire, my cattle, and my bed
Might have been shut together in one shed;
And then had taken me some mountain girl,
Beaten with winds, chaste as the hardened rocks
Whereon she dwelt, that might have strewed my bed

> With leaves and reeds and with the skins of beasts
> Our neighbours, and have borne at her big breasts
> My large coarse issue. This had been a life
> Free from vexation.

The affinity of this to the exaltation by Belarius in the Third Act of *Cymbeline* of his honest freedom in a rocky demesne over the city's usuries and the art of the court is obvious. But it is to be remembered that, although the technical setting of the pastoral is absent from both passages, the 'sweet content' of the country life had formed part of an Elizabethan tradition of pastoral sentiment long before it was handled either by Beaumont and Fletcher or by Shakespeare; and also that there is no especial reason why, as between *Philaster* and *Cymbeline*, the priority should lie with the former rather than with the latter. Indeed, so long as the chronological relations of the two plays are undetermined, the probabilities lie all the other way. Idyll is incidental in *Philaster*; in *Cymbeline* it is an integral part of the design. In the other romances of Beaumont and Fletcher cognate to *Philaster*, with the exception of *The Faithful Shepherdess* which is technically a pastoral, idyll is far from being so conspicuous as it is in *The Winter's Tale* or *The Tempest*, in which the upbringings of Perdita among the sheep-folds of Bohemia and of Miranda in her innocent and sequestered isle afford the closest parallels to the upbringing of the flower-like boys, Guiderius and Arviragus.

The WINTER'S TALE

PURPOSE and structure in *The Winter's Tale* are shaped alike by the canons of romance; if indeed one is justified in using the term canon to denote a principle which is founded on the negation of law. The formula of the play, as of all the dramatic outcome of Shakespeare's sentimental aftermath, is that of recognition; a formula which the *Electra* of Sophocles proved long before to be capable of extremely classic treatment, and which in fact Aristotle distinguished under the name of ἀναγνώρισις as a typical element of classical tragedy, but which in the process of time has generally borne a romantic handling, and has gathered about itself all the associations of romantic interest. The plot of *The Winter's Tale* is woven out of the fortunes of Hermione, who was dead and came to life again, and of Perdita, who was lost and was found again, just as Thaisa and Marina are lost and found again in *Pericles*, and Prospero in *The Tempest* is restored to his lost dukedom, and Posthumus in *Cymbeline* recovers the Imogen of whom he was not worthy. Truth that will out through disguises, wrongs that in the end become rights again, wanderings that lead homeward in the eventide; these are things which have always been precious to the romantic Muse. And in Shakespeare, as elsewhere, the development of such a theme lends itself naturally to the interposition of strange and exciting incidents. Men set sail and are shipwrecked on the coasts of Bohemia, where never coast was; a bear comes opportunely to make a meal of the witness and agent of a crime; shepherds find an infant princess with a casket of jewels that look like fairy gold; a statue steps from its pedestal to become a living breathing woman. Above all, the course of human affairs is swayed and interpreted by the enigmatic utterances of an oracle. Romance gets all the colour and novelty that are its life-blood; and for the philosophy of the universe, that in Shakespeare's later moods lies behind and determines romance, the amazement is converted into the symbol and manifestation of an overruling force working by hidden ways to bring the ends of man to good. The justification of Providence, that, after all, is the conscious intention which informs the romantic theme; and the supernatural intervention of Apollo represents, in accordance with the ordinary use of the supernatural by Shakespeare, an acknowledgment of the ultimate mystery which, in the last resort, the conception of Providence involves.

Nor is the happy issue of the play merely one of external accident. The power that, to the eye of Shakespeare's optimism, makes for righteousness operates not only in the ordering of events, but also in the heart of man; and the material recognitions, which bring the wife and daughter of Leontes back to him, but follow upon the spiritual regeneration wherein he returns from his jealous error, and devotes himself to the lifelong atonement of a 'saint-like sorrow.' Romance, indeed, will not have you apply too searching a psychology. Shakespeare must needs make vital what he touches, and Greene's graceful tale becomes a different thing when the master has introduced into it the audacious roguery of Autolycus and the ripe humanity of Paulina. But art may take its standpoint at more than one degree of remoteness from real life; and the jealousy of Leontes will never bear analysis and comparison, as if it were in the same plane of actuality with that torrent of terrible passion which scourges with eternal tragedy the noble breast of Othello. Were it so, one might wonder whether even the repentance and the sixteen years' penance are quite sufficient to entitle the torturer of Hermione to his ultimate impunity; for, indeed, the plane is not wholly kept, and there are scenes in the Second and Third Acts that touch something too near the quick for romance.

In quite another sense, *The Winter's Tale* declares itself as a notably extreme expression of the romantic temper. Certainly more than any other play of Shakespeare, possibly more than any other contemporary play, it defies the criticism voiced over thirty years before by Sidney, in his arraignment of the artistic ideals, or lack of such ideals, which he discerned in an earlier generation of Elizabethan dramatists. It was the incoherence, the lack of discipline, that offended Sidney; and in effect the disregard of those unities, which played so great a part in the literary disputations of a subsequent age, and which, when all is said and done, sum up in no inconvenient form a considerable body of poetic experience as to the working of the psychological laws that determine the production and maintenance of a dramatic illusion. *The Winter's Tale*, with its bifurcate plot, the two sections of which the poet rather places side by side than takes the trouble to interweave, with its action that shifts from Sicilia to Bohemia and back again, with its light-hearted lapse of no less than sixteen years while a child becomes a woman, sets the unities at nought in a way which it would be difficult not to regard as deliberate, even without the apology of Time, the Chorus, for the use of his wings. It is the utmost liberty that Shakespeare claims for the romantic dramatist; and the issue is made the more clear-cut by the juxtaposition of *The Winter's Tale* with the nearest play to it in point of time, *The Tempest*, in which a story of essentially the same character is presented in a form of perfect classical regularity, as the logical development, in plot and sub-plot, of a single situation, in a single locality, and within the compass of a single day. If Shakespeare 'wanted art' in Ben Jonson's, which was probably the same as Sidney's, sense, it is clear that the lack arose from no incomplete mastery, but from an effort, unintelligible to Ben's more rigid mind, after an unlimited freedom of technique.

In all the plays of the latest group, and to a marked degree in *The Winter's Tale*, the less intense dramatic life, as compared with that of the great tragic cycle which forewent them, leaves the more room for the decorative and episodic elements. There is surely nothing in the whole magic volume to surpass in sheer reach of poesy the lament over Fidele's grassy tomb in *Cymbeline*, or Perdita's exquisite description of the spring flowers that Proserpina let fall from Dis's waggon—

> Daffodils,
> That come before the swallow dares, and take
> The winds of March with beauty; violets dim,
> But sweeter than the lids of Juno's eyes
> Or Cytherea's breath; pale primroses,
> That die unmarried, ere they can behold
> Bright Phœbus in his strength—a malady
> Most incident to maids; bold oxlips and
> The crown imperial; lilies of all kinds,
> The flower-de-luce being one.

Nearly the whole of the Fourth Act, indeed, is an interlude, for its own sake, of delicate and humorous fantasy, which has a function, no doubt, in the disentangling of the plot, but one hardly proportionate to the elaboration with which its details are presented. The blameless loves of Florizel and Perdita serve to bring together once more the fortunes of the houses of Sicilia and Bohemia, and the tyranny of Polixenes as a father may pass for a pendant to the tyranny of Leontes as a husband; but essentially this is Shakespeare's picture of a rustic merry-making, nothing more and nothing less. It is an exercise in pastoral, that traditional idealization of the shepherd's life which the imagination of the Renascence poets, first on the continent and then in England, had built up upon the eclogues of Theocritus and of Virgil, and upon certain *chansons* of love-adventure between knights and village maidens, typical of native French poetry. Sidney himself and Spenser had given the pastoral its vogue at the court of Elizabeth, and it had proved singularly attractive to a literary instinct which already, in the rapidly-growing London of the late sixteenth and early seventeenth centuries, was beginning to feel the irksomeness of cities. It is the poetry of the reaction from civilization, and its tendency, intelligible enough even if illusory, to exalt the simplicity and content of the meadows above the pomps of mortal state finds an echo in Perdita's gentle protest—

> I was about to speak and tell him plainly,
> The self-same sun that shines upon his court
> Hides not his visage from our cottage, but
> Looks on alike.

There are hints and suggestions of pastoral throughout Shakespeare's earlier work, notably in *As You Like It*, that marvellous play with which, in the heart of a middle age whose preoccupations are mainly urban, he opens a sudden window upon the outside world. But never before *The Winter's Tale* had he given himself up to any full indulgence of the vein. It is a dangerous pastime, in dealing with a poet in whom the objective faculties are so highly developed as they are in Shakespeare, to attempt to trace reflections of his personal circumstances upon the mirror of his art. But one is justified in remembering that *The Winter's Tale* is a play of Shakespeare's literary autumn, written possibly after he had already passed into retirement at Stratford, and certainly when the links which bound him to London and the stage had begun to grow weak; and it is difficult not to think of it as influenced by the surroundings, familiar to him in boyhood, to which he had come back in all the freshness of recovered liberty and peace. Speculations as to the legitimacy of horticulture would have their natural origin as he walked with philosophic mind among the beds of carnations and streaked gillyvors in his 'great garden' at New Place; and hard by there was a hundred-acre farm in the open fields of Old Stratford, with another garden and an orchard and twenty acres of pasture, where one may be sure the sheep were shorn with all due jollity at the appropriate season, and the master sat down with his hinds to a homely banquet, in which warden pies coloured with saffron and porridge of prunes and of raisins of the sun did not fail to make their appearance.

Pastoral is never to be mistaken for a transcript of rustic life. Its significance resides, not in any

fidelity to the fact of the peasant, but in its relation
to the state of mind of the world-wearied courtier
or scholar who writes it. And the contrast is
generally brought into the foreground of the
picture. Consciously or unconsciously, the shepherds, or some at least among them, are mas-
querading. So it is in *The Winter's Tale*, where
the rude manners and the open-mouthed simplicity
of the real farm-folk only serve as a foil to the
natural nobility of the king's son Florizel and the
king's daughter Perdita. To the strangers Perdita
is 'the queen of curds and cream' and 'the
prettiest low-born lass that ever ran on the green-
sward.' Even those who are not in the secret will
hardly confuse her with the red-cheeked Dorcas
or the free-spoken Mopsa—

> Nothing she does or seems,
> But smacks of something greater than herself,
> Too noble for this place.

There is all the difference in the world between the
gracious symbolism of her flower-decked courtesy
and the bustling hospitality which the old shepherd
recalls as characteristic of his own wife at shearing-
times; and Florizel woos her appropriately enough
with no rustic compliments, but with dainty
speeches meet for any lady's bower—

> What you do
> Still betters what is done. When you speak, sweet,
> I'ld have you do it ever. When you sing,
> I'ld have you buy and sell so, so give alms,
> Pray so; and for the ordering your affairs,

> To sing them too. When you do dance, I wish you
> A wave of the sea, that you might ever do
> Nothing but that; move still, still so,
> And own no other function. Each your doing,
> So singular in each particular,
> Crowns what you are doing in the present deeds,
> That all your acts are queens.

And Perdita is worthy of his praise, were it only for the exquisite dignity with which she accepts the dismissal that seems the inevitable consequence of Polixenes' discovery of her lover. She will be no burden upon him; he has his place, she hers—

> Will't please you, sir, be gone?
> I told you what would come of this; beseech you,
> Of your own state take care. This dream of mine—
> Being now awake, I'll queen it no inch farther,
> But milk my ewes and weep.

Was it really in the country, one wonders, that Shakespeare found models for these high-hearted ladies, Perdita the unspoilt maiden, and Imogen the constant wife, of his latest plays? They are not precisely the types for which one would look in the pleasure-loving and none too scrupulous court of Anne of Denmark. But in Florizel, the unstained shepherd, there is no doubt a temptation to trace the lineaments of the gallant and too early lost Prince Henry, who seems to have had the gift of touching the popular imagination more effectively than anyone else since the fall of Essex.

The TEMPEST

THE TEMPEST, among Shakespeare's later plays, is a counterpart to the *Midsummer Night's Dream* of his lyric youth. Here, too, is a dream, or, if you will, a fairy tale, in which the protagonists are not men and women but imagined beings, taken partly from folk-belief and partly from literature, to be the symbols of forces dimly perceived by the poet as ruling that life, which is itself, after all, in another degree, but such stuff as dreams are made on. And, like *A Midsummer Night's Dream*, the play must interest the spectator less through a strictly dramatic appeal to his emotions, than by the strange romantic charm of its setting and its sensuous realization of the delicate and the grotesque in the mysterious personages whom it brings before him. It is, in fact, to be classed as dramatic *spectacle* rather than as drama proper, and the elaboration with which it has been put upon the stage by modern managers may be regarded as not, in this case, wholly out of keeping with the intention of the dramatist.

Apart, indeed, from its Ariel and its Caliban, and tried by the too rigid conception of drama which is blind to everything except just the interplay of human characters in action, *The Tempest* certainly fails to answer satisfactorily to the test.

The practical omnipotence which Prospero derives from his magic arts takes all vitality from the plots which he unravels and from the conflict between hero and villains which they represent. And, unless you are sentimentalist inveterate, your emotions will not be more than faintly stirred by the blameless loves at first sight of Ferdinand and Miranda, or by the quite superfluous obstacles, hollow as the property logs that Ferdinand must carry, which are put in their way by the heavy father. The inexperienced but peerless maiden, advancing the fringed curtains of her eyes upon the 'brave new world that hath such people in it,' only to have them dazzled by the first male being that crossed her path; the gallant but patient lover, of whom she very truly says, 'Nothing natural I ever saw so noble'; they have much to answer for, it is to be feared, in the later development of rose-pink drawing-room fiction. Perhaps it would be a little hard to bear them a grudge for this. But even if they are not responsible for their great-great-grandchildren, do they not themselves share something of the colourless insipidity of their great-great-grandfather and grandmother, Daphnis and Chloe? And if you accept Miranda as a 'nonpareil' and 'the top of admiration,' is it not rather because Shakespeare himself, through the mouths of Prospero and Ferdinand, tells you that that is what she is, than because of anything that she says or does as she stands before you? The device is an effective one in the hands of the novelist; but it is less available for the dramatist, who cannot, after all, escape from sooner or later producing his puppets, and making them speak and act for themselves upon his stage. Incidentally, it is a little curious to observe how the type of Shakespeare's women varies at different periods of his career. Miranda, Imogen, Perdita; set them against Rosalind, Beatrice, Helena. Is one to suppose that Shakespeare, like many more recent dramatists, found himself obliged to write 'round' the personality of the 'leading lady,' who starred it for the time being in his company? Or is he merely following the wavering of the modish taste in heroines, a taste set perhaps, as some think, during the period of his final plays, by the senti-mental tragicomedies of Beaumont and Fletcher?

But if *The Tempest* is not exactly a slice cut straight from the red heart of humanity, still less can it be reasonably interpreted as a deliberate and consistent allegory. To prove, for example, in detail that it is not a formal exposition of the Baconian philosophy would carry me into regions of controversy which I do not propose, now or at any other time, to tread. The dream-formula is the true one. The play is no more than a dream, and as such dispensed from any obligation to logical completeness or continuity; an iridescent bubble, shot across by divers threads of symbolism and suggestion, independent of one other, but all re-flecting tendencies of thought and feeling which were dominant in the mind of the poet at the time of its composition. Some of these tendencies may perhaps be indicated without breaking down the filmy texture of fancy by too heavy a burden of external comment.

That the general drift and structure of the play are peculiarly characteristic of Shakespeare's later mood of serene optimism, and that the invincible Prospero, biding his time to charm good out of ill and to make the odds all even, is in particular a kind of concrete embodiment of Providence, have become commonplaces of criticism. I need not labour them, or dwell upon the contrast between the spiritual temper which finds such expression and that which gave birth to the Titanic tragedies of *Macbeth* and *King Lear*. It is one which makes its first appearance in *Pericles*, and dominates *Cymbeline* and *The Winter's Tale*, as well as *The Tempest*. Further, one may readily agree with those who think that the play was written with an eye to the conditions of a court entertainment, rather than to those of the public stage. It is, in fact, a glorified mask. The ship of the first scene represents the 'pageant' of carpenter's work, commonly introduced into such devices, and the dances, songs, and disguises of Ariel and his company are balanced, as in an antimask, by the clumsy revels of Stephano and his reeling-ripe fellows. The character of the formal mask introduced into the Fourth Act suggests a wedding, and at a Jacobean wedding the plainspokenness of Prospero's sermon to the lovers

307

would perhaps be neither intolerable nor uncalled
for. The parallel to *A Midsummer Night's Dream*,
probably performed at a court wedding in 1594
or 1595, and ending with an epithalamium, is in
this point exact. *The Tempest* is known to have
been presented before the Princess Elizabeth,
afterwards the unfortunate 'Queen of Hearts,'
and Frederick the Elector Palatine, during the
festivities accompanying their marriage on the
14th of February, 1613. It has even been supposed
that it was originally written for this occasion.
But the evidence for an earlier performance in
1611, which has now outlived suspicion, would
make this theory untenable, even did Miranda
not still more suggest a portrait of Elizabeth as
she came into her new-washed world from the
seclusion of Combe Abbey in 1611, than a portrait
of Elizabeth after two years of court life in 1613.
It is possible, however, although not, I think,
more than possible, that the play may have been
revised in the latter year, and the hymeneal mask,
which is not particularly appropriate to its place
in the action, inserted as a compliment to the bridal
pair. However this may be, the hunt after topical
allusions in Shakespeare's plays is surely not
pursued with the discretion and saving sense of
humour which it demands, when the escape of
Ferdinand from drowning is interpreted as a
reference to the untimely end of Henry, Prince of
Wales, who died, not by drowning, but from
typhoid fever, shortly before his sister's marriage.

Ferdinand cannot stand both for Henry and for Frederick; nor is it the obvious way of condoling with a father on the death of a son, to point out that somebody else's son did not die. Even less willingly can one be induced to find in the triumphant magic of Prospero a delicate flattery of those political intrigues of James the First which had culminated in the alliance with the Elector. Shakespeare was willing enough, no doubt, to address a passing compliment to the king in *Macbeth*. He had more than once done as much for Gloriana in earlier plays. But the dignified and patient Prospero is no more likely than Hamlet himself to be intended as a full-length portrait of the meanest and least picturesque of all the Stuarts. And so far, indeed, as there is any personal reference in Prospero at all, is it not clearly to one far greater than James the First, namely William Shakespeare himself? I find it impossible to doubt that in the famous address to the 'elves of hills, brooks, standing lakes, and groves,' in which Prospero recites how by their aid he has—

Bedimmed
The noontide sun, called forth the mutinous winds,
And 'twixt the green sea and the azured vault
Set roaring war,

and finally abjures his rough magic, breaks his staff, and drowns his book, Shakespeare is really making his own farewell to the stage and to the arts by which he has exercised a dominion even more elemental than that of the enchanter. This speech gives a key to one at least of the ideas which find expression in the play. Thus Ariel, who from another point of view is the agent and minister of an inscrutable Providence, becomes from this a symbol of the spirit of poetry found pegged in the cloven pine of the pre-Shakespearean drama, brought into the service of the creative imagination, and employed for his term in the fashioning of illusions to delight the eyes and move the hearts of men. And so it is hinted that at the end of the play the insubstantial pageant of the great Shakespearean drama shall fade for ever. Ariel shall have his freedom, and Prospero shall betake himself to the dukedom of Milan—which is Stratford.

Whether I am right in this or not, the scanty evidence available would seem to show that the year 1611, in which *The Tempest* was probably written, was also that in which Shakespeare bade good-bye to London and took up his abode for the rest of his life at New Place. He was then still a comparatively young man, and had been a dramatist for not more than a round score of years. The significance of so early a retirement has perhaps hardly been sufficiently appreciated. No doubt Shakespeare had made money and could afford, like Alleyn, to enjoy his repose and the responsibilities of a landed proprietor. But his willingness to leave London and his triumphs and to bury himself at the age of forty-eight in the smug obscurity of a petty provincial town certainly suggests that his quality of actor and playwright had lost whatever attraction it may ever have possessed for him. The hints of dissatisfaction with the life of the mime, at a much earlier date, in the *Sonnets*, will not be forgotten. Plays and poems are full of these tantalizing glimpses of the man William Shakespeare behind them, and any attempt at interpretation lands one on the perilous ways of conjectural biography. It is, certainly, a merely conjectural reconstruction of the inadequate data when I suggest that Shakespeare as a lad was 'dedicated to closeness and the bettering of his mind,' and felt little desire for the career of a farmer and more or less prosperous burgess, which was that laid open to him by the traditions of his family. He cared not to be Duke of Milan. Literary ambitions, aided perhaps by some event capable at least of symbolical representation in a drama as an intrigue against him, drove him to London. But the actual conditions attending the calling of an actor and dramatist spelt disillusion. Shakespeare was more of a *bourgeois* than he had dreamed. The mayor's son, conscious of his father's coat-armour, rebelled against the disrepute attaching to an occupation whose members were only distinguished by a legal fiction from rogues and vagrants. The prospect of retirement was present to his mind from an early period. He saved money, invested it in Stratford, bought a house there, and, as soon as his affairs permitted, he gladly broke his pen, and returned to his rejected dukedom, to enjoy

311

the dignities of New Place, to dig his garden, collect his tithes, sit through sermons, and entertain the preacher to sack and supper.

May one venture to think that something better and more spiritual than this merely respectable instinct helped to account for his flight? Is it possible that, in 1611, Shakespeare heard Warwickshire calling with a voice that would not be denied? London was a growing city in the early seventeenth century, and a note of revolt from urban life, hardly heard since the day of the poets of imperial Rome, was beginning to steal back into literature. Jonson translated his—

Beatus ille, qui procul negotiis,

although Jonson, if any one, had Fleet Street in his veins; and doubtless many a poet flung himself across a table in the Half-Moon to write an ode about the shepherd's life and its sweet content. But the sentiment was a real one all the same, and there are signs in Shakespeare's latest plays that he shared it. In *The Winter's Tale* it reveals itself in the hints of conventional pastoral, always the townsman's dream of country life. In *The Tempest* it inspires the speculations of Gonzalo, borrowed from Montaigne though these may be, on the golden age and the pleasant liberties of its primitive civilization; and also surely the sweet out-of-doors air of the play, blown through and through with breaths from those voyages of discovery which brought so much romance and such a widening horizon into Elizabethan life.

And so we come to the enigmatic figure of Caliban, about which, it must be admitted, the ingenuity of the commentators has not been idle. I have rejected the temptation to suggest that, just as Ariel symbolizes the spirit of poetry brought by Shakespeare into the service of the creative imagination, so Caliban signifies the spirit of prose, born of Sycorax who is controversial theology, and imperfectly subdued by Shakespeare to the same service. There are some who follow Renan in taking Caliban for a type of Demos, and regard his desire to 'nor scrape trenchering nor wash dish' as eminently characteristic of political ideals which aim at nothing higher than the escape from reasonable labour. Of any political intention on Shakespeare's part in *The Tempest* I am profoundly sceptical; nor do I feel sure that, in the great political cleavage which was beginning to show itself in his day, he would have been so certainly a foe to Demos as is often assumed. Those who believe in his supposed aristocratic and divine-right sympathies, largely on the basis of the Jack Cade scenes in *Henry the Sixth* which he probably did not design, may be invited to compare the demeanour of the boatswain in the storm with that of the crowd of courtiers whose howling proved louder than the weather or his office. Shakespeare, at least, was the dupe neither of a theory nor of a title. 'What cares these roarers for the name of king?'

Browning based on Caliban a semi-ironical

disquisition on the genesis of natural religions and their anthropomorphism. Others have seen in him an anticipation of Darwinian theories as to the development of man. It is not necessary to attribute to Shakespeare prophetic gifts in the region of biology; but he does seem to be endeavouring to adumbrate in Caliban such a general conception of primitive humanity as the expanding knowledge of his day had opened out to him. Caliban is an earthy creature. He has the morals and the maliciousness of a troglodyte, and must be taught the first elements of human knowledge—

> How
> To name the bigger light, and how the less,
> That burn by day and night—

and even the first principles of articulate speech. He will take no print of goodness, and can only be controlled and made serviceable by terror. On the other hand—and here we come back to the cravings after the life according to nature which the play in more than one point suggests—he is akin to earth in another sense. He knows all 'the qualities of the isle,' where the 'quick freshes' are, and where the brine pits; and, in the fervour of his adoration for Stephano, vows—

> I'll show thee the best springs. I'll pluck thee berries.
> I'll fish for thee and get thee wood enough;

and again—

> I prithee, let me bring thee where crabs grow.
> And I with my long nails will dig thee pig-nuts;
> Show thee a jay's nest and instruct thee how

> To snare the nimble marmoset; I'll bring thee
> To clustering filberts and sometimes I'll get thee
> Young scamels from the rock.

And is it upon Caliban or upon the missionaries of European civilization that the irony falls, in his complaint against Prospero—

> You taught me language, and my profit on it
> Is, I know how to curse. The red plague rid you
> For teaching me your language!

or in the Rabelaisian scenes where the monster abases himself in the cult of the *dive bouteille* and confesses of the drunken lackey who holds it—

> That's a brave god, and bears celestial liquor?

HENRY the EIGHTH

ODERN criticism has long ago made up its mind that *Henry the Eighth*, in the form in which it has come down to us, cannot be classed as a complete and unaided work of Shakespeare. It was the acute analysis of James Spedding, the biographer of Bacon, which first assured the existence of a second hand, recognized it as the hand of John Fletcher, and after distinguishing on grounds of general æsthetic feeling between the two elements of the play, succeeded in confirming the result by the more mechanical application of the so-called metrical tests. Subsequent investigations have only tended to support Spedding's conclusions, so far as Fletcher is concerned, and at the present time there does not appear to be any reason to question them. The metrical characteristics of Fletcher's verse, and in particular his extraordinary fondness for the feminine ending, are difficult to obscure at any time; and his fluent style, his easy touch upon the pathetic, and his profound failure to appreciate dramatic values all find ample illustration in those parts of *Henry the Eighth* assigned to him by Spedding. These include the best-known and, from the episodic point of view, the most effective scenes; Wolsey's farewell to his greatness, the death-bed of Katherine, the glorification of

Elizabeth and of James with which the action closes. But there is nothing in these which is necessarily beyond Fletcher's reach, or out of harmony with his genius; and nothing on the other hand so inimitably Shakespearean as to render its attribution to a different writer an absurdity.

But the critical difficulties of *Henry the Eighth* begin rather than end with the establishment of Fletcher; since if there is substantial agreement as to this, there is the widest diversity of opinion as to the relations of Shakespeare to the younger dramatist, and as to the conditions under which their work came to be presented in combination. The production of the play can be precisely dated, because it is clear from contemporary descriptions that it is the 'new play' which was being acted at the Globe under the title of *All is True* on the 29th of June, 1613, when the disastrous fire broke out, which led to the total destruction of 'that virtuous fabric.' By 1613 there is every reason to suppose that Shakespeare had formally retired from the habitual exercise of his art. *The Tempest* was played in 1611, and the autobiographic intention of the passage, in which the wearied Prospero dismisses his familiars and buries his magic staff in the Warwickshire earth, is unmistakable. But such resolutions sometimes have their after-thoughts. The London theatres had been humming in the winter of 1612–13 under the stimulus of the coming of the Palsgrave and the wedding of

Elizabeth. The King's men alone had been called upon for no less than fourteen plays at Court. The visit of the Savoy ambassador had led to a fresh demand in June; and Shakespeare, who is known to have helped Burbage in designing the Earl of Rutland's *impresa* for the tilt on Lady Day, may well also have been called upon to lend a hand to the playwright who had become his virtual successor at the Globe, in the unusual straits to which even his faculties of rapid composition had been reduced by the year's stress of work. It is on the whole a less plausible theory that an unfinished fragment left by Shakespeare on his retirement was handed over to Fletcher for completion. The non-Fletcherian half of the play comprises portions of each Act and touches upon all the various motives, the fall of Buckingham, the rise of Anne Boleyn, the repudiation of Katherine, the disgrace of Wolsey, the intrigue against Cranmer, which succeed each other in the plot. Its scenes are closely dove-tailed into those assigned to Fletcher; and it is difficult to see why, if Shakespeare had started the play independently, he should have selected just those scenes to be written first. You can write a play from beginning to end, or you can write the most significant scenes first and then work round them. But the non-Fletcherian scenes follow neither of these methods, and their distribution seems hardly intelligible except on the hypothesis of collaboration. I do not think that any importance is to be attached to the view that it would be beneath Shakespeare's dignity to collaborate with Fletcher. Those who hold it are imperfectly acquainted with the literary conditions of the sixteenth and seventeenth centuries.

But does the attribution of the non-Fletcherian scenes to Shakespeare carry with it a responsibility for the structure and the meaning of the play? That is a more serious question; for, in spite of its fine rhetorical passages, it would be impossible to maintain that *Henry the Eighth* reaches a high level of excellence. It suffers from the multiplicity of its issues, taken straight over from the chronicle; and in especial from the want of dramatic sense, which spoils the balance of its parts by laying the highest colour upon precisely those elements which should have been kept in the background. The contrast between the overthrow of Wolsey's over-weening ambition and the triumphant emergence of Anne Boleyn, bearing with her the destinies of Elizabethan England, was an effective scheme enough. The Buckingham and the Cranmer episodes are perhaps sufficiently subordinated to the two main motives which they respectively support. But there is almost an ethical obtuseness in the stress placed upon the sorrows of the admirable Katherine, and in the failure to observe that dramatic sympathy won for her could only militate against the dramatic sympathy which the whole purpose of the play made it the duty of the writers to win for her more fortunate rival. And thus the interest is over with the death-bed at Kimbolton, and the closing scenes, which should have clinched the dynastic and patriotic theme, inevitably assume the air of an irrelevant and superfluous pageant. This is just the sort of mistake which it was natural for Fletcher to make. Ungifted with the true dramatist's faculty for seeing his design as a whole, he had the instinct for pathos which led him to lavish his poetry upon Katherine's fate without regard to the havoc thereby wrought in the planes of the composition. Shakespeare had a surer hand in this respect, and if the plan of the play was fashioned about the time of its production in 1613, it is certainly to Fletcher that we must ascribe it. Nor does it bear any such clear impress of Shakespeare's later personality as to make this unlikely. But for such a stray phrase as Anne Boleyn's half-sincere aspiration—

> To be lowly born,
> And range with humble livers in content,

it is difficult to trace any spiritual kinship with the romantic optimism and the pastoral dreams of *The Tempest* and *The Winter's Tale*.

It seems implied that Fletcher, whose strong point was not plotting, took the lead in a collaboration with Shakespeare to the extent not only of writing all the most telling scenes, but also of drafting the plot; but, although this is not inconceivable, it is just possible that there may be another alternative. All Shakespeare's historical plays, apart from *Henry the Eighth*, belong to the

earlier periods of his dramatic career. He seemed
to have worked out the vein with *Henry the Fifth*
in 1599, and one is rather at a loss to imagine why
he should have troubled to return to it, fourteen
years later. Then again, one is haunted by the
feeling that, if Shakespeare had written *Henry the
Eighth* at about the time at which he was writing
Henry the Sixth, its structure would not have been
very different from that of the play before us. This
does not, of course, extend to the manners of
rhythm and phrasing, which, in so far as they are
those of Shakespeare, are clearly those of his latest
and not of his earliest development. But there is
nothing which might not be his early work in the
choice of scenes, in the relation to the chronicle,
or in that want of the finer spiritual insight in the
handling of the emotional issues to which attention
has already been drawn. A good deal in the play
would become intelligible through the conjecture
that it was originally written by Shakespeare during
the early 'nineties, as a play on the subject might
so naturally have been, to take its place in the
series which also contained *Henry the Sixth* and
Richard the Third, and that it was afterwards rewritten by Shakespeare and Fletcher, upon the
old *scenario* but with new dialogue, to meet the
demand of 1613. A date during Elizabeth's lifetime has, indeed, been argued for before now, on
the strength of the compliment paid to her in the
last scene, the expansion of which into a further
compliment to James the First has undeniably the

air of an afterthought. I had arrived at the hypothesis sketched above on *a priori* grounds and
without any idea that there was so much as a
glimmer of external evidence to support it, when,
on turning up *Henslowe's Diary*, I found that there
had been a play, which might quite possibly have
been just the one I was in search of. This was
Buckingham, which was played by the Earl of
Sussex's men under Henslowe's management on
the 30th of December, 1593, and on three other
occasions during the following January. There is
no evidence that it was then a new play, and it
does not appear to have belonged to Henslowe's
own stock. It is quite possible that, like *Titus
Andronicus*, which was acted by the same company
at about the same time, it passed ultimately into
the hands of the Chamberlain's men. It might
have been Shakespeare's, just as *Richard the Con-
fessor*, which comes next to it in the *Diary*, might
have been his *Richard the Third*. I do not assert
that it was. Francis Meres does not include a
Henry the Eighth in his list of Shakespeare's plays
in 1598, but that is not quite conclusive, because
we are not bound to take the list as exhaustive,
especially as regards the earliest journey-work
plays, and in fact it does not include *Henry the
Sixth*.

An elaborate attempt has been made to prove
that Shakespeare had no part or lot in the extant
text of *Henry the Eighth*, but that it was written
about 1616 or 1617 by Fletcher, with the aid of

Philip Massinger, in order to supply the place of a Shakespearean play on the same subject which had been destroyed in the fire at the Globe. So far as the supposed reason for any such rewriting is concerned, this is absurd upon the face of it, since even if the manuscripts of the play and all the actors' parts had been burnt, it would obviously have been easy enough to reproduce the text from what had been committed to memory during the rehearsals. But Massinger might very well have begun his career as a playwright as early as 1613, and have assisted Fletcher in preparing the version of that year. One of the principal difficulties in the way of such a theory, the appearance of *Henry the Eighth* in the Shakespeare Folio of 1623, is no doubt removed by the assumption of an earlier version from the hand of Shakespeare himself, whether it were written in the 'nineties or at any subsequent date, since if such a version had existed, Heminges and Condell, who must have known the circumstances, might quite well have thought the share of Shakespeare, as the original plotter, even in the revised version to be sufficient to justify them in printing it as his. I do not think that the removal of the non-Fletcherian scenes of *Henry the Eighth* from the list of Shakespeare's work would rend many leaves from his laurel crown. It is not notably inspired stuff, although it might quite well be Shakespeare's in one of his less felicitous moods, and perhaps with an old text before him to fetter his imagination. Here and there is a phrase which seems to have the authentic ring, such as—

> Things to strike honour sad,

or the Old Lady's description of Anne Boleyn's 'soft cheveril conscience,' or the picturesque colloquialism of Buckingham's attack upon Wolsey—

> The devil speed him! No man's pie is freed
> From his ambitious finger. What had he
> To do in these fierce vanities? I wonder
> That such a keech can with his very bulk
> Take up the rays of the beneficial sun,
> And keep it from the earth.

Massinger had a receptive talent, and it is quite possible that even at the beginning of his career he may have been able to catch the Shakespearean manner to this extent. But the nearer he approaches to Shakespeare, the more difficult it becomes to find criteria sufficiently subtle to distinguish between Massinger imitating Shakespeare and Shakespeare himself in an uninspired mood; and in the absence of such criteria one hardly sees how such theorizing as has been applied to *Henry the Eighth* can be anything but vanity.

I LIKE to think of Shakespeare, not as when
In our old London of the spacious time
He took all amorous hearts with honeyed rhyme;
Or flung his jest at Burbage and at Ben;
Or speared the flying follies with his pen;
Or, in deep hour, made Juliet's love sublime;
Or from Lear's kindness and Iago's crime
Caught tragic hint of heaven's dark way with men.
These were great memories, but he laid them down.
And when, with brow composed and friendly tread,
He sought the little streets of Stratford town,
That knew his dreams and soon must hold him dead,
 I like to think how Shakespeare pruned his rose,
 And ate his pippin in his orchard close.

1916